Puttin' Cologne on the Rickshaw

BY WILLIAM L. BOUFFARD

Cover design by Tri Widyatmaka

Library of Congress Cataloging-in-Publication Data

Bouffard, William L 1947 –

Puttin' Cologne on the Rickshaw:

ISBN-13: 978-0-9847999-0-9

ISBN-10: 0984799907

Library of Congress Control Number: 2011960287

1 Organizational Behavior, 2 Dysfunctional Management, 3 Servant Leadership, 4 Organizational Culture, 5 Values, 6 Games People Play, 7 Quality of Work Life

TABLE OF CONTENTS

PREFACE

I'VE HAD THIS OVERPOWERING URGE TO WRITE this book for the last ten or so years. A day hasn't gone by without that feeling of guilt that comes when I realized I'm not really accomplishing something that means a lot to me. Some of my friends actually reinforced that feeling of guilt by reminding me I should write a book; they thought my quips describing what it was like in management were hilarious. Maybe they were, but the sad thing is I was only telling the truth. You see I've always prided myself on having an amazing grasp for the obvious.

In his book *Evil Plans: Having Fun on the Road to World Domination*, Hugh Macleod described that feeling best as a "wee voice" that comes from deep inside and is with you day-in and day-out. He says, "Somewhere in the back of your mind will be a feeling that you have something you must give to the world, something that you haven't given yet, something the world needs but doesn't quite know it."[1]

This book, and its predecessor, *Ignore Everyone: And 39 Other Keys to Creativity* are not only entertaining, but inspiring. In *Evil Plans*, MacLeod describes his own journey to escape the corporate world and create his "evil plan"—the name he gives for doing something enjoyable versus struggling to keep your sanity in the modern workplace in a job you despise.

Both these books inspired me to act on that feeling, that wee voice. If you have that same gnawing somewhere inside, or even if you don't, I highly recommend that you take a look at MacLeod's books. They may even nurture that ambition within you that's been silent so far.

Along that same inspirational vein, I also highly recommend Seth Godin's book *Small is the New Big: And 183 Other Riffs, Rants, and Remarkable Business Ideas*. All three books are inspiring for anyone who feels stuck in a go-nowhere career or is working in a hell-hole of a job. They may prove to be just what's needed for you to realize hope after all and encourage you to create your own evil plan.

This book is my evil plan, the culmination of more than forty years of observing, and many times suffering all of the idiotic workplace behavior that you'll read about within these pages. In a way it was my way of putting to good use the misery I've suffered. This book was inspired by a true story—my true story. I'm lucky in a perverted sense as it seems I've had the magnetic ability to find crappy places to work. I'm either a magnet for schlep or maybe, just maybe, all companies are the same.

I've had many bad jobs, but also some good jobs, so I don't want to mislead you to believe that I've only been in bad environments. However, it is important to under-stand all organizations exhibit some, if not all, the behaviors detailed in this book. All organizations have their own brand of dysfunctionality.

In an anticlimactic way, those years of procrastination actually worked to my advantage, because some of the best material for this book was discovered later in my career when I spent time in the upper management ranks. Or maybe it's just that with age, came wisdom—the wisdom to recognize what was really going on in the workplace.

I need to warn you, the reader, that I have not fictionalized anything in this book. Everything you'll read about happens on a day-to-day basis out there in the modern workplace. It was all discovered and learned the hard way—by suffering through it. I've been faithful to the truth and 'told it like it is.'

While this book is about the realities of what goes on in management, some of the behaviors and games we'll discover transcend the executive and middle manage-ment suites and can be found playing themselves out at all levels of the organiza-tion. Whether you're in management or not, reflect on these behaviors, as they may serve as a look in the mirror, and you may discover you don't like what you see.

I've had many different sources from which to draw upon in writing this book as I've had many more jobs than I care to remember, so I feel that sort of makes me an expert at comparing and contrasting the workplaces and behaviors that I've witnessed. The behaviors you're going to discover in the following pages are endemic to them all. This book isn't about just one particularly obnoxious place that I've worked.

In reflection I feel that having had many jobs has been of benefit, because without the experience of seeing the good, the bad, and the ugly side of the working world, I don't think I'd have gained quite the right perspective, perverted cynicism, or the courage to write this book.

So with that in mind, I hope this book can serve a three-fold purpose. First, I hope for all the workplace veterans, who have paid their dues already, that reading this book can in some way serve as a catharsis, that emotional cleansing that we all need after a long career of suffering. Writing this book has certainly been a catharsis for me.

Second, I hope this book can serve newcomers to the workplace in preparing them for what they'll surely experience when they get out there in the rat race. It's like the old saying, "If I knew then what I know now, maybe I'd have done things differently."

Third, for the reader who's working his or her way to the top and may not yet be privileged to be in management, this is your look behind the curtain.

No matter your current position in the pyramid (or the organization chart), this book can provide valuable insight into what makes organizations tick. You can't fully understand how to fend for (and protect) yourself in the modern workplace without fully understanding how the workplace "works." For you youngsters, this book will provide that understanding, so you can develop your evil plan earlier than I did and do something you love versus just blindly following the herd.

This book is a tell-all. It's meant to expose the modern workplace for what it truly is, and that's not necessarily a flattering view. I'm not about to try to put lipstick on the pig.

The modern workplace is brutal. I don't sugar-coat anything. This book is meant to get your attention so you can do something about your life, and career—hopefully, before it's too late.

Harvey Pekar in the 2003 movie *American Splendor* summed it up best. "Life is a war of attrition. You have to stay active on all fronts. It's one thing after another. Wake up! Your whole life's getting eaten away. What kind of existence is this? Is this all a working stiff like you can expect? You gonna suffer in silence for the rest of your life, or are you gonna make a mark?"[2]

ACKNOWLEDGEMENTS

I HAVE MANY TO THANK FOR THE inspiration (and the usable material) that made this book possible. I'd like to first and foremost thank all those past employers (names omitted to protect the few innocents) for providing me the virtual cornucopia of material that fills these pages. I also have to thank all the sociopaths, rude, uncaring, egotistical, narcissistic nut jobs I've endured as they provided proof that what I describe in this book wasn't my imagination.

Despite all the evil doers, I've had the privilege of meeting some truly extraordinary people throughout my career. These are the souls who have suffered along with me as we tried to navigate our ways through the often nightmarish work environment. This book should really be dedicated to them. Maybe it will prove the inspiration for them to act on their suffering and make a change in their careers.

That being said, the first extraordinary person I'd like to acknowledge is Carl Phipps, whose nonsensical quips are exemplified in the title of this book. While working with Carl, I learned many witty sayings, each of which poked fun, in some perverted way, at whatever stupidity we were suffering through at the time.

These Phippsisms provided a brief respite from the reality of everyday work life. Whenever I think of Carl, I remember how important it is to always maintain a sense of humor. Knowing Carl made it worth coming to work every day, and his sayings will stick with me forever and leave me with fond memories of the years we worked together.

Another extraordinary person is Bill Wallace, who provided an exemplary role model for leadership early in my career. In retrospect he was the only real leader I ever worked for during all my years in industry. Bill set a standard for leadership and, more importantly he exemplified how a dedicated coach and mentor can really influence a young person's career.

I'm lucky to have met him early in my career as he provided the model from which I patterned my later management style. His leadership style helped incubate my core values which have provided me the perspective needed for surviving when I encountered the many lunatics in my work life. Needless to say, we became life-long friends. My relationship with Bill negates the old idiom that you shouldn't mix friendship with business.

There are many other characters whom I've met along the way but, alas, they're too numerous to mention here. However, I do want to thank them for the inspiration they provided despite their not knowing it at the time.

I'd like to dedicate this book to my family, who for all those years, had to endure my kick-the-dog behavior as a result of my many bad days at the office.

CHAPTER 1 THE MARCHING MORONS

"I DON'T HAVE TO TELL YOU THINGS are bad. Everybody knows things are bad. It's a depression. Everybody's out of work or scared of losing their job. The dollar buys a nickel's worth; banks are going bust; shopkeepers keep a gun under the counter; punks are running wild in the street, and there's nobody anywhere who seems to know what to do, and there's no end to it. We know the air is unfit to breathe and our food is unfit to eat. And we sit watching our TVs while some local newscaster tells us that today we had fifteen homicides and sixty-three violent crimes, as if that's the way it's supposed to be!

"We all know things are bad—worse than bad; they're crazy.

"It's like everything everywhere is going crazy, so we don't go out anymore. We sit in the house, and slowly the world we're living in is getting smaller, and all we say is, 'Please, at least leave us alone in our living rooms. Let me have my toaster and my TV and my steel-belted radials, and I won't say anything. Just leave us alone.'

"Well, I'm not going to leave you alone. I want you to get mad!

"I don't want you to protest. I don't want you to riot. I don't want you to write to your congressman, because I wouldn't know what to tell you to write. I don't know what to do about the depression and the inflation and the [terrorists] and the crime in the street.

"All I know is that first, you've got to get mad. You've gotta say, 'I'm a human being, goddammit! My life has value!'

"So, I want you to get up now. I want all of you to get up out of your chairs. I want you to get up right now and go to the window, open it, and stick your head out and yell, 'I'm as mad as hell, and I'm not going to take this anymore!'"[3]

In this now famous diatribe from the 1976 movie *Network*, Howard Beale, (Peter Finch), the long-time anchor of the fictitious UBS Evening News, has just learned from news division president Max Schumacher (William Holden) that he has just two more weeks on the air because of declining ratings. The above rant is his reaction, which is broadcasted on live TV.

Beale is being cast aside after a lifetime of devotion and loyalty to an entity that can give none in return. *Network* has become a metaphor for the ways people are treated in the typical workplace–that is; they are used until they're no longer needed, then discarded with absolutely no remorse.

While the movie is a critical look at the inner workings of the network TV broadcast industry, it has many parallels to all of business. It wasn't well received by the industry it lampoons, which shouldn't be a surprise as the truth can sometimes hurt.

Tom Peters, the renowned writer and motivational speaker on business management practices, best-known for *In Search of Excellence*, once said, "The whole secret to our success is being able to con ourselves into believing that we're going to change the world.[4]

Howard Beale, like all of us, thought he was changing the world; however, the UBS network negated all that he'd accomplished. Howard Beale is more than a man who's had enough and just wasn't going to take it anymore. He epitomizes the fate of many an average worker in today's workplace and the TV network depicted in the movie is the perfect metaphor for how businesses treat their workers.

The movie dramatically depicts the way that people treat each other in the management suite. You see a myriad of emotions and behaviors from frustration, fear, ego, narcissism, anger, aggression, and self-righteousness, to downright rudeness and disrespect among the characters. It's almost hard to believe it could be found in one organization, but the fact is it just might be an accurate depiction of many organizations. This book will look at the effect all those behaviors have on the modern workplace and you don't have to look far to find them.

That's because these same behaviors are evident all around us in our everyday life, but most often don't manifest themselves in quite the intensity as the movie depicts. That is except for the last three: self-righteousness, rudeness, and disrespect. I've come to the conclusion that the way people interact in today's world can be summarized nicely using that simple word: *rude*, and the proliferation of rudeness is an epidemic. Self-righteousness and disrespect are just supporting behaviors to the act of being rude.

Rudeness is simply a display of disrespectfulness and incivility. Rudeness in practice becomes both confrontational and disruptive. Rudeness is the antithesis of civility and civility is what seems to be missing in the world today. Make no mistake; civility is not blind obedience to social norms (even if the social norm is incivility), but adherence to respect, or courteousness, to those around you. Thus, true civil behavior is as simple as being considerate of others.

I point this out because, if you haven't already noticed, the world is full of rude, inconsiderate people. You know the people who are thoroughly convinced of their own importance. You bump into these pooterish[5] people during any visit to the grocery store, mall, or when out on the road. You know their ilk; they park their shopping carts in the middle of the supermarket aisle, and act oblivious to your existence as you try to navigate around them. On the road they never use their turn signals. They cut you off and then flip you off; they speed up to block you when you're trying to merge onto the highway. They jabber loudly on their cell-phones in public, providing everyone within earshot a glimpse into their egotistical lives. The list of rudeness goes on.

I'm convinced that with all the rudeness that's out there the world is becoming more uncivil with every passing day. Shannon Bell, in her January 2011 article "Time: Are We Becoming an Uncivil Society?" says it all, "Becoming? Hell, I thought we already were. I mean isn't one of America's favorite pastimes watching a bunch of strangers become stranded in a remote location, subsisting on rodents and snakes, and then spending their days figuring out how to stab each other in the back to win money? You can't get much more uncivil than that."[6]

We're going to find how that phrase, "spending their days figuring out how to stab each other in the back to win money" is not just for people stranded on an island playing in a contest; it just may be an accurate description of everyday life in the modern workplace.

Not unlike the TV show *Survivor*, the workplace is a bunch of people who don't know each other from Adam's house cat, are thrown together, stranded every day for eight to twelve hours in the same place, figuring out how to stab each other in the back for the chance of higher pay, prestige and, for some, the ultimate prize— the chance to suckle at the teat of power.

And day-to-day life at work is not unlike the challenges faced by the contestants on *Survivor*. Their challenges are contests in which they face games of endurance and strength to win status, like immunity from being voted off the island. However, the real challenges are what go on between the formal games—i.e. behind the curtain. Here the players must be adept at showing their true human nature, like dividing and conquering their foes or having no remorse at throwing others under the bus. Players must also be proficient at sneaking and conniving, and instigating problems and open conflict between other players. Like the contestants in *Survivor* and the TV show *Big Brother*, the best personality for success in business is sociopathy.

Since the world is full of rude, un-caring and uncivil people, not only in the work place but everywhere, what's to do? Most people can't just take it in stride and turn the other cheek, instead they must retaliate in kind and thus this evil chain of events keeps unfolding and intensifying.

I've come to the conclusion that this "me" generation thinking is probably not coming to an end any time soon. That's because it's not generational at all, it crosses all ages, race and demographics; all industries and backgrounds. Therefore we must just accept the world for what it is—just plain full of rude people who don't care for anyone but themselves and are oblivious to the havoc they leave in their wake. What we can do, though, is understand the behaviors of this ilk so that we can fight fire with fire.

That being said, if the world is ever going to change from rude and uncivil to well-mannered, it's important to understand what drives rude behavior. I believe the answer is simple—just plain old stupidity. In fact, I think that in today's society we're seeing the results of what Giancarlo Livraghi calls "The Power of Stupidity." In his book by the same name, he details the widespread evidence of the fact that all people have a propensity to do stupid things despite how intelligent they and society may think they are.

As Mr. Livraghi points out; "[large] and small events confirm, every day, the dismal effects of human stupidity. Many problems are going from bad to worse. But what we may perceive as the good old times wasn't as good as [our feeling of] nostalgia [tells us]. Simplistic as this is, it's reasonably practical to assume that we are as stupid as we have ever been. The sheer fact that our species has, so far, survived and expanded in spite of its appalling mistakes proves that we are not completely stupid. But it's painfully obvious that our resources aren't good enough for the state of evolution in which we are now.

"There is nothing new in the abundance of presumptuous idiots. We are just more often aware of their presence (and the results of what they are doing, not only saying).

"For lack of any better criterion, let's stay with the simple 'postulate' that the stupidity factor is a constant in humankind. So human stupidity is growing because there are more of us and, just as infectious diseases and destructive pests travel on airplanes, the contagion of stupidity rides the fast waves of worldwide communication.

"In other words, we are not becoming more (or less) stupid, but the power of stupidity is increasing. The problem is in the vastness of the consequences, that has never been so large and in the speed of their multiplication. We can't uproot stupidity."

Livraghi also points out that he believes the world is caught up in what he calls "The Marching Moron Syndrome." I tend to agree.

"The Marching Morons" is a science fiction short story written by Cyril M. Kornbluth, and published in 1951. The leading character, John Barlow, is a man from the past (1988) who had been put into suspended animation and is revived hundreds of years in the future. Barlow soon discovers that there is a problem with the people of the future; the world has become full of morons. It was explained to him that, due to the fact that while intelligent people weren't having children, excessive breeding by less intelligent people left the world full of morons. There were only an elite few intelligent people who worked to keep order in society.

In the story Barlow eventually becomes the leader of this "intelligent minority." He must provide a solution for the problem of moron overpopulation, so he develops an elaborate plan in which he tricks the morons into thinking they can partake in the vacation of a lifetime to the planet Venus. His plan is then to conveniently lose those spaceships in space. His plan works fine until he becomes a victim of his own scheme.

In the end, Livraghi observes that he believes there's still some hope for the future by telling us that, "It's unlikely that we are heading for any such future, but we are facing some very serious problems caused by human stupidity."[7]

However, I don't share Livraghi's optimism. Interestingly, Kornbluth may not have penned a work of fiction after all and he may prove to be the Nostradamus of the 20th century.

In their controversial 1994 book, *The Bell Curve: Intelligence and Class Structure in American Life*, Richard J. Herrnstein and Charles Murray lay out support for their premise that we will eventually be a society split more along intelligence (IQ) lines than any other factor (race, economics, etc.). For the masses, they detail a dysgenic trend in cognitive ability (IQ) that has been playing out over the past century. From generation to generation, we (society) are getting dumber at a rate of 0.8 IQ points per generation. They further note that the gap between those populating the high end of the IQ bell curve, and the rest of the population, is becoming wider. This "cognitive partitioning" will result in a group at the top of society they call the "cognitive elite" who will rule society while the masses will, in fact, become a population of, what Kornbluth would call, marching morons.[8]

I also will note here that my earlier premise that the world is becoming more uncivil every day is also borne out by this book. The authors observe the growing incivility in American life, and through their data, link that to the ever decreasing IQ of society. Therefore the marching moron syndrome and the rise of incivility are undeniably linked.

I believe that the workplace is just as uncivil, stupid, moronic, and rude as in the wilds of everyday life. Think about it; if regular everyday life is one bout after another with uncivil, stupid morons, then why would we think that our work life can be somehow different? In this book we're going to uncover the facts about why the workplace is just a more subtle (and sometimes not so subtle) form of the incivility we see all throughout society.

I've always thought of myself as a good person, half-way intelligent, with something to offer the world. When I started my career all those years ago, I went to work each day expecting that I'd be treated equitably and with respect. Moreover, I naively believed that my employer, and especially my boss, truly cared for my well-being. I believed that I was part of a team and that we all were in the "good fight" together. In reality nothing could be further from the truth, for as Dennis

Wholey, TV host, once quipped, "To expect the world to treat you fairly because you're a good person is like expecting a bull not to charge at you because you're a vegetarian."[9]

It's depressing, I know, and it's easy to get disillusioned. It's easy to set yourself up in a fantasy world so as to not have to think about how absurd the world has become. It's easy to tell ourselves lies about our situation and fate. We tell ourselves that things will get better once business picks up or we get that new job. It's easy to just resign ourselves to just shut-up and color and ignore the world around us. The fact is everyone lives in some state of delusion, denial or mild depression. Marshall Goldsmith, in his book *What Got you Here Won't get You There*, points out the saddest fact of all, "the most realistic people in our society are the chronically depressed."[10]

Being depressed might not be all that bad actually, for as Dr. Nassir Ghaemi points out in his July 2011 *Wall Street Journal* article, "Depression in Command," "Normal non-depressed people have what psychologists call positive illusion; that is, they possess a mildly high self-regard, a slightly inflated sense of how much they control the world around them. Mildly depressed people, by contrast, tend to see the world more clearly, more as it is. Clinical studies have found that depression correlates with high degrees of both realism and empathy. Psychologists call this the Inverse Law of Sanity."[11]

So if your job has driven you to anti-depressants, you should pat yourself on the back because you have an amazing grasp for the obvious.

For many of us, our only hope is not to end up like Willy Loman, the main character in Arthur Miller's *Death of a Salesman*,[12] who ends up committing suicide. While I truly think that a shitty job is no reason to end it all, I certainly can understand why someone could get pushed beyond their limit like Willy or Howard Beale.

Everyone should read (or at least see the movie) *Death of a Salesman* as, like *Network* and David Mamet's 1984 Pulitzer Prize winning play *Glengarry Glen Ross*, it's another landmark work that has come to stand as a metaphor for the way workplace organizations consume and exploit their employees.

In reality, though, some folks are pushed beyond their ability to cope and resort to venting their frustrations in the workplace in the form of violence. In *Network*, Howard Beale actually threatened to shoot himself on the air. Yes, it was to be self-inflicted, but it's violence none-the-less.

I believe a lot of workplace anger and frustration is actually vented out into the real world. This is good for the workplace, but bad for the ride home. This venting of the frustrations from work manifests itself in the road rage that's become quite a normal occurrence. The only difference between someone involved in road rage and someone who's "had a bad day at work" is that once out in public, the road rage doesn't get you fired, albeit there could be other, more serious, consequences. Other than that, they're one and the same.

Sadly, violence is carried out in the workplace every day. In his September 2010 article "Save Yourself from Workplace Violence," Ben Carlsen offers us some insight. "The extent of workplace violence may surprise you. According to the *Bureau of Labor Statistics* 2008–2009 report on "Fatal Occupational Injuries." assaults and violent acts in 2009 included roughly 521 homicides, 420 shootings, 48 stabbings, and 237 self-inflicted injuries." That's ten a week or two per day. "Deaths by homicide and other violence were the second leading cause of workplace fatalities, behind only highway collisions and accidents."[13]

Despite these seemingly dismal statistics, we still only occasionally hear or read of workplace violence. It still doesn't equal the frequency of road rage because, if you're like me, I witness some form of road rage every time I'm out on the road. A study conducted by the American Automobile Association (AAA) showed that 90 percent of drivers admitted to partaking in road rage with 60 percent actually losing their temper. I'll bet a good percentage of these incidences find their motivation in the workplace. In fact, a 1999 study found that one in four (road rage incidents) occurred during the 4:00 to 6:00 p.m. travel peak.[14] This corresponds to when most people are leaving work for the day.

It's a vicious circle starting with the chronically rude leading the otherwise sane people to retaliate in kind by being callous, rude, and downright nasty themselves. This also circles back to the workplace where everyone ends up abusing each other.

Exposure to workplace abuse leads people to take out their pent-up aggression on the road and against their peers at work which further perpetuates an abusive work environment. More sinister is the secondhand suffering that occurs when victims of road rage, or workplace abuse, vent their frustrations on family members. In urban vernacular it's called the "Kick the Dog Syndrome."[15]

Let's face it, the workplace can be a pretty nasty environment, and statistics support this observation; however, it's not even the possibility of suffering physical abuse (violence) that's the most worrisome. In 2007, The Waitt Institute for Violence Prevention conducted a study of 7700 respondents that showed that upwards of 37 percent of the respondents indicated they had been victim to emotional abuse (including bullying) from bosses and/or coworkers. The results also showed that most abusers were in fact bosses (72 percent). It's also not surprising that men were the perpetrators in 60 percent of the cases. In fairness women aren't exempt from abusing others, as the study showed that women tend to abuse women 71 percent of the time, while men target men only 54 percent of the time. We'll see similar statistics later when we learn about the infamous workplace bully.

Overall abuse (including bullying) is four times more prevalent than discriminatory harassment. According to the Workplace Bullying Institute, stress-related problems were reported in 45 percent of those abused.[16] This makes perfect sense to me because an earlier 2005 study estimated that 10% of the population is on antidepressants. I'll bet the usage is much higher now.

What's more disturbing about the study statistics is that 62 percent of employers ignore abuse in the workplace. Even more interesting is that 40 percent of the abused claim that they didn't report the abuse to their employer because little is ever done about the problem.

I guess it's like any crime: If the laws against it aren't enforced, then no wonder the problem persists. The real problem is that there's no law against emotionally abusing co-workers. It's only a problem if it resorts to violence. That's just plain wrong.

It seems that being rude and disagreeable pays off and is actually rewarded in many workplaces. In her August 2011 *Wall Street Journal* article "Hey You!: Rude People Earn More, Study Finds," Rachel Silverman explains, "A new study finds that agreeable workers earn significantly lower incomes than less agreeable ones. The gap is especially wide for men.

"The researchers examined 'agreeableness' using self-reported survey data and found that men who measured below average on agreeableness earned about 18 percent more annually in their sample than nicer guys. Ruder women, meanwhile, earned about 5 percent more than their agreeable counterparts.

"Nice guys are getting the shaft.

"The researcher's analyzed data collected for twenty years from three different surveys, which sampled roughly 10,000 workers comprising a wide range of professions, salaries and wages. For men, being agreeable may not conform to expectations of masculine behavior, the researchers write in the study. The problem is many managers often don't realize they reward disagreeableness. You can say this is what you value but your compensation system may not reflect that."[17]

So what constitutes workplace emotional abuse or the more popular term: *bullying*? Dr. Robert Sutton, in his book *The No Asshole Rule*, defines it as: "the sustained display of hostile verbal and non-verbal behavior excluding physical contact."[18] Mildred Pryor, et al. in the August 2010 article, "Workplace Fun and It's Correlates:

A Conceptual Inquiry," further characterize it as "repeated and enduring aggressive behaviors that are intended to be hostile and/or perceived as hostile by the recipient."[19] This is a good definition because the problem with detecting abuse is the fact that what one person perceives as abuse, another may not. Some folks have thicker skin than others, so it may not bother them as much. Also it's a crime of degrees. It reveals itself from the subtle to the outright blatant.

Dr. Gary Namie of The Workplace Bullying Institute provides us the more legal definition: "Bullying takes the form of verbal abuse, or behavior that is humiliating; threatening; intimidating; sabotages the target person's work; or exploits a known vulnerability (psychological or physical)." This is the definition that has been codified in the anti-bullying Healthy Workplace Bill being introduced in many state legislatures.[20]

Why is workplace abuse and bullying so bad? Why should we even care? These behaviors poison the whole work environment. And on a personal note, just because you're not being abused right now doesn't mean it won't happen in the future. I'll bet virtually everyone will be abused, in some manner, before their career comes to an end. Anyone who's stuck having to scratch out a living working for someone else should be concerned about the rise in workplace abuse.

Further, Dr. Sutton points out that "[Abuse] has cumulative effects partly because nasty interactions have a far bigger impact on our moods than then positive interactions: five times the punch. It thus takes numerous encounters with positive people to offset the energy and happiness sapped by a single episode with one [abuser]."[21]

It's probably not surprising that the "boss" is typically at the forefront of making people unhappy and disgruntled on the job. From my own experience, I've detailed below a few overarching behavioral patterns that a boss might demonstrate that can foster bad feelings in a subordinate:

- He/she plays favorites (covets protected people or fiefdoms, which we'll learn about later)
- He/she doesn't keep promises (especially at performance review time)
- He/she doesn't listen, interrupts and talks over people
- He/she plays mind games (we'll learn about all the workplace games later)
- He/she doesn't provide ongoing feedback (except at the annual performance review, and then it's always only negative)
- He/she is generally disagreeable, finds fault in everything
- He/she dishes out unconstructive criticism (we'll learn about this in a later chapter)
- He/she is just not motivating (they're not leaders, they're managers; there's a big difference)

The above are only some of the more subtle ways abuse is administered. It can get much worse.

We've seen the statistics on who the typical abuser is and their targets of choice, but how do you recognize them for what they are? The above isn't a very good test because many bosses exhibit at least some of that behavior. However, it's pretty much universal that most true workplace abusers can be categorized to display sociopathic behavior.

A sociopath is a person incapable of feeling empathy, guilt, or remorse for the way he or she treats people. Other major traits of a sociopath are narcissism and egomania. For a true sociopath, business relationships are only seen as a game. Sociopaths view people as objects (tools) to be manipulated, and their narcissistic behavior wreaks havoc on everyone they work with, and especially those who work for them.

The sociopaths are the people who make the average workplace the abusive dysfunctional environment that it is. Frankly, the sociopathic behavior (including bullying) prevalent in today's workplace is nothing short of just plain evil, and we'll discover later how the behavior of these thugs can make work and your life nothing short of a living hell.

Many would like to believe that the workplace is a microcosm of our society as a whole and is governed by the same democratic process. Not true by a long shot. In his book *Images of Organization*, Gareth Morgan explains, "As a citizen in a democratic society, a person is theoretically free to hold his own opinions, make his own decisions, and be treated as an equal. As an employee, he is denied all these rights. His only democratic right rests in the freedom to find another job and move on."[22] How many times have you heard a manager (or your boss) remind you that democracy stops at the front door? Sadly, they're right; it does, and you better get used to it.

Unfortunately, the fact is the typical American business probably can't operate as a true democracy and survive. In his April 2010 *Financial Times* article "Trump Bid Reveals the Myth of the CEO President," Stanford University Senior Fellow Francis Fukuyama points out that "Indeed the evolved corporate governance model of contemporary American business is far closer to East Asian authoritarian rule than it is to anything that comes out of an American democratic tradition. Both corporate America and Asian government are ruthlessly meritocratic; their accountability goes upward, not downwards; and they are measured by their economic performance and not by their ability to satisfy a broad range of interest groups pursuing divergent ends."[23]

Democracy stopping at the front door is an important point despite the above description of American business as a "ruthless meritocracy." Contrary to the definition of a meritocracy, in which people rise to the top based on intelligence, credentials, and education, that's not what happens in the typical workplace. What typically happens (and what we'll learn in this book) is that the sociopathic element will tend to rise to the top. And in a workplace led by sociopathic personalities, their behavior will create a ruthless environment that ultimately becomes little better than a dictatorship, where the accountability is always focused upward, not downwards, and economic performance becomes the sole method of measuring success.

Since I've worked in many a dictatorship it never ceases to amaze me how many organizations have a dictator pulling the strings. You'd think in this day and age that people wouldn't tolerate this type of workplace. On the contrary, as Simon Kuper points out in his April 2011 *Financial Times* article "Superman: the Survival of the Personality Cult." "Many people hate dictatorships, but love dictators. These regimes give people only one pleasure: the sense of having a personal, loving relationship with an all-seeing superman. Then there are the laboriously built personality cults that surround the often ludicrous leaders. If you keep hearing that your leader is a superman, you start to believe it. Seems people will not blame the dictator for how things are no matter how miserable they are in the organization. Many Germans thought that if only Hitler knew what his underlings were doing, he'd put a stop to it."[24]

So how can you recognize one of these sick organizations, which is exactly what they are? Sometimes it's easy, but most times not, because the sickness is typically deep-seated and doesn't always show on the surface. However, the following list may help jog your memory and allow you to focus on your own situation to determine if it's time to fish or cut bait;

- Everyone around you annoys you at some level
- You're mentally exhausted and drained by the end of the day
- You hate getting up in the morning
- Your boss is more interested in the hours you put in than anything else
- You work for a workaholic who also loves to micromanage
- You feel you get no respect

- Nobody communicates
- You don't feel valued
- You feel you have no work-life balance; you're married to the job

If you observe or experience any, or all, of the above telltale signs, then you may be in an evil, abusive environment.

Unfortunately, the truth is, the above describes just about every workplace to some extent. You'd think the rallying cry of most organizations must be "Be Evil." The fact is that evil behavior seems to have become an accepted behavior in today's workplace. It explains why Google adopted the motto, "Don't Be Evil." Sure seems appropriate after reflecting on my forty-year exposure to the American workplace and how much evil I've been subjected to and witnessed. To combat this many companies have developed ethical codes or values as an attempt to try to govern their conduct. Unfortunately, as we'll see later, many don't follow them. Time will tell if Google is one of them.

I believe that if more businesses adopted this "don't be evil" policy, the average workplace might soon become tolerable. Of course I'm making a quantum leap assumption that people actually know the difference between good and evil, or even care. We'll learn how sociopaths don't. This also includes the assumption that a company's leaders would actually live out this motto if they made it part of their espoused values. We'll find out later how the typical visions and especially the values of most organizations are unfortunately just hollow words.

The bottom line, as I see it, is that many workplaces are hellish, evil places to work. As British publisher, poet, and philanthropist Felix Dennis pointed out in his book, How to Get Rich, "Either you learn to go with the flow and change as rapidly as you are able, or you will be left stranded, like the last dinosaur, by the last warm lake, on the last continent the ice age has yet to reach."25 That is, you'll be forced to become one of them to survive.

Why is the typical workplace this way? Since organizations are not inanimate objects but collections of people, people are obviously responsible for making the workplace the hell that it is. It begs the question, why does it have to be like this? Why do people do what they do and why do people treat each other the way in which they do?

In psychology, the short answer is, "because they can." People in the workplace get away with the most rude and outrageous behavior under the guise of "management" and "leadership." For some, management is just another word for a license to abuse. The rude, outrageous behavior and abuse compounds because as writer Eric Hoffer noted, "When people are free to do as they please they tend to imitate each other."[26] Thus, all that's needed is one bad apple and eventually a whole organization will go sour.

I think the answer is that most people are just so wrapped up in themselves that they don't even have the slightest notion of the effect their actions have on those around them. It's ingrained right into the fabric of society that we're all special and that success is guaranteed. In fact, this belief starts way before the typical person even enters the workplace.

In his March 2011 article "The Modesty Manifesto," David Brooks tells us, "A recent survey of high school students found that 70 percent of them believed they had above average leadership skills."[27] This would support my theory that people on the whole, are thoroughly convinced of their own importance, and this attitude starts early in life, so when its brought to the workplace environment, it spawns the sociopathic behavior that's so prevalent.

While researching the reasons people do what they do, I stumbled upon the work of Ernest Becker. His book *The Denial of Death* is a work of psychology and philosophy. Published in 1973, Becker's work is an extension of the original work of philosopher Søren Kierkegaard and psychoanalyst Sigmund Freud.

The basic premise of *The Denial of Death* is that the emotions and behaviors we witness in modern civilization are ultimately an elaborate, symbolic defense mechanism against the knowledge of our mortality. Our behaviors, in turn, become our emotional and intellectual response to our basic survival mechanism. Becker postulates that people are caught between the physical world and the symbolic world of their human psyché.

Thus, Becker believes that because of the symbolic self, man thinks he's able to transcend the dilemma of mortality, by embarking on what he refers to as an "immortality project." Through heroism, a person creates or becomes part of something which he feels will last forever. This eternal state will never die compared to his physical body. Thus the way people treat one another on a day-to-day basis, is a result of their acting out their own immortality project and wanting to be a hero in their own mind. You're heard of someone being described as "a legend in his own mind?" Those are the people who have been successful with their immortality project.

To compound this behavior most organizations reward heroism, so the search for, and rewarding of, heroism pops up a lot in the modern workplace and we'll see many examples later.

In his book *Images of Organization*, cultural anthropologist Gareth Morgan refers to this phenomenon as the "quest for immortality."[28] He explains, "We can understand organizations and much of the behavior within organizations in terms of a quest for immortality. In creating organizations, we create structures of activity that are larger than life and that often survive for generations. In becoming identified with such organizations, we ourselves find meaning and permanence. As we invest ourselves in our work, our roles become our realities, and as we objectify ourselves in the goods we produce or the money we make, we make ourselves visible and real to ourselves."[29]

Another question that comes to mind is why, in this modern enlightened world, do people allow the abuse and incivility that permeates the modern workplace? I think Gary Small and Gigi Vorgan hit the nail on the head in their March 2011 treatise, "Is the Internet Killing Empathy?" They question, "Why the grim curiosity that compels drivers to slow down and gaze at a fatal car crash? We are drawn often by a subconscious fear that the same thing could happen to us. By observing it in other people, we have our own experience of it, but at an emotional distance. The more we observe terrifying events happening to other people, the more they reinforce our sense of denial and detachment that: it can't happen to us."[30]

In other words, people are becoming less and less empathetic to their fellow man.

In his book *Zero Degrees of Empathy*, Simon Baron-Cohen believes that having a lack of empathy is the essence of evil. This process through which people transform from good to evil is what he calls "empathy erosion." He states, "To enjoy the agony one inflicts on another, and to inflict it purely for that reason is part of the traditional notion of evil."[31] This adds a new perspective to Google's "Don't be Evil" motto.

Whether the true underlying psychological reason is denial of death or lack of empathy, there are a couple more simplistic principles in effect here that help explain why people in the workplace do what they do.

First, we all know that to survive workers need to do what their company's management, and above all, their supervisors expect of them. Subsequently, as Eric Hoffer pointed out, they adopt the behaviors of management so when management is uncivil, the workers become uncivil, and this behavior becomes engrained in the organization's culture. And because people identify through the culture what it takes to be successful, the workers then see sociopathic behavior as the way to the top.

This explains why otherwise good, ethical people will be tempted to follow, and mimic, the sociopaths. They'll do that even if it flies in the face of their own beliefs of what is right or wrong. It's been demonstrated many times that people who should understand right from wrong can be induced into performing evil deeds when they are commanded to do so by a person in power.

At Yale University in the early 1960s, a young psychologist named Stanley Milgram began what became one of the most widely recognized experiments in his field. He found that two-thirds of the volunteer subjects for an experiment he was conducting were willing to inflict what they believed were increasingly painful shocks on an innocent person just because the experimenter told them to do so. They did this even when they witnessed the victim screaming and pleading. Luckily the shocks weren't actually being administered and the people targeted were, in fact, actors.

Milgram wanted to demonstrate the relationship between obedience and authority. His study is now known as the famous Stanley Milgram Experiment. The take away here is that this resembles real-life incidents in which people see themselves as merely cogs in a machine, just doing their job, taking orders and doing what they're told. First, they believe that this is what's expected of them, and second, it allows them to avoid responsibility for the consequences of their actions.

In his November 2006 article, "Why Do People Do What They Do," Glen Campbell explains this simply as, "People aren't rational. They rarely do things that make sense for their long-term self-interest." Campbell also shoots down some of the old theories for personal motivation as he explains, "most of the common explanations for human behavior don't really cut the mustard. According to some theories [Maslow], we are supposedly motivated by 'drives'—for food, survival, sex, etc. While these forces certainly exist, they explain very little of the behavior we encounter every day. People are often 'driven,' but usually not by simple bodily goals."[32]

I agree with Campbell; what drives a person is not as simple as Maslow's drives would have us believe. Maslow's work isn't all that profound any longer, as everyone is driven by the basic needs in his hierarchy. There needs to be another discriminator between the behavior of average people and the sociopaths.

Workplace behavior can be better understood when we consider some additional natural human needs that also motivate day-to-day behaviors. In the article "Workplace Fun and its Correlates: A Conceptual Inquiry," Mildred Pryor, et al. offer a more in-depth look at motivation. They claim "There are four things that motivate, i.e., drive human behavior: to acquire or obtain scarce goods (including intangibles such as social status); to bond or form connections with individuals and groups; to comprehend and satisfy our curiosity and master the world around us; and to defend and protect against external threats."[33] I personally like this definition as it serves to explain many of the behaviors that we'll discover in this book.

There's only one thing missing in the above four motivations which, as we'll discover later, is the prime characteristic of the typical sociopath. In a simple word, it is *ego*. Glen Campbell explains this and then takes our understanding one step further, "Most human behavior is propelled by a much more powerful drive; more powerful than food, sex or reason. Each human is seeking to defend his self-esteem. He behaves in such a way as to protect or enhance his apparent personal value. [However] the concept of ego, or the enhancement of one's self-esteem, is only a starting point. Human behavior is [also] motivated by the attempt to avoid shame. From early childhood, humans are shameful, insecure little creatures who are always fighting the spectre of worthlessness. [Thus] human behavior can be largely explained as a reaction to this internal shame."[34]

These are all interesting concepts, and to prove them, we're going to delve deeper into the sociopathic behaviors prevalent in today's workplace, and we'll see why the ego is probably the number one factor in driving workplace behaviors.

All this begs the question, why would we even want to go to work each day? Have you ever really thought about it? Work can be punishing and going to work each day can be as columnist and author Bill Vaughn described "like going daily to the dentist to have root canal surgery on the same tooth."[35] In his *Financial Times* article "Simplicity and the Storm before the Calm," Philip Delves Broughton humorously notes, "For many of us, our days are like whack-a-mole, flailing at problems as they emerge, hoping that one good wallop does the trick but fearing that nothing is ever well and truly solved."[36]

I'll bet the following list captures at least a few of the altruistic beliefs you had when you started out your career:

- The money
- The challenge
- The calling
- Build a reputation and a legacy
- Solve some pressing world problem
- Be part of something larger (quest for immortality)
- Be appreciated

As you progress through your career these vaporize one by one. Many of you will never experience anything close to being completely satisfied with your careers. But you say "If I can't obtain some of these levels of job and career satisfaction, then at least the money is a realistic goal." However, as we'll find out when we tackle the compensation process, even that will disappoint you, as you'll probably never earn what you think you're worth. Why? Sociopathic rule that leads to workplace dysfunctionality, as demonstrated by the bad behaviors seen in today's workplace, is the single reason you might never reach your job satisfaction expectations.

We'll explore how sociopathic, egocentric motives display themselves in everyday workplace behavior. We'll start by looking at the organizational façade that provides the illusion of civility and sanity, to the organizational power structures that foster this type behavior. We'll also delve into all the idiotic workplace behaviors from the rodeo atmosphere exhibited in meetings, the lack of teamwork and dysfunctional communication channels, the backstabbing relationships among peers and colleagues, and all the abusive behavior that lies in between. We'll also take a hard look at the visions and values that most management is deluded into believing, and we'll finish with a look at the most despised practice in modern business—the performance appraisal process.

This book isn't about good bosses, sane colleagues, or normal workplaces. Hopefully you can recognize them when you see them. This book *will* provide you some pointers on how to become a better leader. If it accomplishes nothing else, it will teach you what *not* to do and how *not* to act. You might think of this book as a cross between a survival manual and a leadership primer.

By now you're probably bordering on depression as I have painted a pretty rough picture of the American workplace. While this book only begins the focus on how to change the workplace, I want to be clear that I do believe it can change. It will take people like you, who hopefully become inspired by this book, who are mad as hell and don't want to take it any longer. It's up to you to set out with a different mindset—one that refuses to partake in, or tolerate the bad behaviors. In his book *The Gifted Boss: How to Find, Create and Keep Great Employees*, Dale Dauten reminds us, "You can't get to better without going through different."[37]

I don't pretend to have concrete answers as to how to fend off all forms of workplace rudeness, selfishness, idiocy, and psychological abuse, but hopefully this book will help you to recognize the behaviors, identify them as they unfold, see them for what they are, and help you prepare yourself to cope with them without losing your cool and your mind.

The behaviors you'll experience in the typical workplace will punish you and have a compounding negative effect on your self-esteem as you go through your career. Victor Kiam, entrepreneur and the owner of the New England Patriots football team from 1988-1991 puts it in perspective, "If a punishing work environment is a prerequisite to success in your particular field then my advice is that you're in a game not worth winning."[38]

The book smarts you'll acquire in college and MBA curricula won't help prepare you for what you'll face. In fact, as marketing guru Seth Godin[39] points out, the curriculum isn't even the prime motivation for someone to go to business school. He believes there are basically three reasons. First, he says, "It serves as a screen for potential future employers to pick the candidates they want to hire." And as we'll learn later, most companies are college snobs only wanting to hire the candidates who have attended the prestigious schools (or the school that the head sociopath attended). Students know this and believe that just by attending one of these schools they're guaranteed a good job.

The second reason is so that "the student can establish a network of associates that they can then rely on to help find a job." That and LinkedIn and you're all set.

Last, the prospective students look at "the curriculum and what skills it will offer them." Interesting isn't it, that the last thing people care about is what they can learn.

Leadership books don't help you either. I've read a lot of leadership books and have found that none of them will prepare you for what you'll experience once out in the workforce. I do, however, think that you should read some of the more classic leadership books out there (certainly any book on Servant Leadership), as there are many valuable tips that can help you along your career path.

Your life outside work won't help you either. That's assuming that whatever job, or occupation, you pick will actually let you have time for an outside life. You must face the fact that nothing (except this book) is going to prepare you for what you'll experience in the workplace on an everyday basis.

If you let it, the bad behavior that permeates the workplace will ultimately make you believe it's justifiable and convince you that you must adopt these tactics if you're to get ahead. We are pressured to fold and act like "them" constantly throughout life, and nothing is more influential to this end than the media.

In his September 2010 *Financial Times* article "The Hollywood Boss is No Work of Fiction," Philip Delves Broughton talks about the role-models that the media and real life immortalize. "In *Money Never Sleeps*, the sequel to *Wall Street*, Gordon Gekko tells us that "idealism' kills deals." It's the most pungent line in the film, and a bracing rejoinder to anyone who argues that business is about doing well by being good. In fact, the whole film, like the original, is a perverse homage to appalling behavior.

Broughton says, "But whereas Gekko is fictional, Mark Zuckerberg, the founder of Facebook, is what the all too real central character in *The Social Network*, is not. Mr. Zuckerberg is portrayed as ambitious, a reasonable trait in the founder of a start-up, but also as vengeful, vicious, duplicitous and devoid of even the most basic social skills.

"It is a story we've seen before among the technology greats of the past thirty years. The young Bill Gates, by most accounts, was a similar kind of night-mare, screaming at his staff and elbowing aggressively past rivals as he built Microsoft. When he founded Apple, Steve Jobs was said to push developers to work ungodly hours and to treat both colleagues and competitors with contempt.

"And yet how much of this makes it into the management books? Where is the guru who tells us that the way to get the most out of an organization is to ratchet up the pressure until everyone is desperate and frazzled and then to run psychological rings around them; that to succeed on the epic scale of a Zuckerberg, Gates, or Jobs may require some deeply unpalatable traits?"[40]

To my knowledge there are no leadership books that preach that type behavior as the way to succeed, except for maybe Stanley Bing's highly entertaining book; *What Would Machiavelli do?: The Ends Justify the Meanness*.[41] There are also not any books that prepare you for the emotional abuse that you'll experience in today's typical workplace.

This book is meant to fill that gap.

You can tell yourself you won't get sucked into the madness. All you'll need is skill in your particular field and you can be successful. However, in the September 2010 *Financial Times* article "A Manager's Guide to Obtaining Power that Fails to Match Machiavelli," Morgan Wetzel points out, "Skill does not necessarily have anything to do with being exceptionally knowledgeable or good at one's job. Skill lies in knowing about the levers of power; where they are, how to pull them, and what to do next."[42] Unless you realize that everyone is motivated by power, you'll be relegated to being just a frustrated individual contributor spending your career in hopeless mediocrity. As Ralph Waldo Emerson points out, "Power to him who power exerts."[43]

Morgan Wetzel also cautions us, "If you do not take power over your life, then someone else will. It is up to you to protect your own life, your career, your future; no one else will do it for you."[44]

I don't want to be too hard on leadership books. They'll teach you sound theories and management approaches that can make you a success in leading people; however, getting the opportunity to exercise these theories will be your challenge. You'll find this especially true the higher on the corporate ladder you go. At the senior levels, it truly is a war motivated only by greed, power, and selfish needs and desires.

Expecting to get useful step-by-step instructions from leadership books is, as Oscar Wilde so humorously noted, "Like learning to play the bagpipes; it will sound exactly the same when you're finished as when you started."[45] None of them will result in your being kissed by the muse.

The typical workplace environment will try to stymie you at every turn. The sociopaths will mock you and the bullies will target you because they quickly label everyone who is a threat to their fragile, false persona.

I liken the atmosphere to that of professional wrestling. Have you ever watched one of these absurd contests closely? There's always one contestant who represents good, and one evil. The bad guy never gets punished even for gross violations of the rules, while everything the good guy does is a violation. That's the way it is in an organization led by sociopaths. Have you ever heard the term, "no good deed goes unpunished?" I've heard this sentiment throughout my career, always in a joking context; however, we all know that under the guise of humor there's always truth.

Business life is a virtual war that unfolds every day in every workplace. This stands to reason why a book like *The Art of War* by Sun Tzu is fast becoming the consummate leadership book of the twenty-first century. The Chinese military general Sun Tzu wrote this treatise in roughly 500 B.C. yet its principles are believed to be as relevant today as they were then, and its growth in followers proves that war is the true reality of the workplace and everyone needs to be prepared.

Personally I believe the real management book for the coming century should be the book by Stanley Bing, *Sun Tzu Was a Sissy, Conquer Your Enemies, Promote Your Friends, and Wage the Real Art of War.* As Stanley Bing so perfectly notes, "Why Sun Tzu is appealing to people is a mystery, because his stuff is about as easy to understand as one of those instruction manuals they give you when you buy any product from eastern Europe."[46]

What's really going on in today's workplace is what Bing describes as your typical guerrilla war. "Snipers to the left of you; spies to the right; it's hard to tell friend from foe. The killing has gone on for years; so long in fact that it's hard to remember why the guys in sales want to kill everybody in marketing. Not enough people are destroyed on a day-to-day basis to warrant a white flag or a treaty on either side, but peace just never seems to come."[47]

I do agree with Sun Tzu's quote that business, just like war, "is a matter of life and death, a road either to safety or to ruin."[48] That may sound harsh, but in reality the sociopaths, bullies and, yes, those normal looking co-workers you think are your friends, can and will make or break your career. They'll instill in you frustration, fear, anger, and downright amazement at the shenanigans that they perpetuate in the name of doing their job and trying to get ahead.

Being prepared to identify and combat the events and situations as they unfold is the purpose of this book; for when you can see events for what they truly are beforehand, it always becomes much easier to combat them and rise above each situation to maintain your sanity while everyone else is losing theirs. As Sun Tzu says, "The clever combatant imposes his will on the enemy, but does not allow the enemy's will to be imposed on him."[10]

But you say, "I won't let that type of behavior affect me." Go ahead, be an optimist; but there's a fine line between optimism and pessimism. In today's business world an optimist is someone who brings his lunch to work and a pessimist is someone who also leaves his engine running.

Getting out with your sanity and self-esteem in place will be your modus operandi for each day at work. Despite your efforts, you're still going to have to accept the fact that some days you'll be the pigeon and some days you'll be the statue.

My hope is that this book will take the reader on a journey that's thought provoking, while exposing how strangely humorous the behaviors exhibited in business really are. For those of you who have been around the block already and will probably identify with what you'll read, get ready for some serious déjà vu moments. Enjoy!

However, before we get started, I'd like to share one of my all-time favorite Dilbert comic[49] which exemplifies exactly how you'll feel when working in a dysfunctional organization.

As W.C. Fields once said, "Start every day with a smile and get it over with." And remember as Albert Schweitzer notes, in the end "happiness is nothing more than good health and a bad memory."[50]

From here on, I'll be your Virgil guiding you on a journey through the damnable places.

CHAPTER 2 KAYFABE

THE MAVERICK THINKER R. EARL HADADY SO accurately pointed out once that, "The facts are unimportant! It's what they are perceived to be that determines the course of events."[51]

In Plato's *The Allegory of the Cave*,[52] Socrates describes a group of people who have lived chained in a cave all of their lives, facing a blank wall. The people watch shadows projected on the wall by things passing in front of a fire behind them, and they begin to ascribe forms and meaning to these shadows. According to Socrates, the shadows are as close as the prisoners get to viewing reality.

It's written as a fictional dialogue between Plato's teacher Socrates and Plato's brother Glaucon. In the story, Socrates explains that the prisoners ultimately take the shadows to be real things, not just reflections, and the echoes they hear to be real sounds. The whole of their existence depends on these shadows on the wall.

Little did Plato know, that over two millennia ago he was describing a phenomenon that's common place in the modern workplace—the widely accepted fact that perception is more important than fact. For those poor souls chained in Plato's metaphorical cave, the shadows they saw became their reality, the lens through which they viewed their world. In much the same way, people in the workplace develop their own lens through which they view everything around them and more importantly how they view themselves and their colleagues.

In his book *Images of Organization*, Gareth Morgan tells us, "Reality has a tendency to reveal itself in accordance with the perspectives through which it is approached. We learn that what unfolds in an organization is a reflection of what is in people's minds."[53]

There's a more modern example of this phenomenon called "The Rashomon Effect." *Rashomon* is a 1950 Japanese crime mystery film that exemplifies the effect of the subjectivity of perception on recollection, and therefore reality, emphasizing the subjectivity of what is the truth when seen through the eyes of different people.

The movie unfolds in flashback shortly after a crime is committed on a couple in which the husband, a Japanese nobleman, is murdered and his wife is raped. There are four individuals—the perpetrator, the wife, the murdered husband, and a nameless observer—that witness the horrific crime. Each then recounts the crime with absolute honesty; however, in mutually contradictory ways. The viewer is left wondering which of the four witnesses is telling the truth.

In *The Allegory of the Cave* the captives don't see reality; they only see shadows of what's real, and from this they must fashion what they believe reality to be. It's completely understandable that these poor souls can't distinguish between reality and fantasy. However, in contrast, in *Rashomon* the characters actually are witness to reality, yet they still form a different perception of what reality is. In both cases the participants only perceived what they thought was real.

It's this capacity for people to produce substantially different but equally plausible accounts of shared events that this chapter is all about. People's perceptions of reality become more important than the truth. Specifically, we'll look at how people actively try, and more often than not, accomplish, manipulating the perceptions of those around them for their own selfish purposes.

The subjectivity of perception and how it leads to organizational delusion, and how things are not always what they seem to be, isn't a phenomenon relegated only to the top rungs of the organization. Delusions are created in the minds of everyone within the organization. That's because everyone becomes a player in this game of manipulating each other for their own gain, for the purpose of presenting themselves and the organization as something they are not.

It's a bit like the stagecraft of professional wrestling where the wrestlers assume different ring personas. During the entire performance and in public appearances, they stay in character to maintain the feeling for the fans that the professional wrestling world is reality. It's basically the same phenomenon happening in the average workplace. This delusional state, if you will, is called kayfabe. It's a term that apparently derived from carnival talk for "keep secret." It refers to the practice of maintaining the personas and the illusion that wrestling is 100 percent genuine.

Those same illusions exist in the workplace. It's what keeps the people who slave their lives away, at go nowhere jobs, believing that what they do has purpose. It doesn't just stop there, though. The collective consciousness of the organization as a whole actually has fundamental delusions about itself and how it fits into the larger scheme of the business world. This organization-wide delusion becomes part of the culture, the glue that binds the inhabitants together as they haphazardly work toward the organization's goals.

I guess we all intuitively know that people can be delusional, but how do organizations practice delusion? One of the most common ways for an organization to delude itself is though the phenomenon of "The Halo Effect," a term coined by Philip M. Rosenzweig in his 2007 book[54] by the same name.

"The Halo Effect" refers to the cognitive bias, of the members of an organization, through which their overall perception of their company is framed by a single good quality. For example, people will make a positive judgment of an organization's overall well-being, e.g., their level of customer service, or the quality of their products—even their quality of leadership—solely because of good financial performance (share price, revenue, or profitability). The Halo Effect is definitely alive and well in business; however, it is just the beginning in understanding the delusions that pervade the modern workplace. One of my favorite songs, *What a Fool Believes*, by Michael McDonald and Kenny Loggins says it all in the refrain.

What a fool believes, he sees.

No wise man has the power to reason away.

What seems to be is always better than nothing.[55]

In truth, we know that perception shouldn't be more important than fact; however, it is when viewed from the perspective of the people in the workplace. In this chapter we'll explore why perception becomes their only basis for reality.

Perceptions about events—like The Rashomon Effect—are one thing, but unfortunately, that's not where our perceptions stop affecting our lives. Our perceptions of other people around us can and do dramatically shape our self-concept, self-esteem and our own perception of ourselves. We all embark on a pursuit of happiness—we must meet a standard of success that we've set for ourselves. Additionally, we want everyone around us, our co-workers, friends, and our family to believe we're successful. The reality is that all of us are aspiring to meet a self-conceived image that's probably unattainable. No wonder there's so much frustration and unhappiness that ultimately leads to the incivility we witness in the world.

The real problem with our self-perception is that for most of us we define ourselves only through our career. Most will tell you that they value happiness as the criteria for success, and if they could focus more on achieving happiness, life would be a lot more enjoyable. Unfortunately, most, when asked to define their version of happiness, come full circle and focus on their career. They believe, "If I only get that raise, or that promotion, or that new job, then I'll be happy." Unfortunately, as we'll discover, our measure of success and happiness may be mutually exclusive of the reality of today's workplace.

For most of us our careers even start out under a shroud of deception—not just the lies we tell ourselves to bolster our self-esteem but the lies others tell us. It starts with our first job, whether flipping burgers, or at a professional career level. It starts in the interview process long before we even get the job.

For example, a guy comes home after a couple weeks at his new job, and his wife notices that he's not very happy. His wife asks what's wrong. He tells her that the job is hell, people backstab, belittle, plot, and lie and he's sick of all the games. He hates it. It isn't what he expected. It isn't how they presented themselves during the interview.

She asks, "Well, didn't you ask the right questions at the interview?"

He says, "Yes, but they lied!"

Unfortunately, there's a lot of truth in that made-up story. Lies are a fundamental building block of the modern workplace. As the above example shows, the easiest way to create the image we want for ourselves, or our company, is unfortunately, to perpetuate lies. In this case it's the lies the interviewer(s) told this poor candidate.

Since lies are such a fundamental way in which people manipulate their reality, let's take a close look at them. We start with what's called the "little white lie." In his May 2007 article "Workplace Deception: Paying a Potential High Price," Conner O'Seanery tells us, "They are among the most frequent illusions we encounter at work and are probably the least destructive. In fact, they are crucial for helping any workforce function smoothly." They're inseparable with the culture and politics of the organization. Let's face it, if everyone was completely in tune with reality, life would probably be chaos and we'd all be on anti-depressants. These little white lies tend to serve to spoon-feed us reality because many times it's best we don't know the whole truth.

We even lie to ourselves. When in a crappy job, in which we feel trapped, we tend to rationalize all our negative feelings to be able to cope with the reality of our predicament. This is called "cognitive dissonance," and we all have experienced and practiced it at one time or another.

In his book *What Got You Here Won't Get You There: How Successful People Become Even More Successful*, Marshall Goldsmith provides us with the best definition of cognitive dissonance. "Cognitive dissonance is an uncomfortable feeling caused by holding conflicting ideas simultaneously. The theory of cognitive dissonance proposes that people have a motivational drive to reduce dissonance. They do this by changing their attitudes, beliefs, and actions. Dissonance is also reduced by justifying, blaming, and denying. It is one of the most influential and extensively studied theories in social psychology."

This means that when faced with being in a challenging work environment, we make excuses to justify our inability to face reality. We find some good reason to stick it out and turn the other cheek. We remind ourselves that the pay is good or worse yet, convince ourselves that we need this job because the economy is bad, we're too old to find another job, or we like the people we work with. In this way lies become a foundation of our entire workplace existence.

Conner O'Seanery adds, "We also spread lies to boost our appeal and likeability. The majority of employees in any workplace want to be liked, and lies can do for their personality what joint compound and a can of paint can do for a boring wall: smooth over the defects and create an attractive finish. Appeal-boosting lies tend to be minimally destructive, unless taken to the extreme. Inside every office there lurks one employee who takes it too far. This individual's DayGlo gloss colors every aspect of his being, making it impossible to see him in an honest light."[58]

Lies are just one technique we use to diminish the cognitive dissonance we feel and to try to set ourselves above our reality. The now famous quote by Alison Boulter should bring us back to earth however, "Remember you're unique just like everyone else."[59] Everybody is telling themselves the same lies to get through the day.

Most lies are relatively innocuous; however, the most sinister lies are those that have an ulterior motive behind them. The most common are lies to avoid negative consequences. As we'll see, modern business culture perpetuates the need for these types of lies. Why do we lie? Conner O'Seanery hits the nail on the head "as children, we learn that lies can get us out of trouble, and we carry this comforting knowledge into adulthood."

Close cousins of this type lie are those told to gain an advantage or for personal gain. Again Conner O'Seanery provides us the necessary insight. "Lies for personal gain help boost our standing among the rank and file. They can be used to gain the right kind of attention for ourselves and draw the wrong kind of attention toward others."[60]

Seventeenth century French author Francois de la Rochefoucauld points out another facet of the lying we use to bolster the image that we aspire for ourselves. "We'll even confess our 'little' faults to persuade others that we have no 'large' ones."[61]

Conner O'Seanery warns us, "One of the most frightening aspects of deception is the imperative it creates for more deception. In the workplace, this exponential growth can create an environment in which everyone and everything they do is suspect."[62]

All of these deception methods are perpetuated on a daily basis in business just as in our personal lives. However, one of the most frightening and sinister aspects of deception that plays out in today's workplace are the lies that we create to torpedo our co-workers. It's ironic in a way that the organizations in which this behavior is the most prevalent are most likely to complain that they need more teamwork. The fact is, above all others, this is the behavior least likely to foster teamwork. Unlike the lies to avoid negative consequences, or for personal gain, the practice of lying to impeach co-workers proves to grow exponentially because it's the one lie that requires the impeached to retaliate in kind.

George Orwell said, "In this age of universal deceit, telling the truth is a revolutionary act."[63] Remember the old adage: If you tell the truth, you don't have to remember anything. Few people follow that advice.

Despite all the lying, I'm not so sure it's the most damaging behavior. I'm convinced that people in the workplace just plain bullshit more than lie. I'm so convinced of this that I'll attempt to prove my point. Let's take a closer look at the art of bullshitting, how it compares to lying, and the effect it has on the workplace.

Dictionary.com defines a lie as: a false statement made with deliberate intent to deceive; an intentional untruth; a falsehood; something intended or serving to convey a false impression; imposture; an inaccurate or false statement; the charge or accusation of lying.

In contrast, the dictionary.com definition of bullshit is: foolish, deceitful, or boastful language; something worthless, or insincere; insolent talk or behavior; to speak foolishly; to engage in idle conversation.

Why do I think the average worker partakes more in bullshitting than flat-out lying? First, understand that most people use these two terms interchangeably to describe the typical behavior they see and practice in the workplace. However, when we look closer at the definitions, the difference stands out.

In the definition of lying, the word "false" appears numerous times, yet in the definition of bullshit, it doesn't appear at all. Since a falsehood is defined as an untruth, a lie is therefore the telling of an untruth. On the other hand bullshitting is boastful, worthless, insincere language. There's a big difference. Boastful, worthless, insincere language doesn't necessarily equate to an untruth.

In his essay, "On Bullshit," philosopher Harry Frankfurt presents a very detailed contrast of these two concepts. Frankfurt postulates that the liar, "to tell a lie; in order to invent a lie at all, must think he knows the truth."[64] That's an important point. The liar knows, or thinks he knows, the truth, and then consciously elects to present the opposite.

Interestingly, according to Frankfurt, "a person may be lying even if the statement he makes is false, as long as he himself believes that the statement is true and intends, by making it, to deceive. It is impossible for someone to lie unless he thinks he knows the truth. Producing bullshit requires no such condition." The key is the intent to deceive that's associated with the lie.

While both lies and bullshit can either be true or false, bullshitters aim primarily to impress and persuade their audiences, and in general are unconcerned with the truth or falsehood of their statements. As Frankfurt notes, "this indifference to how things are is the essence of bullshit."

To me, it seems that bullshitting will better serve our purposes, especially when we want to change another's perceptions of us.

Why is my diatribe on bullshit important? Because, as Frankfurt explains, "bullshitting one's way through [life]; not merely producing one instance of bullshit, [but] producing bullshit to whatever extent the circumstances require" is common behavior.

People become masters at this "art," and it proliferates throughout the workplace because "the risk of being caught is about the same in each case; [however] the consequences of being caught are generally less severe for the bullshitter than for the liar."[65]

Frankfurt explains, "bull pertains to tasks that are pointless in that they have nothing much to do with the primary intent or justifying purpose of the enterprise which requires them." In other words they contribute nothing toward the general goals of the organization.

In this way the bullshit flung around the workplace creates an environment that's not based in reality. Frankfurt explains it best: "The contemporary proliferation of bullshit has deeper sources; in various forms of skepticism which deny that we can have any reliable access to an objective reality and which therefore [we] reject the possibility of knowing how things truly are. Convinced that reality has no inherent nature, which [the worker] might hope to identify as the truth about things, [the worker] devotes himself to being true to his own nature."[66]

Because there's so much bullshit flying around the workplace, it clouds reality, and as such, people can't trust their reality and thus become focused only on being true to their own nature. It then becomes the motivation for someone to bullshit in retaliation, thus perpetuating the bullshit syndrome that has overtaken the average workplace. Bullshitting thus becomes one way in which people practice what's called "impression management," since the only thing they can truly control (or so they think) is their own image. We'll learn more about impression management techniques later.

Bullshit becomes the primary factor in defining an organization and molding the culture. In fact, one might say that bullshit is the fuel that powers the engine of business. For this reason, Frankfurt claims, "Bullshit is a greater enemy of the truth than lies are."

In 1928, sociologist W. I. Thomas formulated a theory of sociology called the Thomas Theorem. Simply stated, it says that if men define situations as real, they are real in their consequences. Said another way, if men define their reality through bullshit, then their reality becomes bullshit. This has also been referred to as the "self-fulfilling prophesy."

According to the Thomas Theorem, the interpretation or creation of a situation causes the action. This interpretation need not have any objective foundation, as actions can be and are affected by even subjective perceptions. Thomas stated more precisely that, "Any definition of a situation will influence the present."[67] Not only that, but he claims that after being subjected to a series of these false situations–i.e., bullshit–an individual will gradually change his whole life-policy and even his personality.

This has also been described as "The Tinkerbell Effect," in which there are things (reality) that exist only because people believe in them. Remember in the play *Peter Pan*, Tinker Bell cheats death solely by the audience's belief in fairies. They are thereby successful at restoring Tinkerbell to life. Thus, we hope that if we believe in something hard enough, and with enough passion, it will come true.

A self-fulfilling prophecy is a prediction that directly or indirectly causes something to become true. This is due to the positive feedback loop between belief and behavior. It was twentieth century sociologist Robert K. Merton who is credited with coining the expression "self-fulfilling prophecy" and formalizing its structure and consequences.

According to Merton, in his book *Social Theory and Social Structure*, "[T]he self-fulfilling prophecy is, in the beginning, a false definition of the situation evoking a new behavior which makes the original false conception come true."[68] This means that a prophecy (a statement) that's flaunted to be true–even if, in fact, false–will influence people such that their reactions to this statement will, in the end, make the statement come true. That also applies to the reaction to bullshit. This manipulation of reality is then further perpetuated because the soothsayer of the prophecy will always point out the fact that because the events actually happened, it's proof that he was right.

All the lying, bullshitting, and posturing that go on in the modern workplace serves but one purpose: to try to manage the impression, or perception, that others have of us. We're hoping for our own personal self-fulfilling prophesy, in essence. In sociology and social psychology this is called "impression management."

Impression management is a goal-directed, conscious or unconscious, process in which people attempt to influence the perceptions that other people have about them. They do so by regulating and controlling information, by lying and bullshitting, in their social interaction with other people.

No discussion about impression management would be complete without acknowledging the latest fad buzz word floating around: Personal Branding.

There's been a lot of talk in the last few years about personal branding. It seems everyone is being made to believe it's now a necessity of life to have your own personal brand–a unique and distinguishable appearance, clothing, knowledge,

speech, writing, or behavior–you name it. However, through impression management, people have been actively trying to manipulate what others think of them
since the beginning of mankind. Now we have just another fancy name for it.

In the end, the result of all the impression management we do results in our
personal brand. Everyone has a personal brand, whether they like it not. That's
because people can't stop labeling others; its normal human behavior, and it happens automatically. Our brains are wired this way. We recognize patterns of behavior and then form associations, or stereotypes–i.e. labels–for people based on our
experiences and beliefs. These labels become part of the person's personal brand.
Sometimes all it takes is the first meeting with someone and you're branded for life.
Supposedly just three seconds are sufficient to make a conclusion about someone
you're meeting for the first time.

Some people stumble upon their brand. Others deliberately target a specific type
of image they want for themselves. The game is to get people to label you in the
way you want. For a sociopath, his personal brand is his avatar, and it's his all-
consuming ambition.

People build their brand though impression management; they try to regulate as
best they can the external brand they want for themselves. This is where the role-
playing, lying, and general bullshitting come into play. The higher up the totem
pole, the more intense this becomes.

Those who actively market themselves to build a brand may, in the end, be disappointed that they didn't get the results they set to achieve. For example, a sociopath may actively try to market himself as a servant leader. The problem is that the
innate sociopathic behaviors always shine through. People have probably already
labeled him a sociopath anyway–remember, it only takes three seconds. If you
pay close attention to a sociopath when in public settings, you can identify when
they're trying to posture themselves to be something they're not. It becomes actually quite entertaining.

Whether we call it impression management or personal branding, the key element for people is whether their internal personal brand (what they think of themselves) matches their external personal brand (what others think of them). I guess if your internal brand is stronger (you think higher of yourself than others think of you), you might tend toward sociopathic behavior, but if your external brand is stronger, you just might be leadership material.

There's also a big difference between reputation and personal brand. Reputation is built upon your track record, good or bad. A brand is nothing more than the bullshit flung to see what sticks. People can have brand without reputation. Reputation is all about walking the walk versus talking the talk. I personally feel focusing on building a good reputation should take center stage.

Despite all the posturing to create the image in which we want others to view us, it most likely falls on deaf ears anyway, as the people we're trying to impress probably aren't paying that close attention. They're so preoccupied with themselves that they really don't have time to care about the façade we're trying to fabricate. The author Anaïs Nin said it perfectly: "We don't see things as they are; we see things as we are."[69] Despite that, impression management continues to play out every day in the workplace as most people go through their entire work day focused (consciously or unconsciously) on trying to manage the impression they have on their fellow workers.

To be successful at impression management, or personal branding, and control the perceptions that others have of us, we must develop our own self-presentation methods and techniques. Common self-presentation, or really preservation and self-defense, methods include attacking and plotting against peers and other tactics we'll learn about later.

Tolstoy once said: "A man is like a fraction whose numerator is what he is, and whose denominator is what he thinks of himself or wants others to think he is; the larger the denominator; the smaller the fraction."[70] Unfortunately because it's common practice for most people to try to enhance what other people think of them, they keep making their denominator (ego) larger. This is why ego becomes such a significant player in the behaviors that dominate the workplace.

The big problem with impression management is that it attempts to present people how they desire to be viewed, rather than in an authentic or genuine manner. I'm convinced that people who truly are genuine are a dying breed. Samuel Johnson, the author of one of the first English language dictionaries (~circa 1755) described this best. "Almost every man wastes part of his life attempting to display qualities which he does not possess and to gain applause which he cannot keep."[71]

I've only known a handful of people whom I could describe as being genuine because most people probably don't even know what it means to be genuine. People who are genuine are real or authentic, free from deceit and they sincerely feel for others and can express themselves honestly. We may fool others (through role playing) into thinking we're something other than what we truly are, but most often we're dealing in self-deceit. Most of us forget Shakespeare's famous line from *Hamlet*, "To thine own self be true."[72] As author Nathaniel Hawthorne said, "No man, for any considerable period, can wear one face to himself, and another to the multitude, without finally getting bewildered as to which may be true."[73]

Role-playing isn't just a game played by kids on the playground; adults play it all the time in the workplace. Most people don't even realize they're doing it because it's carried out at the subconscious level. When people role play they participate in what's called The Drama Triangle. The Drama Triangle,[74] developed by Dr. Stephen Karpman, is a transactional analysis model describing a social model for human interaction. It is a model used in both psychology and psychotherapy.

The model posits three habitual psychological roles (or role-plays) which people often take:

- Persecutor; the person who pressures, coerces or persecutes a victim

- Rescuer; the person who intervenes out of an ostensible wish to help the situation, or the underdog
- Victim; the person who's treated as, or accepts the role of, a victim

Dr. Karpman postulates that these roles form a triangle through which we move back and forth during our interaction with others.

Lynne Forest, in her 2008 article "The Three Faces of Victim, An Overview of the Drama Triangle" explains it best: "Whether we know it, or not, most of us react to life as victims. Whenever we refuse to take responsibility for ourselves, we are unconsciously choosing to react as victim. This inevitably creates feelings of anger, fear, guilt, or inadequacy and leaves us feeling betrayed, or taken advantage of by others.

"No matter where we may start out in the triangle, victim is where we end up; therefore, no matter what role we're in, we're in victimhood. If we're on the triangle we're living as victims, plain and simple!

"Each person has a primary or most familiar role; what is called their 'starting gate' position. This is the place from which they generally enter, or 'get hooked' onto, the triangle. We first learn our starting gate position in our family of origin. Although we each have a role with which we most identify, once we're in the triangle, we automatically rotate through all the positions, going completely around the roles, sometimes in a matter of minutes, or even seconds, many times every day.

"Our starting-gate position is not only where we most often enter the triangle, it's also the role through which we actually define ourselves. It becomes a strong part of our identity. Each starting-gate position has its own particular way of seeing and reacting to the world.

"We all have unconscious core beliefs acquired in childhood, derived from our interpretation of early family encounters. These become 'life themes' that predispose us toward the unconscious selection of a particular starting gate position on the triangle.

"In reality, how others see us is not our concern. How we see ourselves is what can bring us transformation. Our challenge is to stay in touch with our true self and allow others the right (and they do have the right) to have their view of us. The two versions—your view and their view—do not have to match for you to be happy. That's a common, but mistaken, idea."[75]

We talked earlier about lying, but only in the sense of people lying to each other. But organizations also lie to themselves, albeit in a more metaphorical sense. This is because, for organizations, the lying, or bullshitting, practiced by the inhabitants has made itself an integral part of the company's culture—The Halo Effect in action.

This self-deception displays itself in the differing levels of either the fantasy or reality state in which an organization resides. Fantasy is where most organizations perceive their reality to be, while true reality is the state in which the company actually resides, yet may refuse to recognize. Fantasy becomes a mask so the corporation can hide from its reality.

In his January 2009 article "Perception v. Reality in the Business World," Ken McCoy talks about the fantasy or reality states that can be found in the modern workplace. While he details their many levels, I will focus on the extremes. However, remember, there are probably an infinite number of fantasy and reality levels in between.

At one end of the spectrum is the state of fantasy in which the organization's management simply refuses to accept any problematic events, especially if those events disagree with the perception they strive for—which is that those issues don't exist. For this kind of company, success may become more luck than effective strategy.

At the other end of the fantasy spectrum is one in which the inhabitants are conscious of their problems, i.e., they realize they're not perfect and to compensate they become overly process-, procedure-, and data-conscious. In this fantasy state there's a preoccupation with metrics in the form of charts, graphs, or presentations that appear to support management's view. However, this organization will use the data as Andrew Lange so humorously notes; "as drunkards use lampposts; more for support than illumination."[76] The bottom line is as Albert Einstein reminds us; "Not everything that can be counted counts and not everything that counts can be counted."[77]

Because most modern workplace organizations dally in that world of actually acknowledging they have problems, the whole metrics fad has become epidemic. In the next chapter we're going to take a close look at metrics and the other myriad fad management techniques that have graced the workplace over the past few decades.

In either of these fantasy states, the result is the inability of the management team to accept anything that doesn't support their self-perceived view of their organization, and not much is ever achieved to make the organization better. The metrics they collect serve as nothing more than an attempt to convince themselves they are striving to be better at what they do.

In contrast to fantasy, we have two ends of the spectrum in the world of reality. The first is the one where employees know the place is screwed up, but are either too afraid to do or say anything, or are tired of beating their heads against the wall and being blamed for things they didn't do. This seems to be where the vast majority of organizations flirt.

At the other end of the reality spectrum, we find what most people might consider true, ethical business behavior. However it may be much rarer than we care to believe. Ironically, this is the only organization that doesn't need to practice self-deception. This is the type organization that most of us will spend our entire career looking for—the one that is able not only to admit to mistakes, address questions, issues, and problems truthfully, but acts like a team with a common purpose. Personally I'm convinced they don't exist.

Ken McCoy leaves us with a challenge, "So look around your place of business. Are they using fantasy or reality levels? I think you'll find many businesses now operate in one of the fantasy levels since it's so much easier than actually doing the work. I think in some cases the Fantasy levels are used because the managers simply don't have the skills to actually accomplish their expected tasks."[78]

In *The Power of Stupidity*, Giancarlo Livraghi provides another insightful look. "[All of us] know that the Earth is round. But our daily perceptions tell us that it's flat. We know that the horizon is limited; we need to climb higher to see farther away. But, too often, we forget to do so in the perspectives of thought and curiosity. We remain confined, without even realizing it, in the restricted sphere of our point of view and our little circle of habits.

"Perception studies indicate that we see things differently not only from the top of a mountain or the bottom of a valley, but also sitting or standing up, or moving a few steps in one direction or another. And the same object, or the same picture, can be understood quite differently depending on how we look at it.

"This isn't just a matter of changing perspective when it's necessary, to free ourselves of shallow conventional perceptions, or to understand someone else's point of view. It is always useful, whatever the subject, to look at it from different angles. It can be intriguing, sometimes surprising, often interesting, to deliberately change perspective.

"It's instinctive, to some extent; unavoidable, sometimes right, to have an 'egocentric' point of view. It is scientifically correct to set the 'center of the visible universe' wherever the observer happens to be. It's obvious that our perceptions are placed at a tiny and ever-changing point of contact between an 'outside' and an 'inside' world. But we need to understand that it's only one of infinite possible perspectives. If we don't learn to expand our horizon, our perceived 'universe' shrinks into a dull mental cubicle of nearsighted boredom."[79]

Depending on where an organization and its employees fall on the spectrum of fantasy or reality, and how they perceive their surroundings, they and their colleagues will mold their environment into the type of culture they desire. Understanding organizational culture is critical to understanding the illusions of stability that every company perpetuates. The organization's culture becomes its true identity, and it sets the stage for all the behaviors, good or bad, that are prevalent. We're going to take an in-depth look at organizational culture in an upcoming chapter, but first we're going to take a look at another realm of fantasy that plagues pretty much all organizations.

As businessman and philanthropist W. Clement Stone said, "Be careful the environment you choose for it will shape you; be careful the friends you choose for you will become like them."[80]

CHAPTER 3 JUMPIN' ON THE BANDWAGON

MOST PEOPLE ARE FAMILIAR WITH THE IDIOM "herd mentality." Sometimes called "crowd wisdom" it refers to how people are influenced by their peers to adopt certain behaviors or follow societal trends. It's a fear-based reaction to peer pressure, which makes individuals act to avoid feeling left behind. It's a term that's been around since the 1800s, when it was first coined by the philosopher Friedrich Nietzsche.

Nietzsche described what he believed were two distinct groups or versions of herd mentality. One was religion-based and the other media-based. It's the media-based version that's pertinent to our discussion. This group includes the poor lost-souls who follow the latest trends or follow what they're told is the right thing to do. Nietzsche believed that both these groups' actions were a form of subservience that found roots in an innate weakness in our human nature. These are the people who religiously jump on the bandwagon whenever some new fad comes along.

Nietzsche also postulated that there was a third group, albeit small, that he called "supermen," because they were able to overcome the pressures of the herd. Unfortunately, there aren't many supermen around in the modern business world.

The phrase "jump on the bandwagon" means to figuratively jump on whatever the latest fad may be, or to succumb to the herd mentality. It was first used in the political arena in the mid-1800s and has been with us since.

Since Nietzsche there's been much behavioral science research on the phenomenon, of "The Bandwagon Effect," and this research demonstrates that it only takes five per cent of the people involved to influence a crowd's direction. The term was first described in the 1950s by Harvard economist Harvey Leibenstein as, "the extent to which the demand for a commodity is increased due to the fact that others are consuming the same commodity."[81]

Colloquially, "The Bandwagon Effect" is defined as; the tendency for people, when presented with a fad or trend that they see others embracing, to adopt it as their own. Witness the growth of social web-sites like Facebook, Twitter and LinkedIn.

As the statistic above shows, all it takes are a few to influence the whole. Thus, as more people come to engage, or believe in something, others will jump on the bandwagon, regardless of whether it's been objectively proven to be worth the time and energy. This need to follow the herd based on the actions or beliefs of others occurs because, people subconsciously want to conform to societal trends and are afraid of being left behind.

As with individuals, it's the same within the collective consciousness of an organization. Companies adopt and engage in whatever fad or trend they see other businesses following. Why? To avoid feeling left behind or (more importantly) to support the fantasy that they are actually being proactive at bettering their organization.

I'm specifically talking about the modern business' obsession with metrics and all the other fads and management trends that have come and gone over the past few decades. These are called, "argumentum ad populum," which refers to a fallacious argument that has been concluded to be true only because many, or most, people believe it. The false logic is that if everyone's doing it, then it must be good.

This obsession revolves around the need for organizations to collect ubiquitous metrics in the interest of hopefully bettering themselves. Somewhere, somehow, someone managed to convince 5 percent of businesses that measuring things ad nauseam was the path to productivity and success. They've been brainwashed into believing that if they just collect the right metrics, or adopt the latest management schema, they'll be kissed by the muse and see the error of their ways and thus be able to improve their efficiency at whatever they do.

We're going to take a better look at the practice of collecting metrics and its close cousin—benchmarking—because we just learned in the previous chapter how organizations can use these to help justify whatever fantasy state they've fabricated for themselves. They're also used pretty extensively in the modern workplace, so they deserve to be understood if for no other reason than to comprehend the uselessness and negative effect they can have on an organization.

In many companies the ritual of collecting metrics is an obsession that most often never leads to any profound improvements in how the organization functions. Processes are quantified and measured, and these metrics are posted for all to see. Organizations have bulletin boards dedicated to their display, and visitors are paraded in front of them to show how "efficient" the organization is. These are the heart of the "continuous improvement" mantra that's typically preached in modern organizations.

The preoccupation with metrics and the latest fad management games is not unlike the cargo cults that developed in remote parts of New Guinea and other Melanesian and Micronesian societies in the southwest Pacific after WW II.

A cargo cult is the religious practice that appeared in these pre-industrial tribes as a result of their interaction with technologically advanced cultures. The Japanese and Allied forces brought in wartime supplies and equipment (cargo) and the tribes became obsessed with obtaining these technologies for themselves.

The tribes used magic and religious ritual to imitate the cargo. The thought was that if they could imitate the cargo, their god would recognize their desires and send to them the actual thing they were worshipping (the cargo).

For example, it was observed that a certain tribe's attempted to construct a radio made of coconuts and straw. An important facet of this cult mentality is that they also imitated behaviors they witnessed. Another tribe was observed marching in formation using rifles made of wood. The irony is that most organizations are doing just that—marching in formation with rifles made of wood.

From an organizational perspective, understanding this mentality is important because an institution mired down in the cargo cult, of collecting metrics and chasing the latest management fads, is actually distracting itself from executing its real and important mission, vision, or goal.

Organizations compile the same metrics that the herd collects, or engage in fads like "quality circles," believing that by doing this, they'll become more efficient, too. That's because the universal mantra in today's typical organization is "increased efficiency." However, it should be "increased effectiveness."

This then becomes the dilemma: Should an organization remain focused on doing things just like everybody else, chasing the elusive goal of increased efficiency, or should it spend its valuable time focusing on being more effective in executing its business plan? Or, as Seth Godin would suggest, "do something remarkable." That being said, we all know the answer. Organizations will continue to follow the herd.

My personal favorites are the quality metrics that measure things like, defects in a product or failures of a product during production, or failures of the product to work once in the hands of the consumer—i.e., customer returns. The interesting thing about these metrics is that if management would just spend more time, energy and resources in the upfront "proactive" work to design a better product, they wouldn't have to measure the effect of their negligence later and then fret about how to "fix" it. Remember what Einstein said; "Not everything that can be counted counts and not everything that counts can be counted."

I've seen virtually hundreds of these metrics in my career. Certainly there's no want for things to measure.

In a way, metrics become a crutch, a way for the organization to delude itself that's it's making progress, so that it can show the world it knows what it's doing—sort of like impression management done at the organizational level.

Metrics are interesting because most often they point right to fundamental flaws in the way the organization carries out its business, yet the company can't or won't see that. It spends enormous amounts of money measuring and tracking product defects and failures, and the associated cost to fix them, yet more often than not will spend little on attempting to put in place preventive measures. This becomes the biggest paradox in modern business: the religious preaching of proactiveness coupled with the useless dedication to measuring things (after the fact) with no intent of acting on the data collected.

I've experienced this over and over in my career. There is never enough time and money committed to prevention by the use of such things as design-to-cost and design for manufacturability, even when it's universally recognized that these are truly proactive activities.

We're going to learn the true meaning of proactive later, but what's interesting is that every one of these organizations knows the most famous metric of all—that it costs much more to fix a problem after it's in the consumer's hands than to have prevented the problem before the product was sold.

This is what's called "hyperbolic discounting." When given the choice to spend money now that won't show rewards until later, or not spend the money and thus keep profits high in the current period, companies will invariably pick the second option. They would rather suffer the expenditure to fix a problem and take a loss in the future than endure an expenditure now that would mitigate the future loss. This is because most management teams can't think past lunch.

Management often believes it can save the upfront costs of being truly proactive because "this time it will be different" and the new product launch won't experience the same problems that its predecessors did. It sounds like a fantasy world to me. It also sounds like organizational insanity which we'll learn about in detail later.

Some companies learn from this lesson, and other companies repeat the short-term savings approach and suffer the same consequences, over and over, yet they never seem to learn. They're effectively lying to themselves. The lying and denying leads to the phenomenon called "organizational amnesia," a condition that plagues organizations everywhere.

"Benchmarking" is another fad phenomenon that some companies dabble with to delude themselves into thinking they own up to their reality. It's right up there with "world-class" and "best practices." In this scheme, the goal is to find out how other companies are doing business, with the intent of comparing themselves, to discover better ways to do things. They then adopt any improvements they might discover. This comparison can be done at the individual process level, the organizational level, or at the individual product design level. Whichever measure, the intent is the same: to learn how everyone else is doing things, so it can be emulated. In other words, so they can jump on the bandwagon.

In his book *Small is the New Big: And 183 Other Riffs, Rants, and Remarkable Business Ideas*, Seth Godin talks about the practice of benchmarking and today's business' obsession with efficiency. He believes that while being efficient at the processes necessary to perform day-to-day business is important, it's more important for an organization to strive to be "remarkable."

As he describes, "In addition to the stress it creates, benchmarking against the universe actually encourages us to be mediocre, to be average, to just do what everyone else is doing. The folks who invented the Mini (or the Hummer for that matter) didn't benchmark their way to the cutting edge. Comparison to other cars would never have brought about these fashionable exceptions.

"What really works is not having every little thing be up to the usual standards. What works is everything being good enough and one or two elements of a product or service being amazing. Instead of benchmarking everything, perhaps we win when we accept the best we can do is the best we can do and then try to find the guts to do one thing that's remarkable."[82]

Metrics, benchmarking, world-class, and best practices are just examples of the fantasy world most organization wallow in. Speaking of fantasy, I remember back in the 1970s when industry was hit with the management fad called "quality circles."

Quality circles were first established in Japan in 1962 and the term was derived from the concept of PDCA (Plan, Do, Check, Act) developed by Dr. W. Edwards Deming. This started the long list of Japan-created methodologies that largely fell flat on their face in the United States. Quality Circles hit the United States hard in the late 1970s & 1980s, followed by "Total Quality Management," or TQM in the 1990s.

When it finally dawned on everyone that all these only attack symptoms, not the underlying problems (which was most likely faulty product design), along came "concurrent engineering." This fad was supposed to attack the design end of the business because making manufacturing more efficient and trying to make the highest quality widget didn't mean a hill of beans if the design was suspect. It still doesn't.

With concurrent engineering, a company's engineering team could supposedly work side by side with the manufacturing team to develop products. In this way the result would be a product that's "producible." This fad didn't work because of a little behavioral problem (and an accounting problem) that nobody took into account: engineering arrogance. Engineers are not going to be told how to design a product by the second-class citizens from the manufacturing floor.

The accounting problem was, as we've seen above, that most organizations weren't ready, or willing, to invest in the practice of being proactive despite their rhetoric. Doing the homework to determine the cost effectiveness of concurrent engineering, you'd think, would be a slam-dunk given all the metrics that most companies compile. However, there is this attitude that companies would much rather spend their money to fix issues than prevent them. This amnesia phenomenon seems to be pervasive in modern organizations and, as such, I've devoted an entire chapter to help understand this infectious plague.

I believe in the concurrent engineering methodology, and it's still around, albeit referred to by other catch-phrases like "produceability" or "design to cost," all under the guise of "new product introduction." However, all these are practiced half-heartedly in most of the organizations with which I'm familiar. Throughout my career the same junk always came out of engineering regardless of the number of concurrent engineering, TQM, or quality circle meetings held or how many half-heartedly conducted produceability studies were performed.

In the 2000s the current fads are "Six-Sigma," and "Lean," and, trust me, they'll both go down in a glorious fizzle because they require teamwork, empowerment, trust, an organization focused on the same overall goals and, of course, the up-front investment. As we've seen so far, those behaviors are only perceived to be real and are not to be found, let alone practiced, in most organizations.

All these fads have, or will, fall out of favor for one reason: Management can't walk the walk, only talk the talk. These fads are just another milestone in what Seth Godin calls, "the relentless race to the bottom."

A final thought on the latest fad movement to hit businesses everywhere: "lean manufacturing." The basic premise of lean is that everything is evaluated as if it were a foregone conclusion that it's wasteful. Anything that's determined to not be of value becomes a target for elimination. In this way processes are streamlined with the intent of increasing efficient use of people and resources.

The concept and methodologies are impeccable, but they'll never universally be adopted because it requires an investment up front in the form of the time for lean teams to conduct their studies and recommend improvements. Also, this only attacks the symptoms of what probably is the real problem–faulty design.

Tragically, what lean really means for most organizations is that management has squeezed (through down-sizing and right-sizing) the headcount so low that there's no other way to describe itself other than lean.

Every company nowadays strives to be certified by the International Organization for Standardization (ISO). This at least gives lip-service to their attempt at effective organization. ISO goes beyond just measuring; it requires a high level of procedural organization. There are many benefits to being certified. The belief is that customers will buy products and services from an ISO-certified organization before they will from one that's not certified. Due to the herd mentality, industry as a whole looks at ISO certification as a badge of acceptance to some perceived elite group. This is akin to calling an action "hot" because it needs to done immediately. Soon everything is labeled hot and as a result nothing is hot.

Everyone somehow believes that if a company is ISO certified that they have their collective act together. However, the thing to remember is that even when you're certified you can still design something that's figuratively (and literally) a piece of shit, then build that piece of shit to the certified processes, yet in the end it's exactly that—a piece of shit. It will still fail once in the hands of the consumer. ISO certification doesn't change that. Just like with lean practices, what ISO certification does do is make sure that every piece of shit produced will be of the same consistent "efficient" quality.

All these are examples of the endless ways for management to delude itself into thinking they're doing the right things to build the business and to continuously improve. Rare will you find organizations that face up to their reality that all the fads in the world won't counteract their bad management, short-term financial perspective, and failure to understand what it really means to be proactive.

As political scientist, economist, sociologist, and psychologist Herbert Simon said, "A wealth of information creates a poverty of attention."[83]

CHAPTER 4 LORD OF THE FLIES

LORD OF THE FLIES **IS A 1954** novel by William Golding about a group of British schoolboys stuck on a deserted island who try to govern themselves with disastrous results. The book portrays their descent into savagery as they're left to themselves far from the structure of modern civilization. Albeit well-educated, the children resort to barbaric behavior as they attempt to live with each other and survive.

The story takes place amid a wartime evacuation in which a plane crashes onto an isolated island with the only survivors being male children below the age of thirteen. Two dominant forces emerge, represented by the two main characters, Ralph and Jack. Ralph is voted chief and convinces the others that their main goal must be maintaining a constant signal fire to lure any passing ship coming near the island. One of the interesting themes of the book is the debilitating effect that corruption has even on good people, which is witnessed by how, by the end of their ordeal, they had all forgot about the need for the signal fire.

In the beginning Ralph means well, but then his obsession with being the top dog overcomes him, and he resorts to bullying to maintain his power. He ultimately fails to conduct himself as a leader, and whatever order he imposed quickly deteriorates.

In contrast to Ralph, Jack has an inherent love of violence. He takes on the role as hunter and eventually becomes a beast like those he's consumed with hunting. Jack epitomizes the worst aspects of human nature when there's no positive societal influence. Like Ralph, Jack appears to be a natural leader; however, unlike Ralph, Jack appeals to all the boy's more innate human instincts. Jack ultimately abandons the group and forms his own group by enlisting most of the boys over to his tribe. Jack's insurrection begins a chain of events that drives the island into chaos.

The central theme of *Lord of the Flies* is the conflict between the two competing drives that exist within all human beings. These are the instinct to want to have order, act peacefully, follow moral standards, and add value for the good of society versus the innate instinct to want to gratify one's own desires and obtain supremacy over others by enforcing one's will on others. It's interesting to note that Ralph starts out as the symbol for goodness, wanting to be a good leader; however, he ultimately falls prey to those innate instincts. Jack starts and remains the symbol of evil. However, in the end both are evil which mirrors how most organizations, however virtuous they start, will devolve into an autocracy.

Lord of the Flies reveals that the human instincts of ego, narcissism, and power are far more fundamental to human nature than any moral or ethical instincts. We are, by nature, evil beings and Golding saw moral behavior as something that civilization forces upon itself rather than being a natural human instinct. That is, the natural tendency of any person or organization leans toward the desire for power rather than the desire for individual equality.

Every modern workplace has this cultural conflict in place, and the evil side will ultimately overtake the inhabitants and drive them toward dysfunction. In this chapter we'll delve into organizational culture to understand how this force manifests itself and affects everyday life in the workplace.

The concept of workplace culture was first defined by Edgar Schein in 1992 in his seminal book *Organizational Culture and Leadership*. His definition included the idea that corporate culture is a philosophy that guides organizational strategy, behavior, and management attitudes. He also posited that organizations also contain various subcultures that are defined by hierarchy, power and/or politics within the organization. Schein further defined workplace culture as consisting of three components: artifacts, espoused values, and basic underlying assumptions.

Artifacts are the organizational structures and processes, while espoused values are those organizational philosophies and beliefs–their core values–that management and the workforce say they practice. Basic underlying assumptions are the real source of organizational behavior and beliefs and are often unconscious perceptions, thoughts, and feelings. All three make up what's called organizational culture.

In his February 2011 *Financial Times* article "Buffett's Exceptional Style of Leadership," Andrew Hill tells us; "Culture, more than rule books, determines how an organization behaves."[84] Thus, the only effective way to understand the behavior dynamics at play in an organization is to first understand its culture.

In his book *Images of Organization*, Gareth Morgan also sets the cultural framework; "When we view organizations as cultures, we see them as mini-societies with their own distinctive values, rituals, ideologies, and beliefs. The fundamental nature of an organization rests as much in its corporate culture as in the more formal organization chart and codes of procedure."[85]

In his 2004 paper "Organizational Culture with Examples of Liar's Poker," Steven P. Borgatti, Management Chair at the University of Kentucky, defines culture as the shared beliefs, values, and norms of a group. It includes;[86]

- Cognitive schemas; scripts and frames that mold our expectations and help us assign meaning and order to the stream of experience

- Shared meanings and perceptions; common interpretations of events

- Prescriptions and preferences; what is the best way to do things; what they want to happen

- Behavioral codes; how to dress, how to act, what kinds of things you can joke about

- Basic values; what is really important; what is evil

- Unmentionables; blacklists

- Myths and legends; stories about the past: Knowledge of the stories identifies you as belonging, and often the stories have hidden points like this is what happens to people who don't follow the rules

- Heroes and heroines
- Emblems, symbols and rituals; objects or procedures that have meaning

In addition to the above, culture is greatly defined by the overall management style of the organization either positive or negative. Is your company's culture positive or negative? It sounds like an easy thing to determine, but if you're not sure, you can tell by asking yourself these questions:

- Is your company a fun place to work?
- Do you look forward to coming to work?
- Are people waiting in line to join your organization or do many of your employees have their résumés on the street?
- Do people trust and respect each other or is mistrust rampant?
- Are layoffs and down-sizing a routine event?
- Is there a high level of stress?
- Is revenue and profit an obsession of management?
- Are revenue and profit on the decline?
- Are customers happy with your product or service?
- Is your customer base on the decline?
- Are many of the games and behaviors that we'll explore in this book played out every day?

Organizational culture becomes the personality of the organization, and the management's style and the atmosphere they create defines the culture more than any other contributing factor. In other words, management sets the overall tone of the organization and thus the culture.

Needless to say, organizations should strive for what is considered a healthy organizational culture in order to increase productivity, growth, effectiveness, and reduce employee turnover and other counterproductive behavior. But what is considered a healthy culture?

A variety of characteristics might describe a healthy culture, including:

- Fair treatment of each employee
- Respect for each employee's contribution to the company
- Employee commitment and enthusiasm for the organization
- Equal opportunity for all employees
- A fair work-life balance
- Strong demonstration of values and ethics
- Strong company leaders
- A strong sense of direction and purpose
- Lower-than-average turnover rates
- Investment in learning, training, and employee knowledge

Good or bad, members of an organization soon come to sense the particular culture of an organization, and new members grow to quickly modify their behavior to fit in. This is why an organization's culture is so hard to change. Even new blood, that identifies that the culture is dysfunctional, will find it hard to influence any change in the entrenched behaviors and beliefs. Thus, to survive they must adapt.

There are different types of cultures, just like there are different types of human personalities, which can be either good or bad. There is much research data available that attempt to categorize the different types of organizational culture. Unfortunately, there are as many competing theories as to the types of culture that exist as there are experts on the subject.

In their 1999 article "Competing Values Framework"[87] K.S. Cameron and R.E. Quinn categorize culture into the following forms:

- Clan culture: known for cohesion, high morale, development of human resource
- Adhocracy culture: known for cutting-edge output, creativity, growth
- Hierarchy culture: known for efficiency, timeliness, smooth functioning
- Market culture: known for market share, goal achievement and beating competitors

All the above seem to describe organizational cultures that appear functional, albeit in their own special way. You might even classify them all as having good qualities—i.e. those that would lead to a successful business. The problem I have with these good descriptions of cultures is they don't reflect the true nature of most workplace cultures. Not all cultures are inherently good (by a long shot).

I know for a fact that there are fundamentally bad cultures out there in today's business. The truth is, even good cultures have their dark side. It's the bad aspects of organizational culture that I want to focus on, because I believe them to be much more prevalent than people might think.

In *Images of Organization*, Gareth Morgan describes one end of the bad spectrum as the "jungle culture." These organizations are ruled by jungle fighters. Morgan tell us, "The jungle fighter is the power hungry manager who experiences life and work as a jungle, where it is eat, or be eaten, and where winners destroy losers."[88] As you can well imagine, this culture likely does not breed good leadership practices and rather than the inhabitants working together to improve the company, politics runs rampant and they fight each other for political turf.

Since financial performance is a driving force in modern business, I want to take a side trip here and focus on maximization of revenue (and profit) and its effect on the culture. Gareth Morgan recognized this as a driving force in molding any organization's culture. "Financial considerations may be allowed to shape the reality of an organization through the routine operation of financial information systems.

Under the influence of these kinds of controls, people or organizational units may be translated into profit centers in nature.

"They can shape the reality of an organization by persuading people that the interpretive lens of financial performance should be given priority in determining the way the organization is to be run."[89]

This financial obsession is the disease from which most modern organizations suffer. In his August 2011 article "Harpagon's Miseries," Giancarlo Livraghi calls this obsession, Harpagon's Syndrome.[90] The syndrome is derived from the main character, Harpagon in the play *L'Avare* (English; *The Miser*), a 1668 five-act satirical comedy by French playwright Molière.

In the play, Harpagon is a wealthy, money-mad old widower. He loves money more than reputation, honor, or virtue, and spends his time watching and guarding over it. It's what destroys his relationships with the world. Fearful of being robbed and killed for his wealth, he buries his money in his garden. As for the real treasures—his children—he marginalizes and dominates them. He deprives them of independence by denying them money.

The best way to describe Harpagon's condition is that he's in such a constant state of fretting about his money that he becomes a tyrant. He commands absolute obedience of those around him and fences in his world to protect himself.

Organizations suffering from Harpagon Syndrome do the same fretting about the financial condition of their business. As we know, modern business is completely motivated by the short-term monetary measures that the market requires of them. I can't blame them, I guess, but what does become a problem is when the harping on financial results affects every other aspect of the organization's day-to-day activities. This is the condition that nurtures the atmosphere that allows all the behaviors we'll discover to exist and thrive, especially the no-surprises mentality.

It's this syndrome that determines whether an organization is being led, or being ruled.

We see parallels in Harpagon's behavior to that of management in a modern organization, the fixation on money being the most obvious. Also, in the way Harpagon treats his children serves as a parallel to how employees are treated. And just as Harpagon withholds money from his children, we see the same behaviors in management, with the tight budgeting and constant search for cost savings.

Livraghi explains Harpagon's Syndrome as "an insidious mixture of fear and mistrust. An initially mild affliction that increases over time, multiplies unreasonable anxiety, tension, and stress that can cause also physical illness, unleashing a vicious circle in which some small doubt grows to become an obsession."[91]

Harpagon's Syndrome probably isn't even recognized as a disease compared to the huge problems that have always been plaguing organizations, but it's nonetheless infectious and spreading. Organizations infected with this condition become unbending in their belief that what they're doing, and the processes and beliefs they have in place guarantees their success. As those processes and beliefs fail to provide the necessary results, Harpagon's Syndrome worsens.

"This syndrome could also be defined as the art of hurting oneself while becoming unpleasant to everyone else, as well as worrying about irrelevant problems while losing sight of those that really need a solution. It also poisons human relations, erodes friendships and affection, destroys trust, and blurs thinking and awareness," says Livraghi.[92] This explains why this condition is so damaging.

It's this financial focus and collective mentality that breeds the jungle environment. However, in today's world this pressure is at work in any organizational culture. In an organization always struggling to make its financial goals Harpagon's Syndrome becomes the disease that could ultimately kill the host. The key is how the members of the organization react to this pressure, which then has a great impact on how the culture evolves.

Back to organizational culture. At the other end of the cultural spectrum, we find what I believe is the most prevalent and sinister example of workplace culture. This is the organization that has a sociopath in the ruling position—not that the jungle culture doesn't—and a team of junior sociopaths who constitute the ruler's courtiers. This extreme culture can be characterized simply as an organization being ruled as a kingdom. If you hang around executive row in any of these organizations, you can literally feel that distinct attitude of omnipotence.

In his 2005 article, *The Kingdom Businesses,*[93] Morris Ruddick details the key to this type culture. He says, "The daily calling for the inhabitants of the kingdom is tied to the throne-room agenda," which is set by the Lord. The courtiers must discern the Lord's agenda as the Lord progressively unveils his wisdom and the steps he thinks are needed to turn his vision into reality. This receiving of the blessing must be accomplished before going about doing their jobs to ensure they don't do anything to bring down upon them the wrath of the Lord.

I find this first-layer of management an interesting breed because they exist in all organizations and culture. These are the organizational sycophants. These courtiers are actually a hold-over from medieval times back when fiefdoms were the norm.

Baldassare Castiglione's *The Book of the Courtier* was published in 1528, yet what's interesting about this work is that it describes perfectly the ilk that usually surrounds the top levels of management in modern organizations.

It serves as sort of a primer for those who wish to become courtiers (sycophants). According to Baldassare, all courtiers must possess a certain *sprezzatura* or the ability to hide what one really desires, feels, thinks, means, or intends. It sounds like the goals of a talented bullshitter.

Sprezzatura apparently was a vital quality for a courtier to have back in the 1500s. Courtiers essentially were practicing impression management on a grand scale to try to create the impression that they were competent. This is interesting when you take into account the Peter Principle. These courtiers had probably reached their level of incompetence; thus the purpose of the sprezzatura was to make him appear to be competent, in control, and a master of himself and his domain, despite the reality. Sprezzatura is also described as being unable to make mistakes or do anything wrong. Later, we'll find how this is a common trait of most top-level management.

Even back in their day, courtiers were reputed as being insincere suck-ups, prone to drama, overly ambitious and lacking any regard for people. Add to that the more sinister part of their duties of acting as the Lord's spies, bringing forward information about the subjects, and you have the model for a modern middle-management sycophant.

I don't think much has changed since the middle ages when it comes to who hangs out with the top levels of management. The courtier's sole duty is to make the boss look good. These jabronis will be looked at in much more detail in a later chapter.

At the middle-management level, the courtier's minions (the junior level of sycophants) also must spend significant time in the presence of the courtiers so that they, too, can progressively obtain wisdom and guidance (marching orders) on the direction to take the organization. The middle managers are then trusted to follow the script and make things happen throughout the organization.

In the modern workplace, the dissemination of these marching orders, to accomplish the organizational vision, usually is proliferated down through the ranks of the organization in the form of staff meetings. Sound familiar? These notorious goat-ropes must be performed by every manager in the organization lest the lowest prole not receive the sacrament. These organizations are pedantic about fostering the illusion that they are communicating to the troops. And an illusion is all that it is.

A cruel irony of this style culture is that the vision and values of this type of organization, while they can appear quite laudable, are usually not followed by the king and his disciples. This type of organization weighs heavy on the occupants and exacts a price, although not readily measurable. According to Ruddick, "The cost of the Kingdom business calling is in the disciplined obedience required to exercise the dynamic of dominion."[94] It's also important to understand the impact this type of culture has on the financial results of the organization. Unlike the jungle culture, it may be touch-and-go whether a kingdom business can repeatedly produce the required financial performance.

Gareth Morgan also touches on these jungle and kingdom types of organizations. He notes; "The basis of day-to-day order in these organizations tends to be autocratic rather than democratic in that the ultimate power to shape action rests in the hands of a single individual or group who typically makes all the important decisions."[95] The problem is those leaders (or a small group) who monopolize all organizational decision-making will ultimately be the ones that orchestrate its ruin.

You can quickly identify this type of culture by how employees welcome the newcomers to their organization. In this organization, they greet new employees with "welcome aboard." This is a dead giveaway of a kingdom-type culture, because just as the captain of a ship makes all the decisions so does the king in a kingdom. It may also mean the crew (subconsciously) recognizes they're on a sinking ship and thus jokingly tries to warn the poor newcomers.

There's also a definite cost to this type of organization in the morale of the workers, for as Sun Tzu pointed out, "By attempting to govern an army in the same way as he administers a kingdom, being ignorant of the conditions which obtain in an army, this causes restlessness in the soldier's minds."[96]

A derivative of the kingdom culture is another dystopian organizational atmosphere called the "fortress culture." This culture is characterized by employees who have doubts about the security and longevity of their jobs and don't know if they'll be laid off or not from day-to-day. They must all keep their engines running.

In the fortress culture there is an overriding atmosphere of fear (for good reason), and these are the organizations that undergo the periodic "reduction in force" (RIF) or reorganization. Because of this they also suffer from high turnover of people electing to leave the organization. In a way these are ruled as a kingdom culture but without the (however dysfunctional) clear communication that's present in the kingdom organization. If there's anything to be said about the kingdom culture it's that the king will always make his wishes known to all. There's no lack of pontification, whereas in the fortress culture the leaders have holed-up in their ivory towers.

The fortress culture develops as such because communication becomes a rare commodity, and this lack of openness causes everyone to circle the wagons to protect their turf. These organizations, by definition, suffer the worst from the fiefdom syndrome and have the least teamwork. For them it's also a struggle every day to meet the business goals of the organization.

So, how does culture actually affect the day-to-day operation of an organization and how does it affect the interactions of the workers who must navigate through their work days? Just like the cultures of different countries, there are rituals that become part of how an organization functions. In his 1991 article "Ritual in Business: Building a Corporate Culture through Symbolic Management," Christian Lange tells us there are basically six distinct cultural rituals:[97]

- The Rite of Passage: This is the process by which a participant traverses the gap between exclusion and acceptance. This is sort of like paying your dues. You'll need to produce positive deeds to progress through this stage.

- The Rite of Enhancement: This is where the organization publicly recognizes the heroes in their culture for the good deeds they've done by presenting them with gold plaques. We'll learn more about this hero mentality in later chapters.

- The Rites of Degradation: These are used to discipline, demote, or to entirely liquidate the social identity, power, and influence of a subject who somehow has wronged the organization. We'll find out later how this can be either a real, or even perceived, wrongdoing.

- The Rite of Conflict Reduction: This happens when there's a conflict between two parties or groups, which becomes unmanageable. This is particularly interesting in an organization that suffers from the fiefdom syndrome or involves a group that has second-class citizen status. The loser here usually finds themselves facing the rite of degradation.

- The Rite of Integration: As the name implies, these are rites that bring together employees within an organization. These are characterized by the need to have team-building events, which is sure fire evidence of an organization that suffers from little teamwork. Another example is the social events where employees are sometimes plied with alcohol in the hopes they'll mellow and get to know each other better. The intent is that maybe some teamwork will develop by osmosis.

- The Rite of Renewal: This concerns restoring and re-vitalizing existing social structure. It also comes from the need to re-focus the business strategy back to the fundamental goals of the organization. This can manifest itself in the off-site meetings in which senior management conspires on the strategic plan du jour yet little concrete, earth-shattering, strategy comes from these management circus events, and the organization, as a whole, sees little value come from them.

Gareth Morgan sums up the effect that ritual has on an organization; "One of the interesting aspects of culture is that it creates a form of blindness and ethnocentricism.

In providing taken-for-granted codes of action that we recognize as normal, it leads us to see activities that do not conform to these codes as abnormal."[98] We'll see later that this is a reminiscent trait found in the cultures that are typically seen in an insane asylum.

No discussion of workplace culture would be complete without acknowledging the existence of office politics as a driving factor in day-to-day deceptive behaviors. Office politics provide yet another tool for management to manipulate and control the perceptions of the workers, to try to align them with what the leadership fanaticizes the values, vision, and overarching goals to be.

CHAPTER 5 ANIMAL FARM

PUBLISHED IN ENGLAND IN 1945, *ANIMAL FARM* is a famous political allegory by George Orwell, the author of *1984*. Allegorically Orwell meant the book to reflect events leading up to and during the Stalin era before World War II; however, it's just as useful when studying the average modern workplace. It's a satire on a dystopian society where pigs have taken over a farm and rule the other animals.

Animal Farm details how politics and class structure develop even in a society that begins by preaching freedom and democracy. *Animal Farm* demonstrates how totalitarian authority can evolve, thus dooming an organization to suffer moral and ethical breakdown.

After the takeover from Mr. Jones, the farmer, the pigs organize the farm with the typical internal structure, or bureaucracy, of a nation: the government or ruling class (the pigs), a police force (the dogs), and a working class (all the other animals). This mirrors the typical workplace organizational structure of top management, loyal sycophants, and the actual workers. In a later chapter, we'll investigate these layers of workplace hierarchy.

Animal Farm depicts the corruption of leaders and how sociopathy, egomania, narcissism, and myopia destroy an organization from within. The parallels it makes to the modern workplace are eerie. The novel portrays how corrupt leadership, coupled with an indifference to that corruption, forms a dysfunctional, autocratic bureaucracy that ultimately leads to chaos.

In his book *The Power of Stupidity*, Giancarlo Livraghi asserts that bureaucracy is at the heart of all organizational demise. "The root of the problem is that bureaucracy is dedicated to satisfying its own idiotic needs at the expense of the service that it's supposed to provide. And it's extremely conservative. It tends to repeat its routines even when they're useless or harmful, ignoring any consideration of practicality or common sense. It behaves like those stupid parasites that continue to pursue their invasive growth even when by doing so they risk maiming or killing the host, and therefore themselves."[99] I find this an interesting take on the sociopathic behavior that typically leads organizations.

The evolution and ultimate demise of the structured society in *Animal Farm* exposes the way in which politics and bureaucracy can be used as an instrument of manipulation and control. The ruling pigs spew their political rhetoric to justify their behavior and keep the other animals under their control. That is not unlike the modern workplace. The story is also about consolidation of power in the hands of a few, and how their evil behaviors actually become the farm's cultural atmosphere. It's the same in the workplace, management behaviors that are subversive and oppressive, that make the working class completely subservient to the ruling class, ultimately will forge the culture.

With *Animal Farm* in mind this chapter is about organizational politics and how it's used as an instrument of domination, manipulation, and control over the workers.

Wikipedia defines politics as: a process by which groups of people make collective decisions and regulate public affairs, including the methods and tactics used to formulate and apply policy. It's also an activity undertaken for political reasons or ends, as in campaigning for votes before an election, making speeches, etc., or otherwise promoting one's policies. The first definition couldn't be further from the truth when referring to office politics; however, the second definition is interesting in light of our earlier discussion of impression management. Politics thus becomes just another term for impression management, because impression management is all about jockeying for power, and that becomes the main focus of organizational politics.

In his book *Images of Organization*, Gareth Morgan tackles organizational politics. "We can analyze organizational politics in a systematic way by focusing on relations among interests, conflict, and power. One way that has particular relevance to understanding organizational politics is to conceive interests in terms of three interconnected domains relating to one's organizational task, career, and personal life. The relationships between these interests provide the personal agendas underlying specific actions and activities."[100]

In his article "Definition of Politics: The Ugly Game of Power," G. B Singh brilliantly noted that office politics really means nothing more than "the game of power that the mighty play to hold their domination over the weak."[101] It includes the pursuit of individual agendas and self-interest without regard to their effect on the organization's ability to achieve its goals or maintain even its fundamental well-being. That is why University of Pennsylvania Organizational Dynamics Professor John Eldred's definition is spot on; "[office] politics is simply how power gets worked out on a practical, day-to-day basis."[102]

The ultimate aim of office politics is just what you may think—the three-Ps (pay, promotion, or power). It is the ultimate tool in impression management.

One way of analyzing office politics in more detail is to view it as a series of interpersonal games. Some are played as the result of management attitudes or policies; for example, the game of "No Surprises," which we'll learn about in detail in a later chapter. It is the fear that management has of any bad news that could upset their apple cart. The result is that all in the organization then withholds negative information for fear of being blamed. This is in response to the fact that most organizations don't handle bad news very well—i.e. when faced with bad news management will typically over react negatively and shoot the messenger. Thus, everyone in the organization is taught to suppress problems until they can't hide them any longer.

Political games are played at all levels of an organization between the management and the employees. One popular game is that of "divide and conquer," where a manager sets his employees against each other with the payoff that none threatens his ego or power base. Politically motivated games are also played between the loyal sycophants jockeying for position under the head sociopath, between middle managers fighting for the next promotion, and even between workers at the prole level looking for a promotion or maybe just a better performance review.

Another popular game that has political ramifications is "Stump the Dummy" (that we'll learn about later), in which the goal is to embarrass and discredit someone. Those are just two of the many games played out for personal, or group, benefit on a daily basis in the average workplace. Once we understand all the games played for selfish personal reasons we'll be better able to truly understand the motivations behind office politics.

In the mean time I want to offer a more in-depth definition of office politics. In reality office politics can be described as the composite of all the attitudes, behavioral traits, personal fears, nepotistic practices, egoism, narcissism, favoritism, protection, hero worship, and manipulation—i.e. all the bad behaviors that humans bring to the organizational table. Politics is how these are all acted out on a daily basis for personal gain (the three Ps). In the end, whatever the game or motive, they only have a negative effect on the workplace culture. Seldom will politic behavior be practiced for the good of the organization.

Office politics can have an even more serious effect on teamwork and communication within the organization. As it is with the games of "no surprises," or Divide and Conquer, when individuals are playing office politics, it interferes with the company's information flow. This especially hurts an organization already struggling to communicate effectively. Due to the games being played, communication most often gets suppressed or manipulated for someone's short-term personal gain, thus you could also say that all the bullshit that's flung on a daily basis is a form of politics. Be it bullshit, or games, they all have a definite negative effect on the organization and are a major contributor to many of the ills that befall an organization.

I prefer to liken office politics to what I would call "planned anarchy," because politics in business can ultimately lead to an anarchical environment. We see it clearly in *Animal Farm* as the farm quickly decays into chaos. Some anarchists define anarchy as "extreme individualism," and this definition tends to lend credence to my view. After all, as we'll find out, the self-centered behaviors found in the typical workplace are usually consciously planned out by the perpetrators and can definitely create anarchy.

Thus extreme individualism, as a way to describe politic behavior, fits nicely when we begin to learn (in later chapters) of the specific behaviors of the sociopaths, sycophants and bullies that populate the typical workplace.

The individuals who manipulate their working relationships for political gain consume the organization's precious time and resources, which contributes to the organization missing its goals. This self-centered behavior creates the communication problem called "the management vacuum," which is the information vacuum surrounding the organization's leaders, created when people withhold important (and usually unpleasant) information, typically because they fear management's wrath. The vacuum also affects how employees interact with others on all matters, thus interfering with the ability of the organization to function effectively.

Ironically, those behaviors actually set the organization up for failure and make it a self-fulfilling prophesy. People playing political games forget that when the organization fails, everyone in it ultimately fails.

It's somewhat ironic because today's business world operates on the old axiom: "failure is not an option." This belief is founded in the fear that arises from the consequences of not meeting personal or organizational goals. In fact, fear is the number one emotional state in today's workplace and it definitely affects the overall health of an organization.

Vault's finance editor, Derek Loosvelt, postulates that fear, over all other political behaviors, is what's running most companies, and he offers us the reasons why: employees fear not being liked; they fear their ideas are stupid; and they fear they'll lose their job. And, of course, they fear being blamed for something, any-thing, even if they're guilty. Because of these fears, they avoid confrontation at all costs. They don't speak their mind in meetings, and during the course of their jobs, they're afraid that, whether right or wrong, they'll be accused of upsetting the fragile status quo. Loosvelt says, they "stifle 75 to 95 percent of their opinions as well as impulses to say something that might otherwise cut through much of the B.S. that is most definitely going on at their company and thus making it not run as efficiently as it could."[103]

Personally I believe a main source of fear in the workplace comes from unconstruc-tive criticism. This manifests itself as the fear of being criticized for something with little guidance on how to rectify the situation. In effect, you're left holding the bag. Ironically, the accusations and lack of constructive guidance often comes from the same managers who preach "don't bring me problems; bring me solutions." However, it's always okay for them to bring *you* a problem without a suggested solution. We'll look at this more when we tackle the dreaded performance review process.

Unconstructive criticism is just one of the many tools that a typical sociopath or bully will use to rule his subjects. I think this is, more often than not, just a symp-tom of typical sociopathic behavior. Sociopaths are so motivated to criticize people that they do this without even thinking that it might be more productive to sug-gest a possible solution to the problem, instead of just hammering some poor slob. In this way they're not able to offer the constructive part of the dialog they're hav-ing with the employee, thus missing a perfect opportunity to make the situation a teaching moment. But doing that would mean actually being a leader, and coaching and nurturing employees isn't a sociopath's strong suit.

The key to coping when you find yourself in this situation is to remember that they have no clue how you should go about fixing whatever their problem might be. Notice I use the term "their" to describe the problem. Obviously if you've really screwed up you should take responsibility and fix the problem you've created. However, as we'll discover later, many of the perceived problems and subsequent blame that a sociopath brings to bear are just that—perceived.

This leads to a universal fear of criticism, and it's powerfully debilitating. When you see people all around you getting hammered for every little thing they do wrong it strikes the fear of God into you, however strong or thick-skinned you may think you are. Sadly, in today's typical workplace, criticism is one of the most overly used methods of managing people. The games of "Stump-the-Dummy," "Divide and Conquer," and of course the performance review process are all forms in which sociopaths or bullies use negative, often unconstructive, criticism to mold the workers into their subservient minions.

The truth is that making mistakes, or flat-out failing at something, has brought successful people closer to their success, but that's a truism that falls on deaf ears in the modern workplace. William Strong, Associate Justice on the Supreme Court of the United States in the late 1800s noted, "The only time you don't fail is the last time you try anything and it works."[104]

How an organization deals with failure is critical to understanding the politics in play in the organization. As we know, the "failure is not an option" mentality is pervasive in business, and this is fine from an overall business perspective, i.e., when trying to meet such goals as product delivery, customer satisfaction, and financial goals; however, few organizations embrace even the remote possibility of failure at the individual level.

This is evident by the fact there's little true empowerment going on in today's workplace. Workers don't know what kind of risks, if any, are acceptable for them to take. The leaders don't empower their employees because, in true sociopathic form, they believe only they are qualified to make decisions. So the workforce then defers all risk taking to the sociopaths and the power elite. This protects them from any possibility of failing and then experiencing the wrath of management. We see this exact process unfold in *Animal Farm*. For most organizations the only empowerment that exists is the illusion in the minds of the sycophants because for them just being close to the powerful is empowering, in a perverted sort of way.

Remember, just like in government, it's so in business that a politician serves that which serves him or her best.

So far we've seen how perception is reality and how an organization's culture and politics play an important role in making the workplace the tortured environment it is. The last area that can affect how an organization is run is through the official organization chart(s). This is where office politics actually finds its way onto paper. In the next chapter, we'll explore organizational structure and the hierarchies that exist within the modern workplace.

CHAPTER 6 FLATLAND

FLATLAND: A ROMANCE OF MANY DIMENSIONS is an 1884 satirical novella by the English schoolmaster Edwin A. Abbott that describes a two-dimensional world, a society rigidly divided into classes. Abbott used the fictional two-dimensional world of Flatland to offer his pointed observations on the social hierarchy of his times. We're going to learn that times haven't changed much.

In the story, 'Flatland' is a society occupied by geometric figures. The narrator is a square, who guides the reader through the implications of life in only two dimensions. Men are portrayed as polygons, whose social status is determined by their regularity and the number of their sides. Females are depicted only as a line. Each male generation adds to its number of sides—e.g. a square begets a pentagon. As sides are added as the generations go on, they approach the shape of a circle, considered to be the perfect shape. Other than females, triangles are the lowliest of creatures, and their status is measured by the angle between their sides. The lowest classes of workmen are triangles with two equal sides and a small angle between the sides. As the angle gets larger, they progress toward being an equilateral triangle, which is considered a tradesman, a respectable class.

For the polygon inhabitants of Flatland, irregularity of shape is abhorred and is considered an affront to society. The crime of being irregular is described as "an axiom of policy that the toleration of irregularity is incompatible with the safety of the state."[105] If an irregularity is more than the acceptable standard, the irregular polygon faces euthanasia. A polygon suffering an irregularity at birth wouldn't necessarily be destroyed, but society would attempt to cure the irregularity to within society's level of tolerance. If the deformity couldn't be corrected, the irregular would be eliminated.

There are a couple of parallels here to the modern workplace, most notably the fact that irregulars are eliminated. If you don't fit into the organization, you're toast. Second, the workplace will try to "fix" people through the performance review process. Should the employee not change to the model dictated by management, he or she will hear that famous line, "I'm sorry to tell you, but you have been eliminated."

Like any society or organization, the main aspiration of Flatland's inhabitants is social ascent–i.e. having their offspring gain sides. The rule in Flatland is strictly controlled by the few positioned at the top of the hierarchy, just like in a typical workplace hierarchy.

In this flat world, freedom and individual equality are oppressed, and the laws are oppressive. Anyone who challenges the status quo, or who may be a threat to the leaders, is eliminated. The leaders of Flatland are so self-important that any attempt of change is considered an insurrection punishable by imprisonment or elimination. Especially forbidden is "to proclaim the Gospel of Three Dimensions to your blind benighted countrymen in Flatland. Death or imprisonment awaits the Apostle of the Gospel of Three Dimensions."[106]

Herein lays the crux of the story. The narrator, a square, has a dream about a visit from a three-dimensional sphere from a place called Spaceland. The sphere introduces him to the idea that there's more to the universe than just two dimensions, that there's, in fact, a third dimension. The square's visit to the third dimension– something he never thought was possible–convinces him that he must try his best to convince the rest of his two-dimensional peers to embrace the reality of three dimensions.

Unfortunately, the leaders of Flatland prescribe the silencing of anyone found preaching the truth of Spaceland and the third dimension. Despite this threat, the square can't contain his enthusiasm and ultimately proclaims the third dimension for all to hear. He is then imprisoned for the rest of his life. This also is not unlike the modern workplace where anyone preaching empowerment, equality, and servant leadership is silenced.

Sociopathically run organizations fear moving into that third dimension, the one where people are treated and paid fairly, trusted, and empowered. The third dimension is just that: all the progressive management practices that would make the workplace a pleasure in which to work. It's the third dimension of life in the workplace that the sociopaths work to suppress.

Individual equality is oppressed in Flatland as in the typical business environment. In many organizations the laws (procedures and rules) are oppressive and sometimes senseless. Like the leaders of Flatland, typical workplace management is self-centered, and they believe themselves to be perfect, and anyone who attempts to change anything is chastised. In the story Abbott addresses this phenomenon. In another dream journey, the sphere also guides the square to the unbelievable world of a space without dimensions, called Pointland. Here they meet the Monarch of Pointland

The sphere describes the Monarch of Pointland to the square, by saying, "he cannot conceive of any other except himself." The sphere further declares, "Behold yon miserable creature. That Point is a being like ourselves, but confined to the non-dimensional gulf. He is himself his own world, his own Universe; of any other than himself he can form no conception; he knows not length, nor breath, nor height, for he has had no experience of them; he has no cognizance even of the number two; nor has he a thought of plurality; for he is himself his One and All, being really nothing."

This sounds surprisingly like typical sociopathic management types. "He cannot conceive of any other except himself."

In the story, the square asks the Sphere if it's possible to change the Monarch of Pointland. He asks, "Can you not startle the little thing out of its complacency? Tell it what it really is, as you told me; reveal to it the narrow limitations of Pointland, and lead it up to something higher."

"That is no easy task," says the sphere, and beckons him to try. So the square tries to explain to the Monarch of Pointland: "Silence, silence, contemptible creature. You call yourself the all in all, but you are nothing; your so-called universe is a mere speck in a line, and a line is a mere shadow as compared with–"

However, the sphere cuts him short. "Hush, hush, you have said enough, now listen, and mark the effect of your harangue on the Monarch of Pointland."

The square notes that the Monarch of Pointland has not heeded his words. The square tells us, "The luster of the monarch, who beamed more brightly than ever upon hearing my words, showed clearly that he retained his complacency; and I had hardly ceased when he took up his strain again. Ah, the joy, ah, the joy of thought! Ah, the divine creative power of the all in one!"

"You see how little your words have done," explains the teacher, the sphere. "So far as the monarch understands, he cannot conceive of any other except himself. Let us leave this God of Pointland to the ignorant fruition of his omnipresence and omniscience; nothing that you or I can do can rescue him from his self-satisfaction."[107]

Just as in the modern workplace, one cannot confront a sociopath and point to the error of his ways and expect to make him a convert.

Why is Flatland important to our discussion? First, the two dimensional characters that inhabit Flatland are just like those that inhabit the average workplace. A two-dimensional object has length and breadth but no depth–the third dimension. Just like the two-dimensional inhabitants of Flatland, the inhabitants of the typical workplace organization are described on the organization chart in the same ways, with geometric shapes. After all, everyone becomes just a box, or square, on the organization chart, right? Thus, two dimensions exactly describe the typical organizational structure, or hierarchy. On paper the organizational structure has height and width only; however, what's missing is the third dimension.

In my analogy, the Monarch of Pointland represents the individual at the top of the organization, and there are many similarities between the Monarch of Pointland and the average sociopathic Lord. The above description of the Monarch of Pointland will become more relevant when, in a later chapter, we learn about the sociopaths that populate the upper crust of the typical modern workplace organization.

The infamous organization chart exemplifies the two-dimensional reality of the organization's hierarchy and, as I mentioned, graphically reveals that the element missing in most organizations is metaphorically that third dimension which represents all the values of morality, ethics, sound leadership, and respect for the individual and workplace equality (just to name a few) that are most often missing in the typical workplace.

So with our visit to Flatland in mind, let's look at organizational charts—the method used to graphically display the organizational power structure and the cultural and political grapevine of the inhabitants in the typical workplace.

From my career perspective, all the organizational charts I've been privy to have varied little from one organization to another. The vertical or functional hierarchy is, and has been, the flagship of business since the Model T rolled off the assembly line.

What I find somewhat ironic, though, is that there's been no revelation over the past century that the vertical design all but guarantees a fragmented workforce, fiefdoms, turf wars, inefficiencies (in how daily tasks are performed), dysfunctional communication and little teamwork. Of course, the most damaging behavior is the command and control management style it perpetrates. These are all the negatives that ensure organizational paralysis, yet businesses seem adverse to any change in how they organize.

The standard organization chart typically seen today is used to show the intended structure of the organization. It also serves the sociopath's ego, because it clearly shows that he's at the top and in control. This formal organization is supposed to reflect the responsibility and authority structure of the organization; however, in reality it only reflects a roadmap facilitating power and the blame game.

The organization chart serves to represent the lines of command and control so common in today's workplace. However, the real responsibility and influence in the organization, needed for it to function, typically doesn't follow the organization chart lines, but follows the lines of communication and politics.

All organization charts typically are pyramidal in shape. They show the person in charge at the top, with the first layer down being the leader's staff. Below that is middle management. As you progress down the chart, people reporting to the middle managers are shown. Individuals shown on the same horizontal level in the organization chart are perceived to be peers within the organization.

The actual working level staff is then shown reporting to each appropriate middle manager. All these are interconnected with solid lines that show how everybody fits into the pecking order.

Sometimes there are even feeble attempts to show the reality of how work actually is accomplished by placing a dotted line from one position to another. This just shows that some poor slob now must serve two masters. This typical structure is depicted in the diagram below.[108]

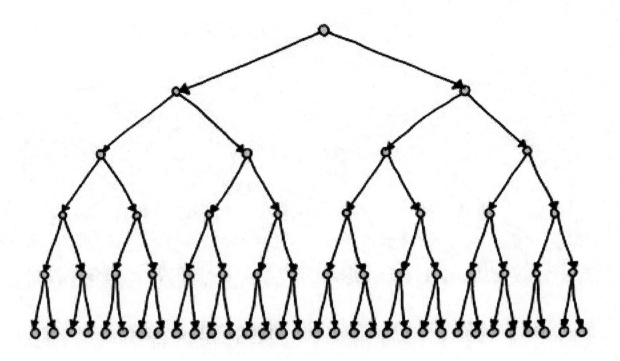

The above chart shows six layers, but some large organizations can even go deeper than this. However, we're going to see later how in all organizations there are effectively only three levels of power and privilege.

Unfortunately, this chart structure doesn't really convey how day-to-day work is actually accomplished. Although that's not entirely true as job titles on the organization chart provide some insight. However, based solely on the org chart for guidance, it's not always clear to the people within the organization, let alone customers, who is really in charge and responsible for day-to-day work. People find out who does what through the culture and the politics. The diagram[109] below depicts how the interaction actually happens on a day-to-day basis to perform useful work.

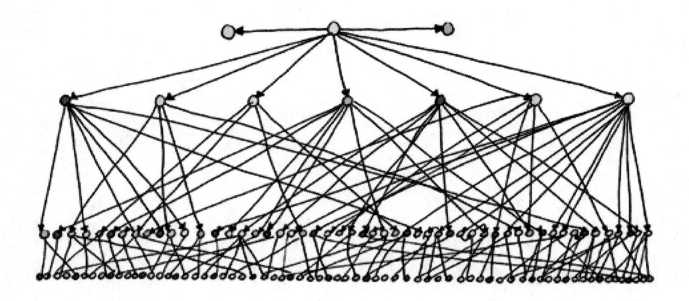

The big problem today is that we forget that organizational charts are just pieces of paper. Management, with its command and control mentality, tries to manage by the chart. Unfortunately, the chart doesn't have much bearing on how an organization actually functions on a daily basis. This fixation on managing to the chart is what cripples an organization.

The biggest problem with the typical organization chart is that its vertical structure implies that communication must go up and down the functional silos, versus laterally across and between functional groups. However, as we see in the diagram above, work is usually performed across the organization, versus solely within a single silo. Thus the structure, by its very nature tends to stifle effective cross-functional communication.

Many sociopathic middle managers reinforce this vertical regimen by promoting a militaristic environment where the chain of command is foremost. Middle managers typically keep their people focused internal to their organizations so that they must always focus their attention upward, toward him or her. To survive, the employee must, first and foremost, understand the boss's directions, and only then weigh that against his job duties and what he perceives the needs of the organization to be as a whole. That scenario is the antithesis of empowerment.

One way managers encourage this internal focus is by pitting employees and groups against one another using the "Divide and Conquer" technique that we'll learn about later. The intent is to keep employees at odds with each other, thus forcing them to suspect one another, and as a result become more dependent on the manager. This results in a constant desperate competition of sorts and enforces the need for impression management to reign free. Such is life in a vertically oriented organization.

The following cartoon sums up best what vertical organizational life is really like. Wherever you go you'll always hear employees bemoaning that they are shit on by management. While it may portray the organization in a non-flattering light, it does reflect a lot of truth.

Because the organization chart emphasizes and magnifies the differences among people at the top, middle, and bottom of the pecking order, it brings out the worst in everyone. Robert Sutton, in his book *The No Asshole Rule* notes that, "Many organizations amplify these problems by constantly rating and ranking people, giving spoils to a few stars and treating the rest as second and third class citizens."[110]

We'll explore this despicable practice in great detail later when we tackle the performance review process, but I will say this here, the ranking process is much like the methods used in shows like *Big Brother* and *Survivor*. At the top of the ranking there are those bestowed the "head of household" status, while at the bottom there are those most likely to be voted off the island. Think of the whole ranking process as a tribal council meeting, except, unlike in the show, you won't get invited to that rodeo, yet this is where the decision is made to either keep you or shit-can you. There's no immunity to win in the heated day-to-day competition called your job and when your time has come to leave, there's no power of veto either.

In their article, "Workplace Fun and its Correlates: A Conceptual Inquiry," Mildred Golden Pryor, et al. sum up the modern vertical workplace environment and the effect this type of organization has on the employees. "A structure which can be the most stifling is a deep vertical hierarchy. In this type of workplace, employees have limited, or no, power, and the organization will typically bestow demerits for bad behavior, and few or no rewards for good behavior. Such an environment has a high potential of minimizing opportunities for fun and creativity. In addition, it may be a source of stress for employees.

"All this breeds negativism and distrust. A toxic triangle exists that is comprised of destructive leaders, susceptible followers, and conducive environments. Yet managers of dysfunctional work environments often contribute to the negativism as they micromanage, abuse power, lack anger management skills, threaten and demean others, and/or engage in other illegal, unethical, or de-motivating behavior. In many organizations a culture of distrust exists among the various constituencies, management and non-management people, team members, horizontally among peers, vertically along the chain of command, and even among organizational members and their customers and suppliers."[111]

So far we've seen how a combination of lies (and don't forget bullshit), a negative culture, office politics, and an archaic vertical organizational structure contribute to a dysfunctional workplace. So what's the alternative?

If you look at most organizational values statements, you'll find that teamwork is either at the top of the list or close to it. However, true teamwork in an organization can best be achieved through a more flat organization in which everyone, regardless of position, has equal vote in the way the organization pulls together to meet its goals. A flat organization effectively eliminates the need for selfish posturing, as there's no hierarchy which, by its very nature, inspires this behavior.

Businesses need to revamp the organizational hierarchy mentality and all the negative consequences it fosters. Organization charts, if they are even needed at all, need to be simplified into a structure in which there's virtually only one level (the team) who are all equal partners in the future success of the organization. This is usually how start-up organizations function.

Here's an approach to accomplishing that structure. First, determine what are the primary goals that the organization most needs to accomplish. Next, organize around those needs, or goals, not around functions, disciplines, or titles. An example of this structure would be a "projectized" organization in which each crucial goal has a dedicated project team. This flat structure is by far better than the traditional functional (silo) organization.

In his blog *Random Thoughts from a Restless Mind*, Dr. Darrell White provides an interesting perspective on the flat organization and how it might operate on a daily basis. In his October 2010 entry "A Tribe of Adults: The Pond Theory of Management," he explains that the key to successful implementation of a flat organization is when the occupants are treated more as a "Tribe of Adults" than how the typical organizational structure treats its inhabitants. As he tells us, "[T]he typical management structure in businesses is not really conducive to fostering this [Tribe of Adults] kind of culture. Pretty much every [business] that I've ever been involved with has been set up as a steep management pyramid; very strict top–down management in a command and control environment. Lots and lots of rules and regulations with an equally dense layer of middle management whose prime objective appears to be applying discipline to everyone who falls below it on the pyramid. Individual initiative is totally suppressed.

"But a Tribe of Adults clearly needs to be managed in a totally different way. A group of people who are willing to take responsibility, not only for the outcomes of their work product but also for their own personal behavior and relationships within the organization, is best managed with as flat a management structure as possible. The ultimate flat organizational chart would be one in which literally no management existed. This is impossible, of course, because at some point someone has to chart the course, lay out priorities, and designate goals. After that a Tribe of Adults shouldn't need much management."[112] Wouldn't that be refreshing to see everyone treated as an adult?

In his book *The World is Flat: A Brief History of the Twenty-First Century*, Thomas Friedman details the flattening of the global marketplace over the past thirty years. This flattening process started with the tech revolution that was spawned when we entered the personal computing age. It was further fueled by the development of the Internet and the World Wide Web and advances in software that allowed the multiplexing of work between companies and across international borders. As the world becomes flatter and more companies outsource and collaborate with one another, the lines truly become blurred among organizations.

Since this is how business is evolving, it only seems logical that within individual organizations there should be a flattening effect also. However, we know that's not the case. Despite the flattening of the business world, organizational structure is still stuck in the vertical (silo) mentality, or the twentieth century mentality. What's wrong with this thinking? It doesn't reflect how business is evolving. Vertical thinking requires the organization to focus on who's in control of each vertical silo. This is the command and control mentality that most businesses still rely on to function. On the other hand, horizontal (flat) thinking allows focus to be on the outcomes (results) desired of the business. This places focus not on who's in control but on how best to accomplish the business's goals. With business so enamored with the results mantra, you'd think this wouldn't be such a tough sell. Aren't results what most organizations preach?

This flat organization is exactly how sports are organized, each team having representatives from each duty or discipline necessary to execute the job and win the game. However, imagine if a sport was organized by position. In football, for example, what if all the quarterbacks were in one department, linemen in another, the receivers in another, etc. and each day they were asked to come together as a team, without any prior collaboration, and win a ballgame? It undoubtedly wouldn't work very well; however, that's exactly what happens every day in a workplace that's organized functionally and vertically.

The problem with vertical organizing is that it forces workers to place their loyalty first to their department and immediate supervisor (they must to survive), second to their own career, and last to the overall organization. The result is an organization with the natural propensity for the Fiefdom Syndrome to take hold. The focus on oneself, over company, spawns the need for impression management and all its associated games. The most damaging result of the vertical structure is that the focus on the overall well-being of the organization comes in last, when, in fact, it should be first. This vertical mentality is what needs to be upended in the modern workplace, yet most organizations don't give an inch in how they think or how they organize.

That said, I don't think that even with a flat organizational structure you'd ever get rid of the negative effects of hierarchy on the organization. Even in an organization that's flat, the command and control mentality of the sociopaths will still rear its ugly head in the form of the politics. Also, as I mentioned earlier, whether the organization chart is vertical, or flat, there is still the problem of the tiered class structure that we'll learn about in the next chapter.

CHAPTER 7 FARCE MAJEURE

AUTHOR ROBERT LINDNER ONCE SAID, "It is a characteristic of all movements and crusades that the psychopathic element will always rise to the top."[113] Just as The Iron Law of Oligarchy suggests that organizations typically end up under the control of narrow groups, most organizations end up with little more than a despot in charge.

While The Iron Law of Oligarchy is a political theory first developed by the German sociologist Robert Michels in his 1911 book, *Political Parties*, it applies to the modern workplace perfectly. The law simply states that all forms of organization, regardless of how democratic they may be at the start, will eventually and inevitably develop into oligarchies. We saw that evolution in *Animal Farm*.

I have witnessed this transformation on a couple of occasions. Land a job at any start-up early in its infancy, and if you stay long enough you'll see this phenomenon start to unfold. Thinking back, it's hard to pinpoint the exact event that sets this in motion because the process is more evolutionary than revolutionary.

I've monitored the start-ups in which I've worked and have found that, years after I left, they had all evolved into highly political, fiefdom-rich environments in which infighting is the norm.

While this chapter is not about the process of organizations turning into oligarchies, it is about understanding the end result of that process and how it affects the company's culture and the people who populate the organization.

Let's start with how a start-up organization typically operates on a daily basis? For one thing, the lines of communication and interaction don't at all follow what a classic organizational chart would dictate. Herein is the recipe for their success.

The diagram[114] below serves up a very good representation of how a start-up environment operates on a day-to-day basis.

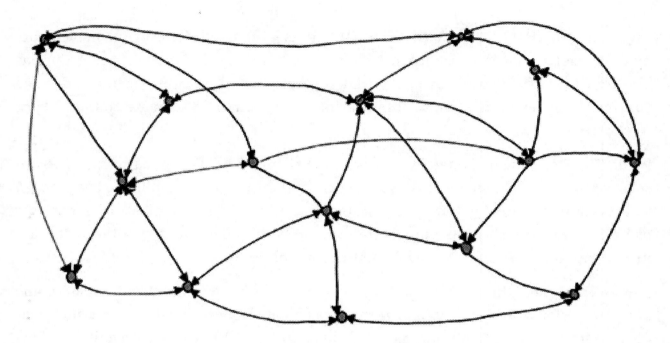

I believe the tipping point—the point when they start behaving like any other dysfunctional organization—for these organizations is when they stop operating and communicating, as the chart above depicts, and feel the need to start managing by the traditional organization chart structure. We're going to look at organizations that have passed that tipping point.

I was planning on titling this chapter "The Inmates Run the Asylum," after the popular idiom that we've all heard many times. However, after reading the treatise by Irving Goffman called *Asylums: Essays on the Social Situation of Mental Patients and Other Inmates*, I decided otherwise. I'll explain why.

After reading Goffman's depiction of the typical asylum, I realized that the old idiom of the inmates running the asylum, despite having a nice ring to it, just isn't right and certainly not what I've personally observed. Goffman convinced me that

I had to take the title, and the chapter, in a different direction. I'm still going to draw a parallel between the typical workplace and an insane asylum; however, I realized that the inmates remain just that—inmates—and they don't run anything. The nut jobs at the top, in fact, run the organization. In this sense the people running the organization should be the inmates. Regardless, Goffman's work is the underlying inspiration for this chapter.

Despite being circa 1960s; *Asylums* is Goffman's seminal work on the subject and is as pertinent today as it was when written. It's been heralded as an accurate depiction and analysis of life in an insane asylum. While comparing the average workplace to an insane asylum may appear an exaggeration, I assure you there are many similarities that this chapter will investigate, and in the end you'll become a believer.

Just like in a true asylum, when you get out there in the workforce, you just might find yourself dealing with a Nurse Ratched,[115] as did Randle McMurphy (Jack Nicholson) in the 1975 movie *One Flew over the Cuckoo's Nest*.

While reading Goffman's work, I came across descriptions, definitions, and behaviors that reminded me so much of life in the typical workplace that if I just replaced a few of his words—employee for inmate, management for hospital staff—his work becomes a treatise on workplace organizational behavior.

Goffman describes an asylum in the context of what he calls a total institution. "A total institution may be defined as a place of residence and work where a large number of like-situated individuals, cut off from the wider society for an appreciable period of time, together lead an enclosed, formally administered round of life.

"Every institution captures something of the time and interest of its members and provides something of a world for them; in brief, every institution has encompassing tendencies. All aspects of life are conducted in the same place and under the same single authority. Each phase of the member's daily activity is carried on in the immediate company of a large batch of others, all of whom are treated alike and required to do the same thing together.

"All phases of the day's activities are tightly scheduled, with one activity leading at a prearranged time into the next, the whole sequence of activities being imposed from above by a system of explicit formal rulings and a body of officials. Activities are brought together into a single rational plan purportedly designed to fulfill the official aims of the institution.

"In total institutions there is a basic split between a large managed group, conveniently called inmates, and a small supervisory staff. Each grouping tends to conceive of the other in terms of narrow hostile stereotypes, staff often seeing inmates as bitter, secretive, and untrustworthy, while inmates often see staff as condescending, highhanded, and mean. Staff tends to feel superior and righteous; inmates tend, in some ways at least, to feel inferior, weak, blameworthy, and guilty. Social mobility between the two strata is grossly restricted." [116]

What's really interesting about Goffman's description of the typical asylum is that he suggests that the notions of deviancy and normalcy are directly related to the context in which the behavior is viewed or performed. In other words, the exact same behavior might be deemed acceptable in one context and unacceptable in another.

What this means is that the definition of insane is dependent on your perspective or frame of reference. The definition of insane within the asylum is the direct opposite of that in the outside, so-called normal world. In the asylum, those who don't modify their behavior according to the behavior practiced by the inmates are seen as the deviants. In the asylum, those who would act normal, by outside standards, are the insane ones. By the same token those in the outside world, whose behavior and actions are like those in the asylum are, of course, considered the deviants.

It's all about how you benchmark "normal behavior." So whether behavior is sane or insane completely depends on what's defined as normal within an organization.

For example, if an organization is mired down in a command and control, socio-pathic management style, then anyone trying to display more servant-leadership management traits would be ostracized as the oddball—i.e. insane.

In his book *Images of Organization*, Gareth Morgan described this phenomenon as "blindness," in that an organization can become so enamored with its rules and standards of behavior that it can't recognize other valid ways of doing things. Thus anyone acting outside its rules is looked upon as abnormal.

There are many similarities between the asylum and the outside world (which would include the workplace) and Goffman recognizes them. "Almost everything that goes on in total institutions happens on the outside, too," he says. "The form and intensity may differ, but the substance is the same. Social interactions occur, rules are promulgated and enforced, a hierarchy is established and functions and people adjust to it. Influence is peddled, bribes are offered and accepted. People intimidate and exploit and are, in turn, treated in like fashion. They form alliances, and they scheme and plot. They display favoritism and they struggle against authority even as they conceal their true feeling and intentions."

Goffman goes on to describe how people are indoctrinated into the asylum which has a direct parallel to employees entering a new job. "The recruit comes into the establishment with a conception of himself made possible by certain stable social arrangements in his home world. Upon entrance, he is immediately stripped of the support provided by these arrangements. He begins a series of abasements, degradations, humiliations, and profanations of self. He begins some radical shifts in his moral career, a career composed of the progressive changes that occur in the beliefs that he has concerning himself and significant others." [117]

Successful survival in an asylum is therefore dependent upon the success of the individuals in making, what Goffman called "secondary adjustments" to thus fit in and not be considered insane. They will quickly learn to internalize and hide those aspects of themselves which are not beneficial for preserving that notion. Goffman also believed that the "official self" is a product of the demands society makes upon the individual, thus the individual learns fast what is expected of him or her and responds accordingly, wanting above all to survive.

Goffman details the right of entrance or initiation into the institution as a series of degradations, performed by both the staff and other inmates that are performed upon arrival of a new recruit. These same degradations parallel what happens throughout the career of the typical employee, from his first day on the job through the day he realizes he must quit.

These induction games Goffman describes also parallel the games as described in the classic book *Games People Play* by psychiatrist Dr. Eric Berne. Later we'll see how Berne's "games" parallel those experienced in the workplace, all with the same goal of controlling the employees so as to make them serve the pleasure of the sociopathic narcissists in charge.

If you want to see the asylum effect in action and how most organizations actually operate, tune into the TV show *Big Brother*. Just like the workplace, *Big Brother* can be addictive. I think that's because what goes on in the *Big Brother* house reminds us so much of our daily experiences at work. Contestants will scheme, lie, backstab, blindside and build fiefdoms and evil alliances. And just like in the modern workplace, the contestants compete to become haves or have-nots. *Big Brother*, and other shows like it, accurately reveals behaviors that can be seen in the typical workplace today. These are the organizations where the lunatic fringe rises to the top and is in power.

So what does the typical dysfunctional workplace asylum look like? As we've seen from our review of organizational chartology, a modern organization consists of layers. It's these layers that form the foundation of the stratification (powerful versus powerless, haves versus have-nots) and the evil behavior that happens in today's workplace, and it's what evolves the organization into an oligarchy. It's these layers and their collective and innate behaviors that have enormous influence on, and form, the culture.

The diagram below presents a compelling representation of a typical workplace oligarchical organizational hierarchy. In a profound way, it can explain the behavior found in today's workplace and the behaviors and games that we'll analyze in this book. The diagram reflects a three-tiered pyramid layering and serves to mimic the typical organizational pathology.

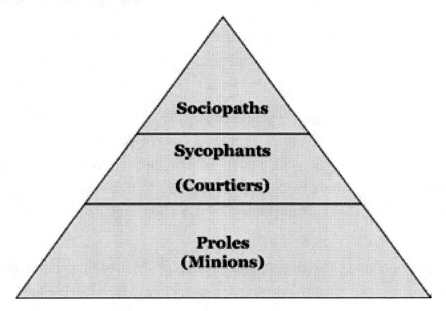

Typical Modern Oligarchical Hierarchy[118]

My organizational pyramid is modeled after a cartoon by Hugh MacLeod, in which he describes the levels as: sociopaths, clueless (my sycophants) and losers (my proles). At the top we find the sociopaths. They're the upper management level of the organization, and they're the ranks starting with the organizational leader and including the first level (senior) staff, although, as we'll see later, sociopaths can, and do, appear in all organizational levels.

The sycophants are the layers of middle management and are the organizational courtiers of the sociopaths. The proles are the rank-and-file minions (the capite censi) with low status that require specific talent to perform their jobs. These are what Gareth Morgan calls the secondary labor market: "a market of lower-skilled and lower paid workers in offices, factories and open-air jobs who are more dispensable and more easily replaced."[119] The proles' position in the hierarchy is the least secure because they are the most likely victims of the routine outsourcing and reductions in force (RIF) that happen in these poorly run junior achievement organizations.

Prole is a term used by George Orwell in his 1949 novel *1984* to refer to the working class of his fictitious super-state Oceania.[120] In the world of *1984*, Oceania is split into three classes: the Inner Party, the Outer Party, and the Proles.

The Inner Party represents the oligarchical upper-class in Oceania, or in the above model, the sociopaths. The Outer Party correlates to the sycophants (the courtiers) in the middle. And since I like the sound of the term "proles," I use it to describe the lower level of the organizational hierarchy. The Inner Party keeps all Outer Party members under close supervision, and they both rule over the proles, or minions.

The members of the Outer Party, not the proles, are really the worst off of the three classes because they are under constant supervision by the Inner Party. Ahh, the price we pay for being a suck-up.

In *1984*, Oceania is a world of perpetual war and pervasive government surveillance and mind control, similar to the workplace. The individual is always subordinated to the state, and it's this philosophy, which allows the Inner Party to manipulate and control humanity.

In his article "The Gervais Principle, Or the Office According to The Office," author Venkatesh Rao describes Hugh MacLeod's prole class of worker—the organizational "losers." While that label may be a bit strong, I agree that his description of the prole, as a loser, is spot on; the losers are the only ones in the organization who "actually produce anything, but are not compensated in proportion to the value they create, since their compensation is set by the sociopaths. They mortgage their lives away, and hope to die before their money runs out. The good news [if you can call it that] is that the losers have two ways out; turning sociopath or turning into bare-minimum performers."[121]

Just like the Outer Party in *1984*, in reality the sycophants are the real pawns in the grand scheme of things. The typical sycophant suffers from the delusion that if he works hard and serves the master well, he will be rewarded. Some will, but most won't, certainly not in recompense for all the degradation they endure.

If they work for a workaholic, these poor bastards will have to put in enormous hours each week and will probably not get much in return. Instead, they'll find they're the brunt of the fury of the sociopaths and bullies when they need someone to blame. The proles, on the other hand, don't really face this fate. They have no delusions about their position. They come to work, perform their function, and go home to a life after work. They're most certainly the only truly happy players in this farce-majeure called the workplace.

This oligarchical organizational structure of the typical workplace isn't unique since it mirrors society as a whole. First there's the top-rung which in *Big Brother* termi-nology are the haves. The sycophant level equates to society's middle class (some-where between have and have-not). And at the bottom we have the proles (the have-nots), or secondary workforce.

Now that we've understood the true basic structure (hierarchy) of the modern organization, we can start digging a bit deeper into how these layers manifest into the dysfunctional organizations that we experience in the workplace.

In his book *Images of Organization*, Gareth Morgan looks at organizations through metaphors.[122] He describes eight metaphors through which we can understand organizations:

- Machines
- Organisms
- Brains
- Cultures
- Political systems
- Psychic prisons
- Flux and transformation
- Instruments of domination

Of the eight metaphors, two are relevant to this discussion: organizations as "psychic prisons" and organizations as "instruments of domination."

An organization that's a psychic prison is one that has gotten trapped in its own thoughts and actions. It involves both conscious and unconscious processes of repression, ego, denial, coping and defense mechanisms, pain, pleasure, dysfunctionality, workaholism, and micromanagement. Morgan says, "This metaphor joins the idea that organizations are ultimately created and sustained by conscious and unconscious processes; people can actually become imprisoned in or confined by the images, ideas, thoughts, and actions to which these processes give rise."[123] That's a fancy way of saying perception becomes reality.

The second of Morgan's metaphors applicable here is his treatment of organizations as instruments of domination. Here the focus is on the potentially exploitive aspects of organizations. He describes them as "organizations that exploit their employees, the natural environment, and the global economy for their own ends."

The essence of this type of organization rests in a process of domination where certain people impose their will on others. Morgan describes these instruments of domination as alienation, repression, imposing values, compliance, charisma, maintenance of power, force, exploitation, divide and rule, discrimination, and corporate interest. Morgan contends that there's an element of domination in all organizations. I also believe there's an element of psychic prison in all modern workplaces. I've personally found both elements to exist side by side in most institutions.

Why do organizations behave this way? What makes people sociopaths or sycophants? What makes an organization evolve into a psychic prison or become an instrument of domination? Is this truly the way the world is, or are these individual behaviors and organizational types merely a product of the modern workplace? This is the chicken-and-egg dilemma; do people and their lunatic behaviors forge the workplace environment, or does organizational life beget the lunatics?

The answer, of course, is both. Sociopathic behavior influences the culture, and then the culture influences the inhabitants. It's a vicious circle. As Venkatesh Rao notes, "Organizations don't suffer pathologies; they are intrinsically pathological constructs."[124] Also, as an organization increases in size and complexity, both sociopathic and sycophantic behavior intensifies. Once sociopathic behavior becomes prevalent, it begins to reshape the culture into both a psychic prison and an instrument of domination.

No discussion about corporate sociopaths and sycophants would be complete without acknowledging the "The Peter Principle." This is the widely held belief that in a hierarchy, people tend to rise to their level of incompetence.

Dr. Laurence J. Peter and Raymond Hull, in their 1969 book *The Peter Principle*, formulated a humorous treatise, which holds that in any hierarchy, members are promoted as long as they work competently. However, sooner or later they're promoted into a position in which they're no longer competent, and there they remain.

This implies that, in time, every job will be occupied by an employee who is incompetent to carry out his or her duties. It implies then that effective work must be accomplished only by those employees who have not yet reached their level of incompetence. This explains why the true work of the organization isn't carried out by upper management, but instead by the proles.

The Peter Principle also introduces the concept of managing up, which says that a subordinate who finds himself working for an incompetent must somehow manage his superior to limit the damage that he will end up doing. Managing up is also a defense mechanism when dealing with a sociopathic boss, especially a micromanaging one.

There's an interesting corollary to the Peter Principle called (not surprisingly) the Paul Principle, a term coined by Paul Armer. This principle also serves to describe the modern workplace. It states that people become progressively less competent for jobs they once were well equipped to handle. This means that if someone is in a position in which he was originally competent, he will, over time, become incompetent in that position. So incompetence comes from either being promoted into it or by staying too long in a single job. This explains why management becomes incompetent sooner or later.

This begs the related question: Who defines competence? I can tell you it's not an objective fair standard of measurement. Dictionary.com defines competence as the combination of knowledge, skills, and behaviors leading to the ability to perform a specific role. The operative words in that definition are "specific role." Rating someone's competence is a whole new can of worms.

Being able to land a job is dependent on your ability to perform the task, as described in the job description, and your ability to bullshit your way through the interview(s). However, once ensconced in the organization, competence is not just the ability to perform one's job effectively. It becomes totally determined by your boss, come review time, based on his subjective perception of your capabilities, which include many highly subjective soft skills.

Most people who fulfill their job duties efficiently will still suffer the wrath of the sociopathic boss when rated on their soft skills performance. The part of the performance review that's the killer is the rating of these soft skills–like problem solving, or creativity, to name a few–that may, or may not, have any true bearing on job performance or competence to perform a specific role. In essence, the performance review process goal is to document how everyone is incompetent. We'll tackle the performance review in great detail in a later chapter.

I'd like to say I have some solutions for this sad state of affairs, but alas, I don't. It's just the way most modern workplace organizations function. It likely can't be changed because it's too ensconced into the business psyche, or DNA. If it weren't, there'd be an exception to The Iron Law of Oligarchy and that's not possible.

To understand the organizational hierarchy as a whole and why the modern workplace is the dysfunctional place that it is, we must first focus on and understand the top layer of our pyramid: the sociopaths.

CHAPTER 8 MAN BITES DOG

THE MOVIE *MAN BITES DOG*[125] **IS A** dark, almost comedic, Belgian film about the escapades of a serial killer. In the movie a film crew follows Ben, the charismatic lead character, on his sadistic adventures recording his crimes for a documentary they're producing. At first they're dispassionate observers, but they quickly become caught up in the addictive violence. More than that, their mere presence incites the lead character to new levels of savagery.

The movie follows Ben as he explains his "craft" to the film crew in great detail. For example, he explains that he prefers to attack old people primarily because they're easier to kill. In one scene, he even screams at an elderly lady, causing her to have a heart attack. As she lies dying, he points out to his newfound followers that this method allowed him to spare a bullet. Ben will target anyone who comes his way: men, women, children, and his favorite victims—mail carriers.

Throughout the movie Ben's violence becomes more and more random and motiveless, and the camera crew, who at first were just accomplices to the crimes, begins to get involved and even take an active part in the murders. In the end, Ben and his cohorts all meet the same fate that they've been metering out. Ben is shot dead by an off-camera gunman, and the camera crew is then picked off, one by one. The last cameraman finally drops his camera to the ground and runs, and while the camera is still recording, it documents his shooting at the hands of the unknown gunman.

Man Bites Dog offers an inside look at our culture and how we make heroes of people who don't deserve it. The movie brilliantly portrays sociopathic behavior and reveals our morbid fascination with this type of behavior. From this movie we can learn much about sociopathic behaviors and also how people exposed to this behavior react to it and how it turns them into sycophants.

Sociopaths are charismatic, and people want to get close to them because they're mesmerized by their decisive and assertive personality. These are the sycophants who get quickly caught up in the sociopath's web of lies and bullshit. The film crew in the movie, just like real-life sycophants, starts taking an active part in the socio-pathic behaviors. Also, the mere presence of the sycophants incites the sociopath to further act in his perverted ways.

One interesting aspect of the lead character is his preference to attack old people versus younger ones. This mirrors the typical organizational sociopath who will focus his attention on those whom he's known a while, and may not be willing to fight back, versus organizational new comers. The sociopath grows tired of people after time, so it makes no difference whether you're performing exemplarily or not; when the sociopath is done with you, you're toast, and he'll then move on to his next target.

Ben's methods of using fear to scare people to death, which allows him to spare a bullet, are metaphoric for how the sociopaths use subtle methods to undermine their targets, preferring this to the more laborious methods, like using the perform-ance review process, to torpedo and eliminate those he's through toying with.

Another telling behavior of the movie's lead character is his admission of random and motiveless targeting of anyone who comes in his way. This ironically includes mail carriers. This is metaphoric for the tendency of sociopaths to always attack the messenger.

Sociopathic behaviors in the workplace are truly a story of "man bites dog." If you find yourself in one of these organizations, the key is to try not to become the dog.

How do these obviously bad people rise to the top of an organization? It defies logic and common sense, yet it happens in virtually every organization. Part of the reason for the sociopath's upward mobility is derived from the fact that he is thoroughly con-vinced of his own importance, which gives him the ability to exude a confidence and decisiveness that few other normal people have. This is a universal trait that we'll see when we learn more about sociopaths later in this chapter.

This decisiveness is why many organizations suffer from the paralysis that ensues, because these top level employees become the only ones in the organization who can make decisions. They believe they know best and are convinced that it's better for them to be in the position of making decisions. They're like the Wizard of Oz, and their unholy organization becomes their Emerald City. In fact, learning a little more about the Wizard might help put the average workplace sociopath in some perspective.

The Wizard in *The Wonderful Wizard of Oz*[126] is this unseen ruler of the Land of Oz who has the characters believing that he rules with an iron fist by the way he manifests himself to them in the story. Depending on whom he's appearing to, the Wizard manifests in different forms—once as a giant head (the omnipotent one), once as a beautiful woman, once as ball of fire, and once as a horrible monster (the bully). His real name is Oscar Zoroaster Phadrig Isaac Norman Henkel Emmannuel Ambroise Diggs. If you shorten his name to only his initials (OZ-PINHEAD) you get a feel for his true nature.

The typical workplace sociopath acts no differently than the Wizard. They can exhibit many personalities that manifest themselves depending on whom they are targeting at the time. To the organization as a whole, they are the giant head; to the loyal sycophants they are like a beautiful woman; to those being bullied they're a horrible monster, and to all others they are a ball of fire.

Where do these nuts come from? First, you must understand that a true sociopath can start in an organization anywhere including among the proles and progress to the organization's top level. However, in the end, true sociopaths are not made; they're born that way.

According to Venkatesh Rao, "The sociopaths enter and exit organizations at will, at any stage, and do whatever it takes to come out on top. They contribute creativity in early stages of an organization's life, neurotic leadership in the middle stages, and cold-bloodedness in the later stages, where they drive decisions like mergers, acquisitions and layoffs that others are too scared or too compassionate to drive. Sociopaths are dynamic and destructive individuals." [127]

Once in a position of power, sociopaths are only looking out for their own best interests. They will protect themselves by promoting those who exhibit sycophantic tendencies into subordinate positions in management. They then become his "Selfish Herd," which we'll learn about later. These sycophants are really just sociopaths in waiting. These junior sociopaths become sycophantic so that they have a reason to be in the debt of the sociopath. I've dedicated an entire chapter to learning about this special (dangerous) type of organizational lunatic.

The sociopath is the most prevalent behavior you'll experience in the workplace despite the fact that experts believe only 1 to 4 percent of people exhibit sociopathic tendencies. On an interesting side note; I've read where researchers at the famous Max Planck Institute for Evolutionary Anthropology in Leipzig, Germany found that humans actually bred with ancient Neanderthals. They discovered this through the analysis of DNA captured from Neanderthal bones compared to modern human DNA.[128] The researchers have estimated that 1 to 4 percent of the modern human genome can be traced back to the Neanderthal.

Because of the negative effect that sociopathic behavior can have on an organization, we'll need to learn more about how to recognize sociopaths and how they typically behave.

The colloquial definition of a sociopathic personality is: a narcissist; someone unconcerned about the adverse consequences on others of their actions; a person with an antisocial personality disorder; pleasure-seeking and remorseless.

Many people think of a sociopath only as a serial killer. The media haven't helped by portraying serial killers as sociopaths; however, they really should be called psychopaths instead. Although most serial killers are in fact sociopaths, most socio-paths lead ordinary lives. Chances are quite good you know a sociopath or are cursed to work for one.

If you're not sure if you work for a sociopath, here are some of their typical traits:

- Charisma; a charming and ingratiating behavior that makes people want to follow them.

- Manipulative; they'll twist the truth to fit their self-conceived notion of what reality should be, which is always in their favor. They see others around them as tools, targets, and opportunities for their own gain. Instead of friends, they have victims, and accomplices (sycophants) who end up as victims.

- Exalted; grandiose sense of self; thoroughly convinced of their own importance.

- Narcissistic; they believe themselves to be superior to all others. They never recognize the rights of others and see their self-serving behaviors as permissible.

- Pathological liars; they have no problem lying, and it's almost impossible for them to be truthful on a consistent basis. They lie; everyone else bullshits.

- The end always justifies the means; they let nothing stand in their way; they will leave a path of dead bodies if they must to get what they want.

- Lack of compassion or empathy; they display a lack of sincerity. They cannot be trusted to be genuinely concerned for anyone other than themselves. They are unable to empathize with the pain of their victims, having only contempt for others' feelings.

- Conniving; they always have an ulterior motive; they love the psychological games we'll learn about later.

- Overreact to insignificant matters; sky is falling mentality, they will create crises out of the most inconsequential problems. They are the true drama queens.

- Surprise adverse; they cannot handle any un-planned problem and they are prone to shoot the messenger.

- No remorse, shame, or guilt for their actions; not concerned about wrecking others' lives and dreams or the damage they do to the organization as a whole.

- Poor behavioral controls; they can be nice one minute and a demon the next, alternating between expressions of feigned love and approval of their targets to outright contempt.

- All-powerful and all-knowing; they are egotistical and will flaunt their skills, knowledge and credentials; they are college snobs.

- Respects no personal boundaries; they have no concern for boundaries. Everything in the organization is their business and fair game for them to micromanage.

Recognize any of those traits in someone you know? Sometimes you find out you're dealing with a sociopath only after it's too late: when he's dropped you like a dirty shirt.

The way they interact with their subordinates is motivated purely by the principle of plausible deniability, which refers to the denial of blame by the upper rungs of management and the subsequent blaming of those in the lower rungs. Sometimes they will blame the proles, but their sycophants most often serve as their fall guys—their selfish herd. Plausible deniability works because the sociopaths have the power and can bully and mob anyone they've picked out as the target for the blame.

So are all people in high positions sociopaths? Not necessarily. As Jennifer Miller points out in her August 2010 article "The Power Trip: Nice People More Likely to Rise to Power," "Contrary to the Machiavellian cliché nice people are more likely to rise to power. [However] then something strange happens: Authority atrophies the very talents that got them there."[129] They then become sociopaths. So yes, all people in high places exhibit sociopathic behaviors to some degree.

This is what's called the cliché of power; the only way to the top is to engage in self-serving, narcissistic and morally dubious behavior. It's also referred to as the "paradox of power." It works because studies have shown that narcissistically driven rude and inappropriate behavior, more often than not, comes from those in a position of power and authority. Unfortunately, starting out nice takes much more time, and in some venues doesn't lead to promotion at all. In fact, most often the sociopaths target the nice people, as they perceive them as weak. So if you want to get to the top fast, become a sociopath first; get promoted. Don't waste time trying to be nice.

Since the characteristic of narcissism appears to be a common thread though all sociopathic behavior, I want to point out that not every narcissist is a sociopath. In today's world everyone is a narcissist to some extent. It might be interesting to delve a bit more into the differences between those displaying pure narcissism versus those that exhibit sociopathy.

Dictionary.com defines narcissism as an inordinate fascination with oneself; excessive self-love; vanity; self-centeredness, smugness or egocentrism. Thus, the dominant interest of a narcissist is himself and his entire image of the world is focused only on himself to the extent that others don't exist or certainly don't matter. This behavior appears to others as complete lack of empathy.

While narcissism certainly is the prevailing behavior displayed in a sociopath, their behavior issues go much deeper. As we've learned, a sociopath is a person with antisocial personality disorder. The Mayo Clinic defines antisocial personality disorder as; "a type of chronic mental illness in which a person's ways of thinking, perceiving situations, and relations to others are abnormal and sometimes destructive. People with antisocial personality disorder typically have no regard for right and wrong. They may often violate the law and the rights of others." This goes way beyond just being self-centered. Note the terms "destructive' and "no regard for right or wrong."

One of the key differences between the narcissist and the sociopath is the degree of their lack of empathy. The sociopath truly could care less for others while the narcissist exhibits lack of empathy as a by-product of their self-centeredness. That is, for the sociopath, his lack of empathy in clearly intentional. For the narcissist, his lack of empathy is really founded in the perception others have of him. Another difference between a narcissist and the sociopath is that, unlike the narcissist, the sociopath's lack of empathy is, in fact, contempt for others. Because of this they are notorious for blaming others for anything that goes wrong. They are consumed with achieving their own success, most often at the expense of others.

As we've seen, one of the main problems with sociopathic authority is that it's completely unsympathetic to the concerns and emotions of the people in the organization. This complete lack of empathy is called the "myopia of power" which is the inability to see the world from someone else's perspective. This is the prime characteristic explaining most of the sociopath's behavior.

The most notorious sociopath is the workplace bully. Bullies and sociopaths rise to the top because society as a whole views them as highly competitive individuals who become strong leaders–just as Ben did in *Man Bites Dog*. This is important to note because it's reflective of how our society looks at its leaders. This societal attitude all but guarantees their presence in the modern workplace.

As sociopaths and sycophants rise in a hierarchy they will do everything they can to change the organization to fit their perverted view of the world, regardless of the often destructive impact it has on the organization. In a sociopathically led organization, as in all organizations, the principle requirement for rising in the hierarchy is sycophancy. This lends some insight into how coaching and mentoring really works. Sociopaths only entertain coaching and mentoring because it boosts their ego to have a fawning underling hang on their every word.

Sociopathic bosses will take their best ass-kissers under their wing and train them to be their next heir apparent. This is why you'll hear a lot about succession planning in modern business. The sociopaths want an official program in place that will justify the nepotistic nurturing of their favored sycophant into a position of power close to them.

If there's a workaholic leading the organization, a certain number of sycophants have no problem jumping on that bandwagon. They'll ignore family, friends and social life to rise in the hierarchy. Sadly, there's a strong societal predisposition to this behavior as we can witness by the vast numbers of ass-kissers (and workaholics) in the workplace willing to sacrifice their lives.

How can such a statistical minority cause such havoc in an organization? It's simple. Once in a management position, their negative influence is magnified. Remember that people will tend to emulate those in power. If that one out of one hundred lands in the top job the whole organization will mimic his behavior. In this manner we get sociopathy by proxy.

How can you know whether someone you work with, or for, is a sociopath? Aside from the list of traits above, you can also make the determination solely on how you feel personally. All you have to do is ask yourself these simple questions:

- Do I often feel that he or she could care less about me?
- Does he or she try to deceive me or make contradictory statements?
- Does he or she not support my needs thus restricting my success?
- Does he or she make me feel guilty all the time?
- Does he or she make me nervous or anxious, especially in their presence?
- Does he or she bring problems to me without any constructive advice?

- Do I dread meeting with him or her?
- Does he or she make me feel like I owe them?
- Does he or she act out any of the games (we'll learn about later)?

If you answered yes to more than a few of these, you might be dealing with a sociopath and there's only one effective solution. You need to quit. Feeling any of the emotions above is just not healthy. I know that's harsh medicine, but there's no changing these ilk. Remember the Monarch of Pointland. It's better to cut bait early than waste your precious career time staying in a sociopathic environment. Even if you're on good terms with your resident sociopath, it's safe to say that eventually you'll turn up on his shit list. Better to leave under your own terms than at his whim.

Many of you may think me an alarmist. That's because as Kurt Nimmo notes, "In America, the criminally insane rule and the rest of us, or the vast majority of the rest of us, either doesn't care, do not know, or are distracted and properly brainwashed into acquiescence."[130]

CHAPTER 9 FEE, FI, FOE, FUM

Fee, fi, foe, fum

I smell the blood of an Englishman

Be he alive or be he dead

I'll grind his bones to make my bread

FEE-FI-FOE-FUM IS THE FIRST LINE OF THE famous classic English fairy tale *Jack and the Beanstalk*. In this story, Jack manages to defeat a dim-witted giant, acquire his wealth, and return home triumphantly. Unfortunately, for most of us, the daily battle we'll fight against the demagogues in the average workplace won't end as favorably as in *Jack and the Beanstalk*.

This chapter is not about how to be Jack and defeat the giant, because the story of Jack's success is only a fairy tale and in the real world you'll rarely defeat the giants that surround you. By giants, I'm talking about the sociopaths and bullies who pervade the modern workplace. If by some dumb luck you do score in the battle against a sociopath, start marking your days because they're numbered.

There's an old saying, "The higher the monkey climbs on the flagpole, the more he exposes his asshole." While that's true, Marshal Goldsmith has a more pertinent view, "The higher you go the more your problems are behavioral."[131] And no one in the workplace acts more like a monkey or an asshole than the organizational bully, this most sinister of sociopathic behaviors.

As of this writing, bullying in grade and high school has received nationwide attention because of the resultant suicides that have occurred as a direct result. However, bullying has also reached epidemic proportions in the American workplace.[132]

A 2011 study, conducted Dr. Gary Namie at the *Workplace Bullying Institute*, showed that workplace bullying is alive and well in the modern workplace and is four times more prevalent than other forms of illegal harassment. And here you thought you left it behind when you graduated high school.

The study revealed that:

- 34.5% of Americans report personally being bullied
- 15.5% have witnessed bullying.
- 49% have been affected by bullying
- 72% of bullies are bosses
- 62% of the bullies are men; 38% are women
- 58% of targets are men; 42% are women
- 81% of employers are actually doing nothing to address the issue
- 40% of employees targeted by a bully never tell their employer
- 45% of people targeted by a bully experience stress-related health problems including debilitating anxiety, panic attacks, and clinical depression

The sheer fact that there exists a *Workplace Bullying Institute*[133] tells you that this is a major problem in today's workplace.

The biggest problem with bullying is that it manifests itself in varying degrees. There isn't a single bullying behavior that all bullies religiously practice, although they all do share many common traits. Also, bullying comes in all sizes and flavors, from the downright verbally abusive, characterized by yelling and screaming, to the more common subtle types of bullying, like micromanaging and forced workaholism. Because of this, sometimes it's hard to convince yourself you actually are working for a bully. By the end of this chapter you'll be able to tell without a shadow of a doubt whether you're under one of their proverbial thumbs.

Here are some sure-fire signs that you're being bullied at work:

- You feel like throwing up the night before the start of your work week

- You can't sleep because you're worrying about what you'll face at work the next day
- Your frustrated family wonders why you act so depressed all the time (or you actually take anti-depressants)
- You try to deny the reality and rationalize your situation
- You have skyrocketing blood pressure
- You feel ashamed because you're being controlled by another person and you don't know how to stop it
- You can't enjoy your time off, and days off are spent exhausted and lifeless; your desire to do anything is gone
- You begin to believe that you actually are inferior and have lost your self-respect
- You constantly feel agitated and anxious, and experience a sense of impending doom

I've felt more than one of those feelings on occasion. That being said, the bully you work for is not the only one you'll have to contend with on a day-to-day basis. There are plenty of people in all the organizational ranks, from top management through the sycophants and even into the proles' class, who act like assholes and can attempt to bully you.

Despite the fact that bullies are sociopaths, they are much more prevalent in today's workplace than the statistics (1 to 4 percent) for sociopathy would predict. While the *Workplace Bullying Institute* statistics above really tell the tale about bullying, we must remember there are also many "bullies-in-training" that may not be full-fledged, high-ranking sociopaths, but they none the less can act like sociopathic assholes. The full-fledged, card-carrying bully, high in an organization, is probably the most often recognized. This is due to the fact that his position will magnify his bullying behavior simply by the influence he can bear on the people under him.

However, you must remember you can be bullied by anyone in the organization that repeatedly acts like an asshole.

In his book, *The No Asshole Rule*, Robert Sutton simplifies the criteria for identifying these assholes. He tells us, "[There are] two tests to use for spotting whether someone is acting like an asshole:

- Test 1: After talking to an alleged asshole, does the target feel oppressed, humiliated, de-energized or belittled by the person? In particular, does the target feel worse about his self-esteem?

- Test 2: Does the alleged asshole aim his or her venom at people who are less powerful rather than at those people who are more powerful? The difference between how a person treats the powerless is a good measure of human character."[134]

Now we have the statistics on who a bully may be, and we know how he makes us feel. Now let's uncover exactly how the bully bullies. Workplace bullying comes in basically four different flavors: physical, verbal, emotional, and cyber bullying. Each will leave a bad taste in your mouth. Let's explore them:

- Physical bullying: This is self-explanatory and is obvious to both the bullied and the casual observer unless the violence spills over onto all who are within rifle range. Thankfully, physical violence is not that frequent in the workplace.

- Verbal bullying: Here the bully will say demeaning or offensive things directly to the victim, both in private or in front of his or her peers and colleagues. This can include indirect methods, like spreading rumors about the target. When conducted in private it makes verbal bullies more difficult to prosecute because it becomes a game of "he said, she said." Of the types of bullying, verbal bullying is frequently the most prevalent. This behavior is exemplified in the games of "Divide and Conquer" and "Stump the Dummy."

- Emotional bullying: Here the bully's, goal involves a concerted effort to make the target unsure of themselves. It manifests itself in how the bully "treats" the target. It can include excluding the target from business functions in which they may, or may not, have a vested interest. This type bullying causes the victim to suffer mental anguish isolating the target from the crowd in a sort of purgatory. A good example of this behavior is "gaslighting.'

- Cyber bullying: Here the bully's tool of choice is e-mail. A classic example is when the typical workaholic bully blasts out e-mails after hours or on weekends, or even when he or she knows the target is indisposed, like on vacation. Not only does the bully have the victim as a puppet on a string, but the bully times the response, comparing it to his perverted notion of a sense of urgency. This is a favored methodology used in the game of "Stump the Dummy."

In all but physical bullying, the practice typically involves more subtle methods, such as intimidation and coercion and through the games that they like to play with their unsuspecting prey. We'll explore some of the subtle games methods in later chapters.

The above bullying methods can be practiced in a number of different scenarios:

- Individual bullying: Here the source of all of an organizations' dysfunction can be traced to one individual who terrorizes one employee after another. This is the most common type of bullying and is especially despicable when it's done by the person at the top level of the organization. This poisons the whole culture and sends the signal that this behavior is acceptable.

- Bi-lateral bullying: This takes place with two people, typically peers or colleagues, who seem to have an ongoing conflict. This is a common phenomenon in the sycophant ranks as they jockey for position under the reigning sociopath. This also has a negative effect on the morale of the whole workplace environment.

- Gang bullying: This is when a number of people gang-up on an unsuspecting target. Yes, gangs exist even in the workplace. The perfect venue for this kind of bullying is a meeting or any group setting, because the bullies add to their joy the pleasure of watching their target humiliated and their reputations going down in flames in a public setting. It usually involves scape-goating and is closely related to the fiefdom syndrome that we'll learn about in a later chapter.

- Workaholism or micromanaging: This is a subtle kind of bullying. Here the bully makes everyone around him miserable because his expectations are that everyone shares his perverted sense of loyalty, urgency, and pedantic control. This is especially sinister when practiced by the person at the top level of the organization. Like all other sociopathic behavior it will bleed down through the organizational ranks.

The effect of bullying and the pressure of having to deal with bully behavior, no matter the technique or venue, cause the general workplace moral, communication, teamwork, and effectiveness to sink to the lowest levels possible. I think the forms of bullying that do the most damage emotionally in an organization are workaholism and micromanaging.

Workaholism has always been a favorite malady of mine, not because I'm a workaholic by any stretch of the imagination, but because I'm intrigued as to why someone would be inclined to forfeit life for the sake of a job. Don't get me wrong, it's good to work long and hard to enhance your career, but I'm talking about the characters that have already made it to the top. I'm not advocating resting on your laurels, but everyone knows that old saying: "Nobody's ever been quoted from their death bed as saying that they wish they had spent more time at the office." I'll bet you know many a workaholic and I'll also bet you never really thought of them as bullies.

Workaholic behavior is a dysfunctional behavior that can be found at all levels of an organization. However, when exhibited by someone in management, with a sociopathic personality, it's a dysfunction that can be quite contagious. This is because, by definition workaholics, and their expectations for those around them, will beget more (albeit reluctant) workaholics. Why? Because subordinates are forced to become workaholics in order to survive.

You probably think this is a threat only if you work for the workaholic, but as we'll see in a later chapter, colleagues who exhibit this malady are not above assassinating you by telling the boss that you're just not pulling your weight. At some level the workaholic is jealous of those who are not addicted. Sadly, throughout the organization, the workaholic's behavior becomes the standard for comparison, and if you don't mimic this behavior you'll be a target.

In management, a workaholic supervisor essentially demands that all his subordinates behave the same. Most will begrudgingly comply because they have no choice. If a workaholic boss spews his workaholic rhetoric onto co-workers and subordinates, it will be destructive to the morale and overall cohesion of the entire workforce. It becomes especially volatile if the head sociopath is a workaholic, because this person's behavior spreads exponentially through the organizational ranks.

While workaholism and micromanagement can exist separately, they're especially horrific when combined into a single personality. If we think hard enough, most of us have been exposed to the passive bullying technique of micromanagement.

Unfortunately, many of these micromanaging workaholics also suffer from pedanticism: a person who's excessively concerned with formalism (process and procedure) and precision. Most sociopaths are pedantic to some extent. You can tell because it's the trait that thoroughly convinces of their own importance.

Many workaholic micromanagers probably don't even think of themselves as bullies. Most probably won't even acknowledge that they're workaholics or micromanagers, and you may not either; nonetheless, it's a form of bullying. They justify workaholism as a sign of loyalty or commitment, implying that if you don't share this sentiment you're not dedicated to the organization's success. They mask and justify their micromanagement behavior by expounding on the old idiom, "trust but verify." The problem is they feel this gives them carte-blanche to run roughshod over everyone. Their definition of "verify" means they will always be in your knickers. In my mind "trust but verify" is an oxymoron. The sociopath feels the need to verify only because he's untrusting.

I believe that most workaholics must actually be miserable individuals. It sure doesn't sound like a very appetizing existence to work your ass off for an organization that deep down inside you know won't show the same loyalty in return. In the end we all have an equal chance of becoming a Willy Loman or a Shelly Levene (*Glengarry Glen Ross*).

The problem is that most organizations tolerate bullying, workaholism and micromanaging when it's concentrated in the management suite. It's believed that this behavior is what makes for the organization's success (The Halo Effect): thus everyone believes they must mimic that behavior if they want to get ahead. If nothing else, tolerating bullies in the organization gives the organization a bad name and, more damaging, it gives everyone the impression such behavior is acceptable.

Once you're on a bully's target list, it's impossible to escape without exiting the company. Once you've been targeted as different and unworthy of their perverted loyalty, you're doomed. As we learned earlier about the typical sociopath, they are thoroughly convinced of their own importance, and as such, as soon as your idolization of them wanes, these pooterheads[135] will mark you for extinction.

Bullying is sinister because the bully usually starts off by pretending to be your friend in an effort to get closer to you. You may be lulled into believing that you're immune to his bullying, but in reality all that's happening is that the bully is scoping out your weaknesses before he pounces. My advice is, if you're faced with this situation run for the door.

If you're not personally the target of a bully, you might not be convinced that bullying can exist in your organization. There are a number of tell-tale signs that an organization is suffering from bullying. They include:

- Reduced organizational effectiveness: The organization struggles to meet even the simplest of goals, or worse, can't meet revenue and profit goals.

- Reduced quality of work, or products: bad product design, shoddy workmanship, unhappy customers, and high rates of product return.

- Low morale, high absenteeism and turnover: I'm not talking about the forced turnover at the hands of management; that only adds to the misery.

- Organizational values statements plastered to the lunchroom wall: that all in the organization view as mere propaganda.

- The eleventh hour mentality: Each day is marked with a crisis du jour.

- Plus, any of the workplace games that we're going to learn about are played out across the organization on a daily basis.

We've focused on how bullies think and act, and how they affect the general workplace atmosphere, but how about the effect on the individual victims? How do people being bullied change in behavior? Behavioral changes of the target can include:

- Becoming aggressive or wanting revenge

- Becoming withdrawn and keeping a low-profile

- Becoming hyper-sensitive to any criticism, however trivial

- Becoming emotionally drained

- Suffering from low self-esteem

- Trouble sleeping

- Suffering clinical depression

As we can see, a bully affects people psychologically. They're quite effective in doing just that. Remember, the typical bully is first and foremost a sociopath and thus, has all the innate sociopath traits. As such, he gets immense satisfaction by making people feel badly.

What's sad is they administer their wrath as a test of belonging. Tolerance to their behavior will elevate one's status to the ranks of the sycophants. Fighting back will mark one for elimination. In a misguided way, they think their behavior is performing a service, ensuring that unsuitable people are quickly identified and eliminated from the organization.

It shouldn't be to anyone's surprise that bullying, like all other sociopathic behavior, is a personality disorder. There are many different types of personality disorders, but they can be broadly categorized into two discrete types called: primary and secondary. Primary disorders are often termed "antisocial personality disorders." Secondary personality disorders are essentially neurotic in nature and generally affect only the person exhibiting the disorder. Thus, I want to concentrate on primary personality disorders that tend to affect others, particularly the bullies' targets.

Psychological theory further divides human behavior into two broad categories called "adaptive" and "maladaptive," or "functional" and "dysfunctional." Simply put, adaptive behavior is normal (by society's standards) and thus not generally disruptive. Maladaptive behavior, on the other hand, can be extremely disruptive and tends to be distressing for everyone associated with the person exhibiting this behavior.

Thus the typical bully can be categorized with primary maladaptive personality disorder. This maladaptive behavior will manifest itself deeply in a person's personality. How it happens leads to that old argument about whether it's heredity or environmental factors that shape the person's personality. The answer is that both shape the person. As I mentioned earlier, sociopath's are born that way, but I believe that, more than heredity, the environment that the person matures in has more damaging long-term effects and nurtures the propensity to become a bully.

In his August 2011 article "Understanding Primary Personality Disorder," Stuart Sorenson sums it up for us, "If we grow up in a loving environment where we are encouraged to feel safe and to explore our world without fear of condemnation, we develop into confident people with high self-esteem. If, on the other hand, we are not valued as children and not taught the value of others we grow up with poor self-esteem and little concern for those around us. This creates a candidate bully."[136]

So I guess it is true then—it's the parents' fault? This fits perfectly with today's societal attitudes where people deny responsibility for their actions because they were supposedly abused or neglected as a child. Unfortunately, unlike childhood bullying, the skills of the adult bully can involve far more manipulative and damaging strategies to the point where psychological and physical health of the targets can be affected.

When bullying behavior is at its most intense, we have the special and serious kind of bully: the "Dictator." This occurs when the bully has mastered the majority of the above noted behaviors plus is in a unique position in management—i.e. he or she is the organization's top dog.

The dictator makes all the decisions about what, where, when, why, and how things are done, and who will do them, and runs the organization as a Kingdom. Employees failing to follow directions are usually severely disciplined or given cause for early retirement. The dictatorial leader traits are;

- All decision-making power is his, including day-to-day decisions at lower levels in the organization
- Is unrealistic in demands, sets impossible deadlines

- Is highly critical of everyone around him
- Is a workaholic and pedantic micromanager
- Uses excessive threat of discipline and punishment
- Digital personality, you're either in his graces or out—no in between
- Does not allow others to question his decisions or authority, surrounds himself with fawning yes-men—his courtiers

That is, his only tool is a hammer, so he sees everyone and every problem as a nail.

Another insidious trait of the dictator (or any sociopath for that matter), especially when found in the top of an organization, is the habit of reaching over the management layers below him to interfere with the mid-level managers and even the proles.

There are no boundaries between the dictator and anyone in the organization. His or her reach can go right into the depths of the organizational structure. Chain of command means nothing.

The diagram[137] below serves up a very good pictorial of how a sociopathic dictator operates on a daily basis:

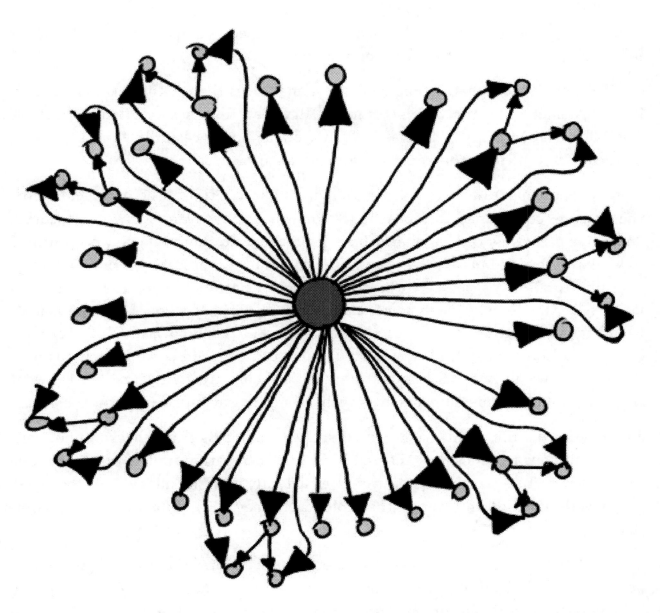

No discussion on dictators would be complete without mentioning the infamous "Napoleon Complex," a term describing a type of inferiority complex affecting usu-ally men who are short in stature. The term is also used more generally to describe people driven by a real or perceived handicap and try to overcompensate in all that they do. This is derived from the belief that Napoleon compensated for his short height by seeking power through war and conquest.

While there's some research that tends to validate this theory, there are more studies that demonstrate that it's just a myth. However, from my experience, I believe this phenomenon is perfectly valid when viewed, not necessarily from stature or physical size but, from the perspective of moral turpitude.

When people repeat George Santayana's famous quote, "Those who don't learn from the past are condemned to repeat it,"[138] known as "Santayana's Law of Repeating Consequences, "they certainly must have been thinking about people who continue to work for horrific bully bosses. The fact is that most organizations, run by a bully, continue to allow its people to be abused and do nothing about it. In fact, they rationalize the perpetrator as some exalted genius without whom the organization would crumble—remember cognitive dissonance and the Halo Effect—all the while hoping, subconsciously, that this will all come to an end in some miraculous way. However, as we all know, human nature just isn't going to change, no matter what wishful thinking we delude ourselves with. The only way out is through the exit.

Just like in real life, bullies come in all shapes and sizes, ethnic background, gender, or religious leanings, but they all have one sociopathic trait in common: they think their shit never stinks. However, they actually stink up all levels of the work-a-day world right down through the prole level. They leave only a trail of disgruntled employees.

In his May 2009 article, "Pointing Fingers," Peter Vajda, offers up a question to ponder. "These 'big fish' were at one time 'small fish.' When did the inappropriate behaviors they exhibited on the way up begin and how did the degree of inappropriateness increase? Taking their first drink, the alcoholic never dreams of becoming an alcoholic. Eating a first dish of ice cream, the slim never dreamed of becoming obese. Making an initial furtive glance, the innocent never envisioned having an affair. But they all have their 'stories' that rationalize a next drink, a next dish of ice cream and a next glance, and more. These individuals concoct a 'story' that allows them to rationalize and justify their immoral or unethical behavior; a story each uses to absolve themselves of blame or guilt so that they can create their own so-called truth and not own their inappropriate behavior. Thus, their 'I did nothing illegal' story or some flavor of it is simply a ploy to evade self-responsibility."[139] There's that cognitive dissonance again.

Workplace bullying is proliferated in the modern workplace despite how barbaric this behavior seems to sane people. However, remember, behavior is measured sane, or insane, by the norm in the organization. You'd think in the modern world we would have evolved beyond this.

The biggest problem is that organizations actually find themselves nurturing this behavior. This happens because even an organization can suffer from myopia, or blind spots, when it comes to their leader's behavior. According to Robert Sutton, there are three major blind spots[140] that organizations fall prey to that explain how the bullies remain on power:

- The jerks succeed despite, rather than because of, their vile ways. They erroneously conclude that this nastiness is crucial to their success.

- The assholes confuse the tactics that helped them gain power with the tactics that are best for leading a team or organization.

- The defensive measures that experienced victims use to protect themselves from cruel and vindictive actions are the measures that have the side effect of shielding assholes from realizing the damage they inflict.

If you're in a toxic workplace, don't fool yourself into thinking you can accomplish much by fighting the bully. You'd be better off just acknowledging that the organization is infested with sociopaths and bullies, and go find a better place to work.

David Chapman, in his article "Are you Being Bullied at Work? Would you like to Fight Back," offers us the bottom line, "a highly skilled bully usually has the dedication, focus, and business acumen to create success, or at least the appearance of success. Then he is honored and promoted, held up as an example of a company-centric leader. He is rewarded while the frustration builds among the targets of his bullying and intimidating, backstabbing, and manipulating. For them, life has become an upside-down hell [their Divine Comedy]" [141]

Next we're going to explore the life of the pitiful sycophants who, in some perverted way, idolize these sociopaths and bullies.

CHAPTER 10 EDDIE HASKELL

EDWARD CLARK "EDDIE" HASKELL WAS A FICTIONAL character on the *Leave It to Beaver* television sit-com, which ran from 1957 to 1963. Eddie played the quintessential suck-up and has become an archetype for insincere sycophantic behavior. Look around you and at your colleagues, and I'll bet you can identify an Eddie Haskell or two in your midst. They exist at all levels of an organization, whether at the top levels of management or in ranks of the proles, and they are constantly sucking up to their boss.

One of my favorite leadership quotes is "If you think you're leading and no one is following, then all you're doing is taking a walk." It is supposedly an Afghan Proverb, and in my opinion, no truer words were ever spoken regarding leadership.

However, the problem in today's top-level leadership ranks is that with the existence of sycophants even bad leaders have followers. In today's typically sociopathic organization, the sycophants will exist no matter how abysmal the leader. In fact, it might be argued that the more sociopathic the leader the more devout sycophants there'll be, because sociopathic behavior attracts this type individual like a magnet. Remember the movie *Man Bites Dog*. Thus, a sociopathic leader without followers is virtually impossible because today's workplace is infested with sycophants; a special type of sociopath.

It's been said that all that is required in America to be a success is great sycophantic skills. From my experience I'd have to say that's true.

Even good—and by that I mean non-sociopathic—leaders have a group of Eddie Haskells following them. It's a given because even good leaders can fall prey to the schmoozing of these leeches and promote them into the positions close to them. For the bad leader, the sad fact is that the sycophants are the only true followers they have. Their narcissism won't let them recognize that the rest of the organization's population is only following because of the fear that is proliferated down through the ranks. They certainly aren't following because of the sociopath's leadership abilities.

In this chapter we're going to explore the world of the organizational sycophant, so let's start with the dictionary.com definition. A sycophant is: a servile self-seeker who attempts to win favor by flattering influential people. Of course Ambrose Bierce, great American editorialist defines it best. He says a sycophant is: "one who approaches greatness on his belly so that he may not be commanded to turn and be kicked."[142]

Sociopathic behavior encourages and actually creates the sycophantic ranks within the organization, as it did in the movie *Man Bites Dog*? Despite the fact that the sociopathic mentality is one in which people loathe each other and have no respect for each other's skills or feelings, sociopaths nurture the sycophantic behavior because of their narcissism. The relationship between the sociopath and his adoring sycophant really becomes a love–hate relationship.

From his article "Sycophants: an Analysis," Paul Wallis describes sycophancy spot on. "Sycophancy is a career move for those who lack talent, intellect, and basic human instincts. The 'team' mentality in which people who loathe each other and have no respect for the skills of their colleagues has been a fertile mating zone for sycophants.

"Becoming a sycophant is easy. All you need is:

- An IQ lower than plankton
- A total lack of any need for self-respect
- An endearing belief in anything convenient
- The ability to spot morons who hire sycophants

- A reputation for being able to support anything from genocide to economic collapse

- A genetic history of undiluted hypocrisy

- The sensitivity of Styrofoam

- The social instincts of a cockroach

"From this inspiring basis, the sycophant can develop a self-image based on being clever and a true can-do person."[143] Despite their courtier heritage, most modern-day sycophants don't have that *sprezzatura* so valued back in the 1500s.

If an organization's leaders are sociopathic, there will always be an entourage of followers who are sycophantic. This is also true if the leaders are really leaders; however, a true leader will know how to temper this behavior. I call this "Haskell's Law:" In any organization, there are those who are willing to please leaders in exchange for power and privilege, or even the outside chance of proximity to power and privilege. These two groups, the sociopaths and sycophants, become symbiotic.

This symbiosis is much like the goby fish that lives together with the shrimp. The goby fish is one of the largest families of fish, with more than 2,000 species. Gobies are bottom-feeders and they are distinctive because of their disc-shaped sucker. They can often be seen using the sucker to adhere to rocks and corals, and in aquariums they'll happily stick to glass walls of the fish tank.

On the other side of the symbiosis, the shrimp is in charge of digging a burrow in the sand in which both the shrimp and the goby fish will live. Since the shrimp is almost blind, it's vulnerable to predators when out of the burrow, so in case of danger, the goby fish touches the shrimp with its tail to warn it. When that happens, both the shrimp and goby fish quickly escape into the burrow. That's much like the sycophant—the goby—keeping watch over his idol—the sociopathic shrimp.

The relationship between the sociopath and the sycophant is really just another example of the stupidity that runs rampant in the modern workplace. However, the relationship is much more complex than simple stupidity would explain.

As Giancarlo Livraghi reminds us "We must assume that the general concept applies: there are just as many stupid people in power as there are in the rest of humanity, and there are always more than we think. But two things are different: the relationship and the attitude.

Livraghi says, "Power is an addictive drug. People in power are often led to believe that because they have power they are better, smarter, and wiser than ordinary people. They are also surrounded by sycophants, followers, and exploiters enhancing their delusion.

"The power syndrome isn't only a disease of powerful people, but also of their followers and of most of the people they know or meet, or who are trying to get into their environment. It's a known fact in all human communities, and at all times in history, that the people in the service of power (or wishing to be) thrive and prosper in a stupid symbiosis with the powerful, which tends to increase and complicate the stupidity of power.

"The victims of this intricate mechanism aren't just the 'ordinary people' who are subjected to the whims and abuse of the intermediaries as well as those of the powers above. They are also, quite often, the people at the top, who become prisoners of their entourage."[144] Thus, sycophancy is a dangerous career path, for both the sycophant and the target of his admiration, because it's a relationship that's founded only in the power that's vested in the sociopath which can be fleeting at best.

In reality, an organization needs the proverbial goby fish—those who will give up all self-respect just to be close to power. In fact, it's actually good that they exist, as they most often divert the sociopath's attention from the rest of the innocents.

These two groups share much in common, as they complement each other and are necessary to each other's success.

In fact, there's another basic reason that the sociopathic management will surround themselves with loyal sycophants. I mentioned earlier that sociopaths surround themselves with a "selfish herd." Thus, "The Selfish Herd Theory" describes the symbiotic behavior between the sociopath and his loyal sycophants. In practice, the behavior the theory describes is like that of the goby fish and the shrimp "escaping into the burrow" when trouble ensues. When the sociopaths retract into protection mode, their line of defense becomes plausible deniability, and they will throw under the bus an expendable sycophant to save themselves.

The selfish herd theory was proposed in 1971 by British evolutionary biologist W. D. Hamilton.[145] In our context it means the risk of an individual (the sociopath) being blamed for something is reduced if that person places another individual (the sycophant) between himself and the accuser (or the problem itself). This is why the sociopaths like having an entourage (the herd) of sycophants; it reduces any risk that their position can be jeopardized. Just like in the wild where the weakest are pushed to the outside edge of the herd, so they become expendable when a predator attacks, so do the sociopaths place their sycophants out at the edge of the herd.

The good news for the sociopaths is that there's an unlimited supply of people who make a career out of sycophantic behavior. It's their only way to succeed.

In the hiring process, organizations generally don't screen for sycophantic traits, and this allows this ilk to infiltrate the organizational ranks. I've yet to see a résumé in which the candidate listed "effectively sucks-up to management" as a skill. They don't advertise themselves. Of course, this is equally true for a sociopath; they don't add egomaniac, narcissist, workaholic, and micromanager to their list of skills on their résumés.

They infiltrate because during the interview process the unwitting organization is sold a bill of goods by the sycophant's self-confidence. The problem is compounded because once a sociopath gets his foot in the door and infiltrates the management level of an organization; he will tend to hire those most like himself. This isn't a unique behavior. Most managers hire people much like themselves; it's one of our innate human tendencies. In this way, sociopathy and sycophancy spreads like a cancer. Once in place they then set the new hires up as their stoolies; thus the sycophantic ranks are populated.

Unfortunately, all of us have the propensity to become a sycophant because we're taught sycophantic behavior early in our life. As children we learn fast that power has its privileges and benefits. We're also taught that we must look out for ourselves—nobody else will. It instills in a person the "me" mentality that the latest generation has been rightfully accused of having. It also explains why the world is becoming so uncivilized. Intolerance of the views and rights of others is an indicator that sociopathy and sycophancy is at work.

Oddly enough, there's an inherent dichotomy in the fact that most organizations suffer with sycophancy. Marshall Goldsmith tells us of a recent study which looked at the leadership profiles at more than one hundred major corporations. He tells us, "Not one profile included the desired behavior that read 'effectively sucks up to management.'"[146]

"Almost every company says it wants people to 'challenge the system,' 'be empowered to express their opinion,' and 'say what they really think.' Companies say they abhor such comically servile behavior, and so do individual leaders. Almost all the leaders say that they would never encourage such a thing in their organizations. There's no doubt that they are sincere. Most of us are easily irritated, if not disgusted, by ass-kissers. Which raises a question: If leaders say they discourage sucking up, why does it dominate the workplace?' Marshall Goldsmith provides us the simple answer as: 'We can't see in ourselves what we can see so clearly in others."[147]

In his March 2009 article "The Sycophantic Culture," Henry Pelifian explains, "Once an adult takes his or her place within an organization, public or private, the dynamics of human interaction and reaction begins based as much on human emotions, weaknesses, and biases than on fairness, objectivity, and merit. The expression 'go along to get along' is almost an unsaid national slogan for many Americans. [Thus] sycophants do not make waves or criticisms. A sycophant will never criticize or correct his superiors, being careful to be fawningly pleasant. The stakes are high: paychecks, pay raises and promotions."[148]

For sociopaths and their sycophantic followers, the status quo is primary and paramount. They don't embrace any change, as real change or reform may well mean a loss of their power or position. As we'll see in a later chapter, this explains why the "no surprises" mentality is so pervasive throughout business.

Anyone criticizing will be seen as undermining their authority. They stifle criticism because they believe they make no mistakes, and when they do, they conveniently blame someone else, which is how "plausible deniability" works. Remember "The Selfish Herd Theory"—the sycophants are there to absorb any criticism to shield the sociopaths. In the end, criticism is the antithesis of sociopathic and sycophantic thinking.

From my experience, criticism is usually unwanted by most institutions despite what they say or whether they're led by sociopaths. When criticism is focused up the organization, it is usually not tolerated; however, as we'll learn later, criticism starting at the top and working down the organizational ranks is an everyday occurrence and one of the favorite games of the sociopaths and bullies.

This is because their balance, on the pedestal they've fashioned for themselves, is too precarious to tolerate criticism. Thus, the funneling of criticism (and blame) down the organizational ladder is the defense mechanism to maintain their balance.

People who do criticize are quickly labeled complainers or whiners (and jokingly drama queens) and set up as a target for the sociopaths' and bullies' wrath. This distinction ensures that they end up at the bottom of the next ranking, come performance review time. While there's certainly a difference between a perpetual complainer and someone who voices displeasure with something concrete, many sociopathically led workplaces stifle any kind of communication that casts a negative view on the workings of the organization. Remember the culture of fantasy that many organizations reside in.

Unfortunately, organizations that don't like criticism are hard pressed to face up to their shortcomings, and this can only lead to their downfall. This makes the prospect of any kind of positive change in these organizations virtually impossible. This contributes to the phenomenon of organizational amnesia. We'll delve deeply into this behavior later, as it's an important aspect of a dysfunctional workplace.

Another pervasive trait of the average sycophant is a propensity to lie. In trying to please the sociopaths and garner acceptance, a sycophant will be untruthful or deceitful, if necessary, and blow smoke up the skirt of his or her target idol. Recall all the myriad lies (and bullshit) that pervades today's workplace; it's all done under the guise of self-preservation. This can also lead to the gaslighting behavior we'll learn about later.

In her October 2010 *Financial Times* article "Power Posing and Flattery Beat an MBA Any Day," Lucy Kellaway tells us why sycophancy works so well. "A recent article described a study done by Jennifer Chatman at UC Berkeley. She set out to discover whether there was a level at which flattery stops working and found that there wasn't one. You can lay flattery on with a trowel; or even a spade or wheelbarrow; and it still does the job."

Kellaway further tells us, "[Chatman] decided to put this theory to the test. [She] picked six colleagues and plied them with praise in increasing quantity. [She] finished off with 'I just don't know how you do it. You're a total genius.' In each case the smile got wider as the dose increased, and there was a flush of pleasure across the [person's] face. In three of the cases the subject told [her] in return that [she] was also a genius."[149]

In his book *A Man without a Country*, Kurt Vonnegut said, "[Sycophants] exist because they are presentable and because they don't ever rock the boat. And unlike normal people, they are never filled with doubts, for the simple reason that they don't give a shit what happens next. Simply can't."[150]

The sociopath and sycophant together become a self-fulfilling prophesy of doom for any organization. And if you don't want to be around come judgment day, my advice is to quickly identify the known sycophants in your organization and avoid them at all costs. They're not your friends, regardless of how friendly they appear on the surface.

Before we delve into the many consequences of sociopathic and sycophantic behaviors, I'd like to quote Will Rodgers who put into perspective why sycophants exist. "We can't all be heroes because someone has to sit on the curb and clap as they go by."[151]

CHAPTER 11 OATH OF FEALTY

DURING THE MIDDLE-AGES, FEUDALISM WAS THE LAW of the land, the basis by which the upper nobility class maintained control over the lower classes. It was a rigid structure of governance consisting of kings, lords, and peasants. This method of governance was the foundation of the overall society and defined the culture at the time. The kings all believed that they ruled their land by divine right, and then passed this on through their heredity.

The feudal structure was necessary due to the geography of the large amounts of land each king had under his control. The problem was there was no physical way for a king to govern all his land effectively because there was no communication system other than horse and rider or carrier pigeons. Since it could take days to travel from one part of a kingdom to another, the kings needed a way to maintain control over their lands, even if indirectly.

The solution was that each king formed a contract with his barons, who were each entrusted to govern large portions of his land. The mini-kingdoms were known as fiefdoms. In return, the barons paid homage to the king by giving their support to the king at all times. This promise of faithful service to the king was called the "oath of fealty."

The only problem with this system was that the barons had the same problem the king had. Because they often had to govern large amounts of land, they further divided their land up and made the same type of agreement with their underlings that the king made with them. In this way, they created even more (smaller) fiefdoms ruled by even more mini-barons. Sometimes these smaller fiefdoms were divided up again into even more fiefdoms.

The king and his barons—and others who ruled the fiefdoms—made up the nobility class, a distinction they believed made them much superior to the common peasants, or serfs. As a result, these lords usually were merciless to their peasants and demanded much from them and gave little in return. Just like in modern times, the barons and peasants believed that the harder they worked, the more of their effort they gave to the Lord, and the more they served him and blew smoke up his skirt, the better life would be for them. It is here we find the humble beginnings of sycophancy.

Over the course of my years in the workplace, I've come to realize that the workings of the ancient feudal system describe exactly how most organizations function today. In Medieval times you had the humble beginnings of the three levels of today's organizational hierarchy. Now, instead of Lords we have top management; instead of barons we have the middle-management sycophants, and despite all the advances of mankind, the workers are still treated like the peasants were in medieval times. These three-tiered structures, coupled with the stove-pipe vertical organizations that are common place in business, provide the exact impetus needed for fiefdoms to form in the workplace.

Robert Herbold was the first to identify the fiefdom phenomenon in business and give it a name: the "Fiefdom Syndrome." He describes it as a condition in which "Individuals and groups tend to isolate themselves from the larger organization and worry more about defending their turf and protecting the status quo than moving the organization forward. Such behavior is called the Fiefdom Syndrome."[152]

Does the following sound like your organization?

- Senior management reviews and approves nearly all actions and decisions
- Management micromanages the day-to-day activities to minute detail
- Meetings are at epidemic frequency and are needed for even the most inconsequential action to be taken or problem to be solved
- There's very little, if any, focus on customer satisfaction

- People who do try to make changes or innovate are chastised or removed from the organization

- Each group executes on their own objectives with little teamwork or coordination between groups or thought of whether it supports the overall organizational goals

- Organization-wide goals (like mission or vision) that requires coordination between groups suffer

- Alienation and suspicion exist between people and departments

Any of these conditions are indicative of an organization suffering from the fiefdom syndrome.

In his book, *The Fiefdom Syndrome*, Herbold details the behavioral reasons that the fiefdom mentality grabs a foot-hold in an organization and begins to thrive and evolve:

- People have an innate need to control the data or information that reflects on their work

- People have a natural desire to be independent and in control of their destiny

- People have a natural tendency to exaggerate the quality of their work and its importance to the organization

These natural human tendencies coupled with sociopathic and sycophantic management styles, make it easy to see how fiefdoms become a natural occurrence in the workplace landscape. While one can observe fiefdoms in a huge variety of organizational situations, Herbold tells us they generally fall into six major categories: personal, peer, divisional, top-tier, group, and protected.[153]

- Personal fiefdoms (or the fiefdom of one) can affect co-workers, work groups, entire departments, and even the actions of the entire company, if the person's impact is broad. Personal fiefdoms can control information, stifle creativity, and inhibit positive change. An example would be the organizational bully.

- Peer-level fiefdoms: similar groups in an organization each operating as a fiefdom

- Divisional fiefdoms: prevalent in larger organizations with multiple operating divisions or product lines where each organization ends up acting as its own entity. (Some corporations actually foster this)

- Top-tier fiefdom: one of the easiest fiefdoms to spot, and the most difficult to alter, in that the people at the top (senior staff) of the organization become immune to the realities of the business

- Group fiefdom: perhaps the most harmful and common fiefdom in business today formed when there's a group (function or department) with a common responsibility or objective

- Protected fiefdoms: these are groups that are favored by the top management sociopaths. All others become second-class citizens in this organization. It occurs when a top executive harbors, or even creates, a fiefdom and provides long-term protection of that fiefdom by sheltering it from financial or strategic scrutiny and, in general, ensuring a hands-off approach to it

Other than the personal fiefdom revolving around the top level sociopath, a protected fiefdom is probably the most sinister of all and the one that has the most negative impact on the overall organization. It's different from a top-tier fiefdom—although the top-tier fiefdom is also protected—in that, with a protected fiefdom, the fiefdom operates as it wishes with full acknowledgment and blessing of the top management. As such, when the top-tier sociopaths allow protected fiefdoms to exist, they enable the continued growth of other fiefdoms. In fact, other fiefdoms grow as a natural survival response.

A protected fiefdom is the product of the phenomenon of collective narcissism, a condition in which a group has an inflated image of itself. This, coupled with validation from the top management, is what sets the group above all others in the organization. Because this group is sanctioned from above, they're viewed as untouchable, which sets up the perfect environment for the second-class citizenship syndrome to set in. This is a condition in which all others are treated with indifference regardless of their contribution to the function of the organization. As you might imagine, this results in animosities and resentments permeating the workplace atmosphere.

The following diagram[154] reflects how an organization would look with a protected fiefdom.

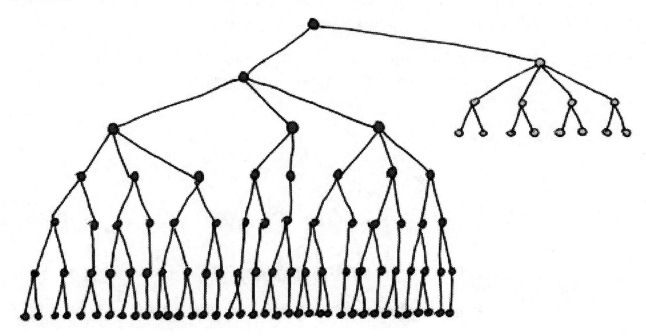

The second-class citizenship syndrome affects everyone and every group outside the protected fiefdom. They're treated as inferior and, as such, not critical to the success of the overall organization. This also creates an environment ripe for selective amnesia to take hold, because the protected group usually does no wrong in management's eyes, so their mistakes are never viewed as systemic problems that need addressing. As such, the protected fiefdom goes on making the same mistakes, and the organization repeatedly ignores them without anyone ever taking the group to task.

Probably the most common fiefdom environment, however, is the group fiefdom. It's been the most common certainly from my own personal experience and affects all organizations to some degree. These are organizations that are splintered with each sycophantic middle manager ruling his department just as the feudal barons did centuries ago. These fiefdoms have their own sociopath/sycophant hierarchy. In fact, the power structure and pecking order within a group fiefdom often mirrors the power structure of the overall organization—just look at the organizational chart. In these environments, departments, or groups, despise each other.

So how does an organization suffering from the group fiefdom syndrome look and actually operate on a daily basis? The diagram[155] below says it all.

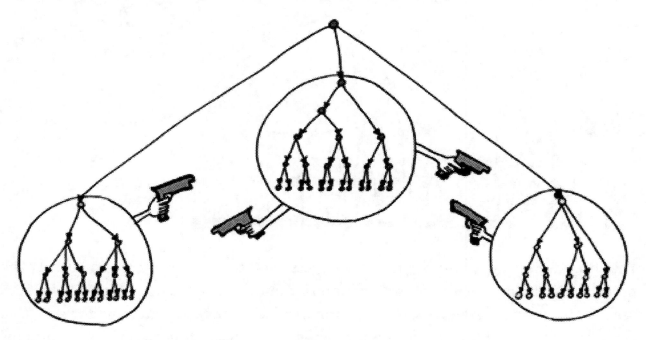

There's another kind of pseudo-fiefdom (not on the above list) that can be found in most, if not all, sociopathic organizations. It's actually more of a clique than a fiefdom. I use the word "clique" because it's a small group of people with shared interests and work history or experiences who elect to spend time together and exclude others. A fiefdom, on the other hand, is the estate or domain of a feudal lord—i.e. an organization in which one dominant person (or group) exercises absolute control. Since this clique really has no formal leader per se, it doesn't fit the fiefdom definition.

This is the group of people in the organization who are considered to be inferior or lower in social status or have fallen out of grace with the sociopaths or sycophants. They are the organizational losers. These are the people who populate the next layoff list.

Unlike in a group fiefdom, the members of this clique of losers can come from all layers and any of the formalized fiefdoms in the organization. The group's sole reason for existence is to form a support group for those suffering at the hands of the maniacs. These are the poor souls who feel contempt or disapproval for the sociopathic regime in power most often because they have been the target of the sociopath's wrath. As such they are targeted for exclusion by the sociopaths and sycophants. Therefore, as you can imagine, they must meet secretively. Their meetings are in secret because the members have to constantly protect themselves from exposure, because if the sociopaths got wind of the group's existence there would be hell to pay. Sociopaths do not tolerate anyone conspiring behind their backs.

One might call their meetings bitch sessions; however, they do serve a purpose in helping the members survive their captivity. Think of their meetings more as therapy sessions for the down-trodden in which they get to commiserate their situations at the hands of the sociopaths and bullies. These are the poor slobs probably also labeled the organizational drama-queens.

If you don't already belong to a clique, consider yourself lucky. And if you don't believe they exist, look around you. You'll see this clique meeting at company social events or in clandestine groups in the workplace. That group of people you catch standing in the corner and whispering to each other is a dead giveaway. The closed door sessions of just two or three people in which only muffled mumbling can be overheard is another sign that there's a clique of the oppressed. If you're living in an organization steeped in sociopathy and sycophancy, you'll probably know who the people are because they have targets on their backs. These are the poor souls you can see being openly ridiculed by the sociopaths even in public venues.

So when you fall from grace in the eyes of the sociopathic elite, as you surely will, look up the local loser clique in your organization and join. They may even recruit you once word gets around that you're not the apple of the sociopath's eye any longer. If nothing else, you can all connect on LinkedIn and serve as references for each other.

Each of the above categories of fiefdoms results from some basic human behaviors or tendencies—the need of all individuals to control data, the perceptions they want others to have of them, or simply as a defense mechanism. We learned about personal impression management techniques earlier, but the fiefdom can actually adopt these behavioral techniques as if they were a single entity.

Ironically, as Herbold told us, fiefdoms exist simply because the majority of people want to do well in the workplace, and to demonstrate that they're doing well, employees naturally look for ways to control the information about themselves that could be used to evaluate their success. However, a dichotomy exists because it's this desire to do well that's the exact behavior that seals the fate of the organization to hopeless mediocrity. Herbold explains, "Fiefdoms emerge when people place more energy and emphasis on demonstrating that they're doing well than on changing their behavior to improve their actual performance.

"It's not that people who exhibit fiefdom tendencies are mischievous or unethical. These behaviors are simply natural human tendencies that emerge as people try to exercise control over their workplace environment, protect their domain, and avoid change that might upset the present order."[156]

It goes without saying that in any organization, it's important to share key information and data across the enterprise. When the right information is widely available, the leaders of the organization know what's going on and can make appropriate strategic decisions. This is not the case in a fiefdom-rich organization. The proliferation of fiefdoms in an organization actually promotes much of the sociopathic behavior at the top, especially micromanagement. If information flowed like it should, the bosses wouldn't have to go searching for it. I'm not saying that micromanagement is good or that it's the fault of the workers; it still is a destructive sociopathic disorder, but the Fiefdom Syndrome exacerbates this behavior.

As a result of the Fiefdom Syndrome and the partitioning perpetuated by organizational charts, middle managers will do everything they can to keep their people focused internal to their fiefdom. In his 1996 article, "Leaders of People: Some are Wonderful, Some are Clueless, the Rest are Somewhere in Between," Peter Scholtes explains, "Their people direct their attention upward, needing a deep daily understanding of the boss's needs."[157] Remember the kingdom culture? Managers foster this internal focus by encouraging employees to compete with one another for pay raises and recognition. The employees take the bait because they know that if they don't, it will affect their rating and ranking on the lay-off list.

One reason fiefdoms survive is that people convince themselves that their work, products, and services are better than they actually are. They exhibit an overconfidence of their abilities. This is called "organizational arrogance," and it's quite prevalent in hi-tech organizations. Protected fiefdoms usually suffer from this fate. It's also an example of the Halo Effect. When we tackle the performance review process we'll learn how this is an innate human tendency.

Fiefdoms cause fragmentation and redundancy and can be destructive to an organization. Each organizational group, like finance, human resources, manufacturing, procurement, IT, and other disciplines or business units, will tend to want to develop their own departments to make their group as independent as possible. Needless to say, this is not the most cost-effective situation for any organization to find itself. Ironically though, many large companies actually foster this redundancy by design.

How do you combat the fiefdom syndrome? Probably the toughest fiefdom behavior to break down is defensiveness. It's extremely destructive to the organization as a whole. It's especially tough to break in the typical sociopathic-led, blame-oriented organization which, by its very nature, promotes defensiveness.

Most often the defensiveness is the result of differing opinions on how something should be done. This is not unlike the situation described in Dr. Seuss's 1984 *Butter Battle Book*. The *Butter Battle Book* tells the story of a land where two hostile cultures, the Yooks and the Zooks, live on opposite sides of a wall and dispute between them what side of the bread to butter. The Yooks eat their bread with the butter-side up, while the Zooks eat their bread with the butter-side down. While the *Butter Battle Book* is actually a parable about arms races (nuclear weapons in particular) and mutually assured destruction, it pretty humorously mimics the absurdity of many of the things that cause friction among competing groups (fiefdoms) of a single organization.

Other than the obvious stifling of communication and defensiveness, there is another effect that fiefdoms have on the organization that actually jeopardizes their very future. As Herbold explains, "Fiefdoms can eat away at innovation. Why? Those who inhabit fiefdoms usually see no reason to shake the status quo." Organizations with little propensity for improving are doomed to eventually go out of business. It's that relentless race to the bottom.

This all sounds kind of hopeless. How then does an organization combat the natural tendency for fiefdoms to spring up? Recall the recommendation made in the chapter on organization charts. The answer is to organize people around a task, or project–i.e. a flat structure–not around strong functional organizations. When workers get too attached to a group, the problems begin. This also will affect the individual project teams, but this can be overcome by making periodic changes in the composition of these teams.

Herbold offers a few additional tips:

- Delegate and empower your people. Creative people need to feel they have responsibility for their ideas and plans. Measure effectiveness and progress, but keep the organization lean.

- Encourage independence. Often it's the individual who marches to a different drummer, who is the most creative. Yet these are often the very people management wants to put constraints around.

- Skip the training. While education's important, all-day seminars sometimes lead to navel-gazing and ritual, which can lead to fiefdoms.

- Keep it simple. Streamline the trip from idea to marketplace, and you'll be less fiefdom-fertile.

- Melt meetings. While it's true that collaboration can boost creativity, multiple meetings and memos are often the stuff of fiefdoms. Too often in organizations, things get proceduralized to an excessive degree. Never rank process above product.[158]

The Fiefdom Syndrome is the biggest inhibitor to teamwork that can plague an organization, and I believe the major problem in today's workplace. This is because of management's failure to realize the essential and simple truisms about fiefdoms and how they negatively affect the organization's ability to meet its goals. Until they are realized, the modern organization's management team has a long, hard uphill battle ahead if it wants to combat and eliminate the fiefdom syndrome from infecting their organizations.

CHAPTER 12 NATTERING NABOBS OF NEGATIVITY

"IT'S AN UP AT DAWN, PRIDE-SWALLOWING SIEGE," said Tom Cruise's character in the movie *Jerry Maguire*.[159]

We've learned that life in the average workplace can be akin to being in one of Irving Goffman's Total Institutions. In a previous chapter we concentrated on a special total institution, the asylum, and in this chapter we're going to delve deeper into the behaviors that are exhibited in the typical workplace asylum.

Anyone who's seen the 1975 movie *One Flew over the Cuckoo's Nest* can attest that's it's not easy to survive an asylum. What we may not realize however, is that we sentence ourselves to a type of asylum every day when we shuffle off to work.

An asylum is a dog-eat-dog environment, and Goffman showed us how the typical workplace is much the same. Remember, Goffman asserts that each institutional environment determines what's considered sane, or insane, behavior and then molds the inhabitants to whatever behavior is accepted as the norm. In this chapter we're going to start delving into the behaviors prevalent in the workplace asylum and learn how organizational life molds the inhabitants' behaviors until they become conniving and devious personalities. In particular we're going to focus on one especially heinous behavior (game) called "Divide and Conquer."

In the movie *One Flew over the Cuckoo's Nest*[160] the main character, Randle McMurphy, played by Jack Nicholson, describes what he calls a pecking party. He describes this as a situation in which chickens see blood on another chicken and start pecking at it, and each other, like crazy. They do this until they end up killing each other.

McMurphy describes how Nurse Ratched's "Therapeutic Community" meetings are like pecking parties. In these meetings Nurse Ratched would strike one of the inmates to reveal his weakness (and metaphorically draw blood), and all of the patients would follow her lead, pecking at the man. This would set off a chain reaction, setting them all against each other instead of against Nurse Ratched. Her goal of keeping them all feeling weak and divided was achieved.

These pecking parties are not unlike the 'Divide and Conquer" behaviors you'll experience in the typical workplace. So how does one survive in an organization that practices this devious version of the pecking party? You'll find yourself asking that same question if you find you're unlucky enough to land a job in Winkie Country, in the land of Oz. Unfortunately, you won't have Dorothy's option of eliminating your Wicked Witch of the West by melting her using a bucket of water.

Business consultant Rick Brenner said, "While most leaders try to achieve organizational unity, some do use divisive tactics to maintain control, or to elevate performance by fostering competition." In his July 2005 article, "Devious Political Tactics: Divide and Conquer," he introduces the concept of "confidential aspersions." This is the practice of bringing someone into confidence with the intent of using him or her to achieve one's own goals or aspirations. Typically, this technique is applied in private, prior to asking someone for some information, or for a special favor or to use that person as a divisive influence in the organization.

He tell us, "This is just one of a family of political tactics that implement a strategy of 'divide and conquer,' which has been used for thousands of years in war and politics. Today, managers and others use it in the workplace. Confidential aspersions are very damaging. Using the tactic sets an example of denigrating colleagues, which can contribute to formation of a toxic and conspiratorial atmosphere."[161]

Dr. Berne's game version of "Divide and Conquer" is called "Let's You and Him Fight." He uses the example of a woman luring two men into fighting, with the implication that she'll surrender to the winner. In his example the woman sets up the competition, and then escapes with a third person. In the workplace this is exactly how the game is played and is a favorite of sociopaths and bullies. The only problem for them is that when they set one of these conflicts in motion, the winner may not be the player they wanted or expected.

Sociopaths use games such as "Divide and Conquer" and other tactics ("Stump the Dummy" and "Pyromania" which we'll cover later) to maintain control over the workforce. "Divide and Conquer" is alive and well in today's typical workplace, and its affect is to motivate people to scapegoat, stereotype, and discriminate against anyone who they see as competition or as a threat to their careers.

Spiro Agnew called these types of people "nattering nabobs of negativism."[162] This is a sort of metaphor for people with a grandiose sense of their own importance, who constantly find fault in others, like to pit people against each other, and generally love to stir the pot.[163]

"Divide and Conquer" is actually a strategy and tactic that has been used for thousands of years in war and politics evidenced by the fact that Sun Tzu even offers it as an offensive technique in *The Art of War*. It's apropos because work life is, after all, a war and politics runs rampant in most organizations. It has become a favorite tactic of the sociopaths and serial bullies in the modern workplace.

In the "Divide and Conquer" strategy, one power tries to break up an existing power structure or prevent smaller power groups from allying together. This serves as another major contributor to the fiefdom syndrome.

In a fiefdom-rich organization, "Divide and Conquer" can be focused on whole groups, but I've personally witnessed it most often being used on individuals. When used against individuals, the purpose is to destroy one or both individuals so that they can't team up against their attacker. Frankly, I think it's used as much for the sheer sport of it as for any ulterior personal motives.

The "Divide and Conquer" strategy typically involves a sociopath, or bully, denigrating one person, or group, by confiding in a third party. The goal is that he hopes the person he's confided in will feel like they've been included in his confidence and thus will look unfavorably on that person (or group) that's been targeted. This in turn sets up a sort of animosity. The underlying goal of this game is to pit people against each other by fostering distrust within the organization.

If the sociopath can keep people fearful and cautious of each other, they'll remain reliant on him and will unknowingly feed this evil game by always going to him when they have any problem or issue with one of their colleagues. Thus the sociopath has any and all negative information funneled through him, thus providing him the ammunition to continue to maintain a hold over his targets. We'll learn later how this also feeds the game of "Stump the Dummy."

Typically, this technique is applied in private, but derivatives of this game can easily be used in an open forum such as a meeting, especially if the sociopath is also a bully.

The sociopaths use this technique to maintain power and influence by keeping smaller departments, functions, or people from uniting or working together. In fact, the use of the principles of the "Divide and Conquer" strategy is more common than you may think. You'd swear that management wants fiefdoms to form and teamwork to fail. It may be hard to believe, but the fact is they must. Sociopaths love seeing people in conflict, as that way they keep the pot stirred and they can stay in ultimate control. They want the organization in constant crisis. Sociopaths who use "Divide and Conquer" are also prone to be pyromaniacs, as we'll see in a later chapter.

"Divide and Conquer" is a strategy for domination and has a storied history. In *The Art of War*, Sun Tzu writes, "The art of using troops is this: when ten to the enemy's one, surround him; when five times his strength, attack him; if double his strength, divide him."[164]

How does this method manifest itself? According to Brenner, here are some of the forms the 'Divide and Conquer game" takes in the workplace:[165]

- The three-legged race. Some supervisors assign responsibility jointly to two people who are already at odds. This tactic can be a simple error, or even a misguided attempt to give them a chance to work things out, but often its purpose is to keep the warriors in conflict, to protect the supervisor. If you really want harmony, work on the difficulty directly, possibly with professional guidance. Worries about your own position are better addressed by working on your own performance. Foster unity, rather than divisiveness, in your team.

- Delaying the decision. When subordinates contend for the same promotion or for some other desirable assignment, some supervisors delay their decisions, on the theory that competition creates superior performance. Although performance might improve before the decision, this tactic can damage relationships permanently. And that could depress performance permanently after the decision, for the winner, for the loser, and for the entire group. This tactic is a good example of how a manager can sabotage the career of his subordinates.

- Lying. One approach to dividing an alliance, or to keeping trouble alive, is to tell lies to one or both parties. Lies, either of omission or commission, can create the impression that one party threatens the other. Disinformation of any kind is risky, and it's especially risky to its source. After the immediate benefit fades, the disinformation can remain, limiting future options.

- Delegating for conflict. Delegating authority generally enhances effectiveness, but some managers delegate to create conflict by delegating different responsibilities to two people, in such a way that they must cooperate to succeed. Since neither is fully responsible, the delegator is free to play one against the other. This tactic damages relationships and depresses organizational performance. Costs are high and repairs difficult, because they involve both reorganization and replacing people.

- Maintaining differences. When managers have promised to retain employees in mergers or acquisitions, keeping organizational elements intact can be a divide-and-conquer tactic. Managers can then systematically discriminate in allocating resources and opportunities. A typical goal might be to drive up voluntary turnover in acquired units. Indirect subversion of the promise to retain employees is still subversion. This tactic is unethical and therefore risky. If the promise to retain was sincere, subverting it could subvert a key strategy of the combination.

"Divide and Conquer might be effective on the battlefield, or when subjugating whole populations, but in the workplace it is ethically questionable. Managers who use it risk conquering only themselves."[166] You can't scare a sociopath by pointing out the illogical errors of his ways, so this is a behavior that you must learn to cope with.

"Divide and Conquer" is not just used to pit two people or two groups against each other. It is also used to pit a single person, or group, against themselves. Sociopaths do this by setting up what's called a "double bind."

A double bind is a dilemma in which an individual, or a group, receives two or more conflicting messages, in which one message negates the other. This creates a situation in which a successful response to one message results in a failed response to the other, and vice versa. Thus, the person, or group, will be automatically wrong regardless of response. For example, your boss tells you to do a job, but doesn't allow enough time for you to do it, and he also threatens that you may lose your job if you don't perform. Another would be, you're given an assignment, but denied the resources to successfully carry it out.

This double bind scenario is also called a "Morton's Fork." A Morton's fork is a choice between two equally unpleasant alternatives that lead to the same unpleasant conclusion. It's analogous to the expression, "between a rock and a hard place."

Another variation of the three-legged race is when the boss gives the same task to two different people; however not telling either one that the other has also been told. By allowing them to find out on their own, the perp has instilled in both a sense that the boss doesn't trust them. And we wonder why trust is such a scarce commodity in the modern workplace.

The "Divide and Conquer" game only creates stress, frustration and certainly arguments among members of the organization. Like the "Chicken Little Syndrome" that we'll learn about later, it produces the "student body left–student body right" syndrome. It plays both ends against the middle to try to make people compete with each other to achieve an advantage. It's one of the most evil behaviors you'll find in today's workplace.

CHAPTER 13 TOGETHER, EVERYONE ANNOYS ME

I'M SURE YOU'VE SEEN IT MANY TIMES: You're driving past a road construction site and one guy is actually working while three others are standing around holding shovels watching him. Most often these are municipal workers, thus we laugh about the typical bureaucracy of government, but forget how that same lack of teamwork is alive and well where we work. At work, we may fail to even notice the organization's dysfunction and, worse yet; we're probably actively contributing to it and the demise of teamwork.

We all intuitively know that when everyone is working individually and not as a team, the overall goals of the organization will most likely be missed. This is why the game of "Divide and Conquer" and the Fiefdom Syndrome have such a damaging effect. Workers may be efficient in their jobs, yet ineffective in meeting the organization's vision and strategic plan because they are divided and cannot, or will not, pull together for the common good. When you consider just what we've learned so far, the deck appears stacked against teamwork ever working.

Too often teamwork is envisioned as some small close-knit group assembled to solve some specific task or problem—e.g. a Skunk Works type environment. That's not really the kind of teamwork I'm talking about and certainly not the global teamwork that organizations need to survive and be competitive. The reality is that, for most organizations, teamwork usually means that commitment has been gained only because it allows people to blame someone else when things go wrong. This is not the brand of teamwork that will set aside an organization as world-class. In today's workplace, team usually means "together, everyone annoys me."

This chapter is about the lack of true teamwork in the modern workplace and the characteristics of the typical workplace environment that's counter to teams forming or working effectively. However, before you can have any hope that your teams can be effective, you must first understand and overcome the natural aversion to relationships that develop between workers.

Some people were born to work on a team while others find it unnatural as they actually have personality traits that are counter to team development. Aside from having an introverted personality, the propensity to shy away from team situations is universal to all individuals. In his July 2010 article, "Teamwork in the Workplace," Dr. Dale Roach describes the typical factors that teamwork-adverse people exhibit:[167]

- The Super Ego Factor: This super-human doesn't need the help of anyone else to accomplish the task or at least this is what he or she thinks. If you're super-human, teamwork makes no sense to you.

- The Isolationist Factor: This is the Lone Ranger of the work place. He does his own thing without asking the advice or input of anyone else. Teamwork makes no sense to this person.

- I'm Smarter than You Factor: These people are the Einsteins of the group. They're so smart that simple communication with anyone on the team is an absolute waste of their time and energy. They seek out the highly intellectuals, and anything or anyone not in that camp is a second-class citizen.

- The Moody Factor: This is the Incredible Hulk. You just don't know what his temperament will be.

- That Was My Idea Factor: This is the Spoiled Brat team member. Everything has got to go his or her way. These types of people have such a severe case of being introverted that they simply can't see beyond themselves. Their lack of teamwork is so severe it is difficult to get these people to see the big picture.[168]

All of the above strangely match the characteristics of the typical sociopath.

CHAPTER 13 TOGETHER, EVERYONE ANNOYS ME

In his book, *The Five Dysfunctions of a Team*, Patrick Lencioni has a different take, and details the reason that teamwork is such a difficult concept for many organizations to grasp. "There's a natural absence of trust between workers. Working as a team requires that each team member be willing to open up to other team members and show their vulnerable side. This acknowledgement of weaknesses allows the group to build trust between its team members, and collectively create the structure that minimizes ineffectiveness through the foundation of trust."[169] However, as we've seen, *trust* is probably the rarest commodity in the workplace.

Of course, the behavior described in the previous chapter does nothing to promote teamwork. In fact, all the behaviors and games we'll explore do little to foster teamwork. All these games encourage an environment of conflict and, coupled with the fact that most people have an innate fear of conflict, the chances of teamwork incubating on its own is almost nil.

For all the negative behaviors to stop and for teamwork to flourish, individuals and group leaders, need to be willing to address conflict head-on in a constructive manner. Make no mistake; conflict can create debate and discussion which can be a good thing. Conflict shouldn't be completely avoided as it can help identify opportunities for improving the effectiveness of the organization. However, in most organizations, peaceful debate and discussion is impossible due to the innate behaviors we're learning about.

The key to controlling conflict, and using it in a focused manner and not allowing it to run rampant through the organization's day-to-day workings, is the biggest challenge facing most organizations. Most organizations just elect to ignore conflict as if it doesn't exist. "In a group setting, conflict that's ignored or deemed unimportant will eventually fracture the effectiveness of the group and potentially dig a hole that is nearly impossible to climb out of," writes Lencioni.[170]

In his book *Death by Meeting*, Lencioni provides another teamwork-killing problem evidenced in many organizations: the lack of commitment. "This happens when people do not have the opportunity to air their concerns and participate in the decision-making process or feel valued by the company. It is not necessary to always achieve consensus as long as each team member understands that his/her input was appropriately considered in making a decision. This approach drives commitment and minimizes the possibility that individual staff members will undermine the group's decisions."[171]

Additionally, there's the whole accountability problem that most organizations suffer from. In an organization in which blame is really the operative work for accountability, people often won't hesitate to call-out their peers or teammates on actions and behaviors that seem counterproductive to the good of the team. They'll do this in the proactive interest of making sure that any team failing doesn't get blamed on them. This is probably one of the few times that proactiveness exists.

To combat the propensity to find blame, any well-run and successful team must have individual and collective responsibly for the success of the team. However, when there's the fear of being blamed for any mistake, even the best-intentioned team will self-destruct. Team members must be willing to challenge each other, and be challenged themselves, without fear of retribution.

Another factor inhibiting teamwork is organizational inattention to results. "This occurs when individual needs take precedence over the needs of the business team. If team members are focusing on whether or not they succeed, irrespective of the collective performance of the business, the group is at risk for achieving long-term, sustainable success. Individual success comes from group success by paying attention and focusing on the overarching goals of the group," says Lencioni.[172] We'll see later that the typical performance review process sets the stage for this behavior.

Lastly, I'd like to add to what all the august experts believe are the reasons teamwork fails. My theory is that one of the basic reasons that teamwork doesn't work, or if it does get a foothold, it can't hold on for long, is our old friend plain old stupidity.

In his book *The Power of Stupidity*, Giancarlo Livraghi asserts that teamwork often fails due to the inability to meld the collective intelligence into one consciousness that can accomplish the team's goal. This is because in a group environment stupidity takes over.

He tells us, "The combination of intelligence in different people is more difficult than the combination of stupidity. This isn't only because the power of stupidity is generally underestimated and its consequences often unpredictable. There are multiple and complicated causes of this problem.

"Stupidity is brainless; it doesn't need to think, get organized, or plan ahead to generate a combined effect. The transfer and combination of intelligence is a much more complex process.

"Stupid people can combine instantly into a super-stupid group or mass, while intelligent people are effective as a group only when they know each other well and are experienced in working together.

"The creation of well-tuned groups of people sharing intelligence can generate fairly powerful anti-stupidity forces, but (unlike stupidity bundling) they need organized planning and upkeep, and can lose a large part of their effectiveness by the infiltration of stupid people or unexpected bursts of stupidity in otherwise intelligent people."[173]

Since effective organizations need intelligent teams, this explains why teamwork is so hard to nurture. It's doomed because bringing together intelligent people into a cohesive group takes real work to effect. Mr. Livraghi does have a good point regarding the magnetism of stupidity. It may completely explain the fiefdom syndrome.

Any group, or team, however intelligent they are or view themselves, will have members who say or do stupid things thus undermining the effectiveness of the team. And nowhere can stupidity flourish more than at the top of the organization.

The senior staff management team sets the tone and example of teamwork for the entire organization. A dysfunctional senior staff, doing what the populous believe are stupid things, will result in inefficiencies rippling throughout the organization and a loss of concentration on the mutual goal. Also, the inefficiencies intensify as the stupid behavior spreads down the organizational structure. From my experience, most executives rarely think that organizational inefficiencies start with their own management team's stupidity.

Teamwork is also stifled when management has not clearly communicated their vision and strategic plan to the organization as a whole. Everyone's not singing from the same hymnal, so to speak. Herbold writes, "American business has a problem with leadership. This failure has to do with management's inability to impart to its employees the desire to see the big picture. This management failure minimizes effectiveness and does not allow natural ability and desire to work with others to flourish."[174]

From my experience, if you ask various members of an organization from the proles up through the ranks what are the objectives of their business, you'll get a wide variety of responses. For the factory worker, it might be producing quality products. Marketing will undoubtedly be focused on good customer service. For senior management, it's providing favorable financial performance, profit margins, and managing expenses. As you can see, they're all focused on different things, albeit all important to the organization.

All of these different goals are vital and valid, but the problem is that the individuals who focus on their own goals miss the opportunity for true excellence that only cross-functional teamwork and unity of purpose can bring. They're not seeing the true big picture. Products might be delivered (sometimes even on time) meeting the factory workers' goal, but somehow the satisfaction level of customers is not good. Maybe because the product design is faulty or marketing promised something to the customer that the product can't do or maybe the customer doesn't feel he got value for his money. This is why customer satisfaction—truly the big picture for most organizations—may be the only metric worth keeping.

One of the most important teams is the pseudo-team that's created when everyone in the organization is aligned to, and working toward, the organization's common goal or vision. They don't need team meetings to accomplish their goals; everyone just does their job and works toward that common goal. This is the real challenge for top management teams: reconciling the individual group's goals into one cohesive top level goal. This is where the performance review process could help, but sadly it isn't recognized as a tool for advancing the big picture, only for setting individual goals.

A lack of concerted focus on the same goal or vision becomes the true definition of organizational dysfunction, and it's what leads to a dysfunctional workplace. Mechanically, this dysfunction will manifest itself both vertically (from the person at the top, to the senior staff, to department heads, to employees) and horizontally (between the department heads and between their respective staffs). Some examples of vertical dysfunctions include:

- Unhealthy attitudes toward the risks facing the organization (The Halo Effect)
- Slow decision-making, or decision-making that's concentrated at the top of the organization
- Breakdowns in communication down the organization
- Lack of follow-through on initiatives (selective amnesia)

Some examples of horizontal dysfunctions include:

- Internal competition (fiefdoms and "Divide and Conquer")
- Lack of trust
- Lack of collaboration and teamwork

- Criticism, and negativity (sociopathic rule)

All the above contribute to what I'll call a dysfunctional workplace, where the critical relationships and teams needed to create organizational successes just don't form.

The organization's leadership and front-line managers can talk ad nauseam about the importance of teamwork at every level of the organization, but the teamwork that's most critical to ensuring that an organization runs effectively is the one-on-one relationship between a boss and each of his or her subordinates. That's what is copiously missing in most organizations. Try that if your boss is a workaholic, micromanaging bully.

You have to ask yourself, if teamwork is so hard to orchestrate, why do organizations cherish it so? Hugh MacLeod sums it up best: "Since the modern scientifically-conceived corporation was invented in the early half of the twentieth century, creativity has been sacrificed in favor of forwarding the interests of the 'Team Player.' Apparently it's felt that there's more money in doing it that way; that's why they do it. There's only one problem. Team Players are not very good at creating value on their own. They are not autonomous; they need a team in order to exist. So now corporations are awash with non-autonomous thinkers.

"I don't know. What do you think?"

"I don't know. What do you think?"

"And so on...

"Creating an economically viable entity where lack of original thought is handsomely rewarded creates a rich, fertile environment for parasites to breed. And that's exactly what's been happening. So now we have millions upon millions of human tapeworms thriving in the Western World, making love to their PowerPoint presentations and feasting on the creativity of others.

"What happens to ecology when the parasite level reaches critical mass? The ecology dies."[175]

I'm not convinced that the kind of euphoric team environment that most organizations preach and strive for is really achievable, and I don't think it will bring the riches and successes expected. Instead, organizational management should strive first for that simple relationship between boss and employee. Once you master that, move on to eliminating conflict and building trust in the organization. This approach is called going "back to the basics." However, too often, organizations try to legislate or dictate teamwork.

"It is amazing how much you can accomplish when it doesn't matter who gets the credit," said President Harry S. Truman.[176] In the end, teamwork is nothing more than completing your job on time so someone else can complete theirs.

In our look at teamwork, we've only touched on communication, or lack thereof, but in the next chapter we'll take it head-on and see how dysfunctional communication affects the modern workplace.

CHAPTER 14 WAITING FOR RIGOR MORTIS

IN HIS BOOK, *GAMES PEOPLE PLAY*, Dr. Berne postulated that in everyday interactions, each person will demonstrate one of two basic unconscious predilections, or life plans, that he calls "scripts." Dr. Berne believes that the games people play in everyday life are driven by these scripts that are either destructive or constructive; there's no in between. This, he claims, is basic human nature and forms the basis for all interpersonal communication.

The title of this chapter is the term Dr. Berne has coined for what he calls the "destructive" or "tragic script."[177]

Dr. Berne believes you can identify what script is at the heart of a person by the way he acts toward others. One who is constructively driven will be pleasant to deal with while one who is destructively driven will play the more disagreeable games. It is fairly obvious which script the average sociopath follows.

This chapter is meant to address workplace communication, or lack thereof. We're going to delve into Dr. Berne's book *Games People Play*, for I believe it is the key to understanding dysfunctional workplace communication.

In his book *Games People Play*, Dr. Berne dissects the whole process of interpersonal relationships, and is one of the founding works in the field of Transactional Analysis (TA). Understanding the basics of TA is a great place to start if we want to explore communication in today's workplace.

As a prelude to detailing and understanding the games people play, Dr. Berne first breaks down and explains communication by its elemental component parts. He starts with the most basic, what he calls the "stroke."

"A stroke denotes any act implying recognition of another's presence. Hence, a stroke may be used as the fundamental unit of social action. An exchange of strokes constitutes a 'transaction,' which is the unit of social intercourse. A transaction happens if two or more people encounter each other in a social aggregation, and sooner or later one of them will speak or give some other indication of acknowledging the presence of the other. This is called transactional stimulus. Another person then says or does something which is in some way related to the stimulus, and that is called transactional response."[178]

Thus, we have communication. Communication happens through repeated stimulus–response transactions. Unfortunately, communication among competing players in the workplace is never that easy. Let the games begin.

According to Dr. Berne, games are categorized according to the situation, or context, in which they're most likely to occur. They include:

- Life games
- Marital games
- Party games
- Sexual games
- Underworld games
- Consulting room games
- Good games

A game does not necessarily imply fun or even enjoyment. On the contrary games are dead serious business. So how does Dr. Berne define a game?

"Games are a recurring set of transactions, often repetitious with a concealed motivation, or, more colloquially, a series of moves with a snare, or gimmick. There are two chief characteristics: their ulterior quality, and the payoff."

Dr. Berne was certainly not an optimist when it came to people's' behavior, and as you can see, he believed that every game is basically dishonest, and the outcome has a dramatic, (mostly negative) effect on those playing. The payoff is key–the resulting benefit to the player perpetrating the game for whatever sinister motive.

Another important component of communication is what Dr. Berne calls the "ego state." He tells us, "An ego state may be described phenomenologically as a coherent system of feelings, and operationally as a set of coherent behavior patterns. The repertoire can be sorted into the following categories: an ego state which resembles those of parental figures; an ego state which is autonomously directed toward objective appraisal of reality, and those which represent archaic relics (still-active ego states which were fixated in early childhood). Colloquially their exhibition is called Parent, Adult, and Child."

- Parent: the same state of mind as one of your parents. You will thus respond as he or she would, with the same posture, gestures, vocabulary, and feeling

- Adult: an autonomous, objective appraisal of the situation. When in this state, you're using thought processes, the problems you perceive, or the conclusions you've come to, in a non-prejudicial manner

- Child: the intent of your reaction is the same as it would have been when you were a little boy or girl

As noted earlier, communication is a function of repeated stimulus–response transactions and according to Dr. Berne, "[T]he first rule of communication is that communications will proceed smoothly as long as S/R transactions are complimentary [parallel across ego states, e.g., parent to parent, or adult to adult, etc. and its corollary; that as long as transactions are complimentary communication can, in principle, proceed indefinitely.]

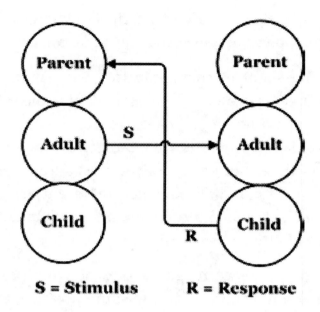

S = Stimulus   R = Response

"These rules are independent of the nature and content of the transactions; they are based entirely on the direction of the vectors involved. [That is] communication is broken off when a crossed transaction occurs. The most common crossed transaction, and the one which causes and always has caused most of the social difficulties in the world, whether in marriage, love, friendship, or work, is the transaction depicted above."

This is the case where a conversation starts as adult-to-adult, and in response, one of the players reverts to a child. This forces the other to become the parent.

The crossed stimulus–response transaction depicted is the fundamental component of communication within the game and can happen many times in the typical conversation. Often a conversation begins with complimentary stimulus–response and as the games proceeds, it degrades into the crossed transaction mode were the game ends with either one or the other side on top, so to speak.

Like any business acumen, the players in these games become increasingly adept with practice. Wasteful moves are eliminated, and more purpose is condensed into each move. In other words, the games become much more intense and deadly serious and the players become more skilled at perpetrating them on their unsuspecting peers.

In chapter 12 we detailed "Divide and Conquer" which is the first of the games that we needed to understand if we're to survive the workplace. Later we'll look at other sinister games that have become common in today's workplace. Games played in the workplace can come from any of Dr. Berne's earlier mentioned categories, and I urge the reader to pick up a copy of his book to become familiar with all the games he describes.

I need to point out that on the surface, the majority of communication in the workplace, certainly at the professional business level, is conducted (albeit sometimes forced) in adult-to-adult transactions; however, when that communication takes on an ulterior motive and the conversation starts to cross the ego states, that's when they become games and that's when communication breaks down.

So other than the games that are constantly played out every day in the workplace, what other aspects of group and interpersonal communication pose problems? Ironically, the information age and the technologies its born has certainly contributed to the demise of effective communication.

Robert Sutton explains, "When groups work mostly through e-mail or conference calls rather than face-to-face, they tend to fight more and trust each other less; people don't get the complete picture that comes with being there, so the groups develop incomplete and often overly negative views of one another."[179] This is the curse of the modern connected workplace and the globalization of business in general. Gareth Morgan also talks of this, "The strength of [an] organization is now being undermined by developments in information technology that erode hierarchy and introduce new organizational power bases."[180] Morgan's last two points just may be good news; we need to breakdown hierarchy and introduce new power bases if we want the workplace to ever change for the better.

Personally, I believe that the electronic communication age has proven a godsend for the world of business if for no other reason than it provides the Pearl Harbor files necessary for most people to avoid being blamed when things turn sour. That said, I do think that e-mail has made the workplace more bearable by reducing the need for meetings. Mass communication becomes just a click away.

Unfortunately, the true purpose of e-mail, and a sure sign of the lack of trust that's prevalent in a blame oriented culture, is evidenced by the number of people typically cc'd on e-mails. The more people brought into an issue, the more who can share in any inevitable blame.

It's not at all easy, and it takes a lot of determination, but making an effort to remove the barriers to communication that stand in our way, whether tangible or intangible can be the key to building relationships that really work. It's certainly a prerequisite to expecting teamwork to take hold. To do that, we need to first understand those barriers.

In his February 2006 article "Seven Barriers to Great Communication," Eric Garner points out that, "Communicating is straightforward. What make it complex, difficult, and frustrating are the barriers we put in the way."[181] According to Garner, there are seven top barriers to communication:

- Physical barriers: These are the empires and fiefdoms into which strangers are not allowed; separate areas for people of different status, working areas or working in one unit that is physically separate from others.

- Perceptual barriers: The problem with communicating with others is that we all see the world differently.

- Emotional barriers: One of the chief barriers to open and free communications is the emotional barrier. It's comprised mainly of fear, mistrust and suspicion. As a result, many people hold back from communicating their thoughts and feelings to others.

- Cultural barriers: When we join a group and wish to remain in it, sooner or later we need to adopt the behavior patterns of the group. These are the behaviors that the group accepts as signs of belonging.

- Language barriers: Language that describes what we want to say in our terms may present barriers to others who are not familiar with our expressions, buzz-words, tech-speak, and other jargon.

- Gender barriers: There are distinct differences between the speech patterns in a man and those in a woman. This means that a man talks in a linear, logical, and compartmentalized way, whereas a woman talks more freely, mixing logic and emotion.

- Interpersonal barriers: There are six levels at which people can distance themselves from one another:

  o Withdrawal: an absence of interpersonal contact. It is both a refusal to be in touch and wanting to spend time alone

  o Rituals: meaningless, repetitive routines devoid of real contact

  o Pastimes: fill up time with others in social but superficial activities

  o Working: those tasks which follow the rules and procedures of contact, but no more

  o Games: subtle, manipulative interactions about winning and losing (rackets and stamps)[182]

  o Closeness: the aim of interpersonal contact, where there is a high level of honesty and acceptance of yourself and others

Another key obstacle to good communication within the organization is when, functional or dysfunctional, the communication only filters down through the organization from the top–i.e. vertically. Thus, people must be at the right place at the right time, or in the "in"-crowd to know what's going on. This is because in most kingdom businesses information only filters down on the day staff meetings are held. Also, communication breaks down when all the employees don't share in the organization's vision and strategic plan for the future, because it has not been effectively communicated down from on-high. Of course fiefdoms don't help either, because most have their drawbridge up and the moat is full of crocodiles and information is laundered before it leaves or enters.

When a company is small, particularly in the start-up environment, communication is usually not at all complicated. Recall the start-up organization chart in Chapter 7? Everybody knows each other, they wear many functional hats, and there's usually a close relationship between everyone and management. It's when an organization grows and the organizational chart starts taking typical vertical form and bourgeons that problems begin. The lines of authority become clear but not the communication channels; thus cross-organizational (horizontal) communication becomes something that falls by the wayside.

Any horizontal communication difficulty the organization experiences will become amplified, especially during any tough times. When this inevitably happens The Fiefdom Syndrome becomes more entrenched and the result is individual groups adopt a "circle the wagons" posture and attitude. At the individual level, fear and anxiety run rampant, trust is non-existent, and communication shuts down. Also, as an organization grows, good management—employee communications become much more important yet more difficult to ensure, becoming the number one problem facing the organization.

In his July 2005 article "Bad Communication: Is it Holding You Back? —Learn How to Break Free," Andrew Schwartz tells us, "Poor communication and ineffective human relations are the major causes [of workplace problems]. Effective communication is talking and listening to create an understanding between two people or groups. The end result is to get things done in a way so that you and the organization will all be satisfied. Poor communication with your boss or your peers and/or employees means the job won't be done well. It will mean friction and frustration. It can also result in foul-ups, misunderstood orders and wasted time."[183]

Understanding boss-to-subordinate communication, I think, is the key to effective communication, and the first building block to teamwork within an organization. Even when employees are generally good at communicating with each other, an organization can still be quite communication bankrupt, because the relationship between boss and subordinate is non-existent. As we'll see later when we tackle the performance review, communication between boss and subordinate is usually only one-sided.

Whether good boss-to-employee communication is even possible I believe lies solely on the back of the leadership and management team. In a typical organization, steeped in sociopathic behaviors, it's all about how the boss treats the underlings and those around him in general, which sets a positive or negative stage for communication to flourish.

In his book *What Got You Here Won't Get You There*, Marshall Goldsmith describes twenty traits that he's discovered in the typical leader.[184] He describes these as the behaviors that a leader must shed before being able to move to the next career level. I think they also have pertinence when discussing how communication and teamwork can break down in the typical organization. The specific behaviors are:

1. Wanting to "win" too much
2. Adding too much value
3. Passing judgment
4. Making destructive comments
5. Starting with "no" or "but" or "however"
6. Telling the world how smart you are
7. Speaking when angry
8. Negativity
9. Withholding information
10. Failing to give proper recognition

11. Claiming credit that we don't deserve

12. Making excuses

13. Clinging to the past

14. Playing favorites

15. Refusing to express regret

16. Not listening

17. Failing to express gratitude

18. Punishing the messenger

19. Passing the buck

20. An excessive need to be "me"

From my own experience I can attest that any of these can be a communication show-stopper when you're dealing with someone who's guilty of these behaviors. In fact, I could make the case that many of the above could be viewed as subtle forms of bullying. When bosses practice the above behaviors, you can rest assured that communication and teamwork within that organization will be negatively affected.

Nowhere is communication tested more than during conflict, which is unfortunately a normal and natural part of our workplace and personal lives. In fact you could even define conflict as communication gone badly, because conflict usually starts and ends with poor communication. I know I've already talked about conflict in the workplace and how it undermines teamwork; however, it's also pertinent to understanding the effect conflict has on communication in general.

First we must remember that conflict can be helpful in making necessary changes within the organization; however, unresolved conflict results in many employee morale issues like job dissatisfaction, general unhappiness, hopelessness about career, and ultimately exodus from the organization. This then results in individual behaviors such as depression, withdrawal, indifference, and even aggression. This is why organizations with high levels of conflict have high employee turnover. Communication is both the cause of, and the remedy for conflict.

We all know that conflict is a normal part of life, but in no place is it more rampant or more influential on our lives than at work. Even in a well-run, team-spirited workplace, conflict will arise. When people are thrust together all vying for the same piece of the pie, conflict becomes inevitable. It's simply human nature.

The job of an organization's management is to recognize and address the factors that foster conflict within their organization, and this is where the ball is typically dropped. Companies do a lousy job of this, partially because the leadership itself fears conflict.

In the context of communication, conflict can best be described as a clash between people's personal agendas. If everyone's personal agendas were in sync, there would be no conflict. This is why aligning the organization to the overall vision is so important; however, even then personal conflicts will still arise. Conflict is magnified ten-fold in an organization suffering from the fiefdom syndrome. The existence of fiefdoms means there is constant conflict. Open communication between silos is stifled, and this starts at the top between the fiefdom leadership.

Before one can effectively counteract and attempt to avoid conflict, you must know the types of conflict that can be found in the workplace. There are fundamentally only two types of conflict in the workplace:

- Substantive conflict
- Perceived (personality-based) conflict

To anyone embroiled in a personality-based conflict, it is all-consuming and tough to resolve equitably. It's these personality-based conflicts that plague the average workplace. The substantive conflict can be dealt with fairly easily by just addressing the specific problem that's caused the conflict.

As we'll learn later when we explore the performance review process, the real problem for effective communication lies in the personality-based conflicts that arise between a boss and his subordinates. These become no-win situations typically for the subordinate. These are the clashes over job duties and performance issues that become exacerbated during the performance review process. Personality-based conflicts also arise between employees and are the natural result of all the games played in the workplace in the interest of furthering personal agendas.

Leadership teams need to nurture a culture that minimizes personality-agenda- and fiefdom-agenda–based conflicts, as these disputes are truly counter to effective communication and teamwork.

The first way to eliminate conflict is to get everyone in the organization singing from the same hymnal on the organization's vision. If everyone understands and buys into the management's vision for the organization, communication might find a common ground. Also, management needs to foster an open culture where people are rewarded for teaming to solve issues versus escalating them in conflict. This is done by eliminating the blame orientation and "shoot the messenger" mentality prevalent in so many organizations.

That said however, I'm not so sure that personal-agenda–based conflict can ever be eliminated. As we've seen, the propensity for people to practice impression management, to lie, bullshit and play games will always be present and will always create conflict.

Plus, there's a problem with expecting that management will take action to nurture a culture that doesn't tolerate conflict and rewards civil communication. From my experience, management always seems to be the last to realize, if ever, that there's indeed poor communication within their organization despite all the conflict around them. Why? This, ironically, is a direct result of the poor communication.

There's also another factor that works to inhibit communication. We learned how people, when thrust together, begin to all act alike. This can be explained by what's called the "reciprocity rule of human behavior." Simply stated, it's the phenomenon that, over time, people come to share, reciprocally, similar attitudes toward each other. An example is that if I think lowly of you, you'll eventually develop a low opinion of me. It's that sixth sense we all have about each other. The irony is that these type feelings arise despite any positive accomplishments on the part of either of the parties.

This phenomenon is also called "cultural transmission." British evolutionary biologist Richard Dawkins studied this process and published his theory in *The Selfish Gene* in 1976. He coined the term "meme" as a concept for explaining the spread of ideas and cultural phenomena. Meme identifies ideas, behaviors, or styles that spread from person to person within a culture.

The concept comes from the analogy that as genes transmit biological information, memes can be said to transmit ideas and belief information. Author Malcolm Gladwell tells us, "A meme is an idea that behaves like a virus; that moves through a population, taking hold in each person it infects."[185] In the example above, one person might hate another, and that person responds with hate; then hatred quickly spreads through the organization via memes. Thus we have a communication breakdown.

Many companies try to counteract this phenomenon (and their communication problems in general) through training. I've sat through many a communication and team building seminar, yet despite these goat ropes, workplace communication and teamwork never got any better. The expectation is that if management can only get the employees together and "teach" them how to communicate, they'll begin to respect each other, work together, and the problems will miraculously go away. The problem is that the underlying reasons people don't communicate are never admitted or addressed.

As we well know, when organizations are mired down in politics or are culturally bankrupt, information becomes stove-piped within single organizations (fiefdoms), and dissemination becomes impossible. Commitment at the highest management levels to implement and enforce omnidirectional information sharing (without games being played) is required before there can be meaningful information exchange and communication.

As I mentioned many times, the most critical team is that forged between boss and subordinate. I think the more basic and simple reasons communication, between boss and subordinate, is such a tough commodity can be found in Steve Tobak's January 2010 article, "Why Your Boss Doesn't Always Listen to You." He explains that "Most leaders, managers, entrepreneurs, and overachieving types in general, have one thing in common; they think they're right most of the time. This leads to the classical communications problem of not listening." Recall #16 on Marshall Goldsmith's list of bad behaviors.

Tobak recalls countless times when his boss didn't listen to him and explains, "Getting snubbed by your boss or, even worse, a top executive or CEO, is a real demotivator. It's especially true for people who take their ideas, job, and the company's success very seriously."[186]

However, the typical sociopathic leader is only interested in his own opinion. Therefore, in the typical boss-to-subordinate interaction you can bet the boss is barely listening. For a sociopath listening really means that he's only listening to himself. In fact, most sociopaths look at any interaction with a subordinate more as a threat than an opportunity. This may explain why coaching and mentoring is such a lost art.

Tobak presents a unique perspective on the listening issue and why the boss doesn't always listen to you or your ideas:

- Low priority: Your ideas, while good, aren't a priority.
- Bad leadership: Most senior managers aren't strong enough leaders to know how important it is to take the time to hear a middle-manager's, or employee's, views and share his perspectives.

- Narrow view: What might seem important to you may not be important or such a good idea, one or two levels up.

- Dumb idea: It's such a naïve or otherwise idiotic idea that he doesn't know where to begin to explain it, so he just nods politely and waits for you to go away.

- Bad timing: There's always some crisis going on and they're distracted or can't be bothered.

- Politics: Often the answer is an ugly truth that some executives don't want to admit to you or, worse still, don't even want to think about themselves.

- You're intimidating: They can't handle this, especially if you're inflexible and never back down. This happens a lot, believe it or not. Just because he's the boss doesn't make you any less of a pain in the butt.

- Dysfunctional management: Your boss and/or the entire management (senior staff) team are dysfunctional. Some management teams just don't know how to function right.

- Not in his/her job description: Bad leadership; obviously isn't a servant leader. In all likelihood, his annual compensation plan doesn't have a line item that reads "Listen to Bob."

Tobak also offers some additional good advice, "so, the next time your boss doesn't listen to you, try to get a little perspective and, above all, don't take it personally. And if you are 'the boss,' investing time by explaining your views can go a long way toward inspiring a young up-and-comer."[187]

Listening just may be the universal key to good communication. If more listening were to take place and less trying to talk over everyone, the workplace just might become bearable. You'd swear the rallying cry in the modern workplace must be "stop talking while I'm interrupting." Talking over one another is a major reason meetings are so horrific and little ever gets accomplished.

In the next chapter we're going to take a much closer look at conflict in the workplace and, in particular, the conflicts that arise between individuals.

CHAPTER 15 THE RED QUEEN EFFECT

DO YOU EVER FEEL LIKE YOU'RE BEATING your head against the wall or just not getting anywhere at work no matter how hard you try? If so, you probably are the victim of "The Red Queen Effect."

In 1973, evolutionary biologist, Leigh Van Valen of the University of Chicago, devised what he called the "Red Queen Principle" (also called the "Red Queen Effect") from Lewis Carroll's *Through the Looking Glass*. It's based on the Red Queen's comment to Alice that: "in this place it takes all the running you can do to keep in the same place."

In the workplace, Van Valen's Red Queen Effect suggests that competing people will have to allocate more and more resources into fighting one another for even a modest, or negligible, increase in benefit.

The Red Queen Effect is a zero sum game that dictates that an improvement in one person's situation must/will lead to a decrease in another's. It's a pretty simple principle actually. If one person develops a competitive advantage that allows that person to capture a larger share of the organizational resources, prestige, or praise from the boss, this will, in turn, lead to a smaller share for other people, thus they suffer a status decrease. The only way that they can survive is by learning how to increase their own status, so that they can regain their share of the resources, prestige or praise. The Red Queen Effect especially plagues sycophants as they jockey for position under the sociopaths.

Take, for example, a rabbit. As it evolves to run faster, it has gained a competitive defensive advantage over its predator, the fox. In turn, the fox then must compensate for its loss of advantage by learning how to run faster. And so on, back and forth. However, the difference between the rabbit and the fox and the average employee is that in the workplace people hardly ever look at themselves as the source of their problems and realize they must change to gain a competitive advantage. It is much easier to just torpedo your competition than change yourself. This game of jockeying for position is played out every day in the workplace.

I'm sure everyone has heard the term "thrown under the bus." It seems to have entered the business vernacular like gang busters. While quite childish, in a way it serves as the best description of the workplace behavior displayed by people toward one another and provides proof of the Red Queen Effect.

Have you ever heard the old idiom, "If you want the biggest house in the neighborhood you can either roll up your sleeves and build it, or you can tear everyone else's house down?" This chapter is about how workers tear each other's houses down.

The urbandictionary.com defines "thrown under the bus" as sacrificing some other person, usually one who is undeserving or at least vulnerable, to make a personal gain. Someone is said to have been thrown under the bus when he or she is made the scapegoat for something that may have gone wrong. Throwing someone else under the bus is a classic method for covering-up your own mistakes or diverting any focus from yourself. It's also used to simply torpedo your competition.

"Thrown under the bus" is the perfect metaphor for the act of positioning someone to be flattened under the wheels of the ever-moving organizational machine (the bus) of one-upmanship that plagues the modern workplace. You're either on the bus or you're under it. From my experience, in today's workplace there is almost no in between.

The archaic term for this behavior is to set up a patsy. There's also the old term "throwing someone to the dogs (or wolves)." When the shit hits the fan, someone is going to be blamed, and to ensure that it's not you; you select a candidate, some unsuspecting poor slob to feed to the dogs. Remember the rite of degradation? When top management practices this it's called plausible deniability or the selfish herd theory.

Throwing someone under the bus is an effective strategy in a couple of ways. First, it can be used as a diversionary tactic serving to distract the attention from the main culprit (you) onto some other poor nincompoop, allowing you to completely duck the blame. This is quite useful in an organization notorious for witch hunts. In fact, mastering this technique is more a matter of survival in one of these types of organizations.

Second, it can be used, just as the Red Queen Effect predicts, to deflower your colleagues to set yourself up in a better position with the boss. I know what you're saying; *I'd never resort to that kind of sinister behavior*. It's a noble attitude, but I'll let you in on a secret: people who are *on* the bus typically get paid more than those perpetually found *under* the bus. So if you can keep your colleagues perpetually *under* the bus, you set yourself up for a bigger share of the spoils come performance review time.

What if you find yourself the target? Confronting someone who has just thrown you under the bus is tough because the typical practitioner has probably become a master at this diversionary tactic. In fact, you may never even know who tripped you up. A skillful practitioner is able to do this stealthily. Don't even try to find out because the sociopaths and sycophants are in bed together and cover for each other, so nobody's going to snitch.

If you're lucky enough to actually know your accuser and you try to call his bluff, I guarantee he'll do whatever he can to effectively change the subject. People skilled at this game will lie, or bullshit, whatever it takes to focus attention either back on you or onto some other related or even tangential issue. This is called "strategic diversion." They have a whole slew of them in their back pocket for just such occasions.

It really doesn't matter anyway, because the damage is usually already done to your credibility and reputation. Sociopaths have both a short attention span and the tendency to never get both sides of the story before they act. Once they've been told about your failing, you're guilty, so don't expect your day in court.

You can't take your nemesis to the woodshed, so your only recourse is to play the game "what goes around, comes around." Thus the workplace becomes like a battleground in a bus depot.

This behavior has also been described as the "prisoner's dilemma." The prisoner's dilemma demonstrates why two people might not cooperate even if it's in both their best interests to do so. It was originally framed by Merrill Flood and Melvin Dresher working at RAND Corporation in the 1950s.

The classic version of the prisoner's dilemma, and the one used most to describe it, is as follows: Two suspects are arrested by the police. The police have insufficient evidence for a conviction of either one, and in the interest of obtaining a confession they separate the prisoners so they can interrogate them separately. They offer each of them a deal. If one testifies against the other, he can go free. If both remain silent, there's a chance both will be acquitted, but they don't know that. If each betrays the other, they both receive a prison sentence. Each prisoner must choose to betray the other or to remain silent. Each believes that the other won't know about the betrayal. For each, their only concern is maximizing their chance of freedom, without any concern for the other prisoner's fate. Thus, in the interest of assuring their survival, they rat on each other.

This is because people typically base their behavior on the assumption that others won't act as they do, or that the other person isn't as smart as they are–the "holier than thou" mentality. However, in an organization in which this behavior is condoned, everyone eventually learns (the hard way) that the best thing they can do for their career is sacrifice their co-workers. This results in a highly dysfunctional organization full of politics, in-fighting, and defensiveness. Personal fiefdoms abound as a way for people to defend themselves.

Another variant of the "thrown under the bus" game is the one perpetrated by the workplace pyromaniac, whom we'll learn about later. This brand of pooterhead will actually throw an entire organization under the bus.

Diversion and evasion on the part of your accuser, and your crucifixion, are the aim of this game. It's accepted that the person using this tactic has absolutely no intention whatsoever of taking any responsibility for his behavior or actions. Rather than be accountable and responsible, the finger-pointer advances his agenda at the expense of yours—impression management at its finest.

The closest of Dr. Berne's games would be "courtroom." Although his courtroom game is typically a three-handed game with a plaintiff, a defendant, and a judge, "thrown under the bus" (TUTB) can be played with only two players—the accuser (the plaintiff) and the target (the defendant).

In Dr. Berne's game, the judge serves the purpose of either vindicating or condemning the defendant. In TUTB the defendant doesn't have the option of deferring to an impartial judge. When you're thrown under the bus, there's no chance to defend yourself. There's no arraignment, bail, or trial. There's no jury of your peers to decide your fate. And most of all, you're guilty until proven innocent. According to Dr. Berne, this game is typically played by siblings, which explains why it's such childish behavior.

There's a deviation of TUTB that closely resembles Dr. Berne's courtroom game. We have the same plaintiff–defendant interaction, but in this instance the plaintiff also brings in your boss as the judge, jury, and executioner. The way this works is one of your colleagues, intent on positioning himself higher on the scratching post than you, goes to your boss to share a problem, and in this game you are the problem. Your colleague then spills to the boss the details of your screw-up, ineffectiveness, or failing in some way.

What happens next is the critical part of the game. The bully boss listens to the plaintiff's side of the story and, because he's a sociopath who's driven to make an immediate decision and couldn't give two-shits less about justice, takes the plain-tiff's side without even listening to your side of the story. His quick—everything is urgent—decision is that you must be guilty.

Most often these "rat" sessions are held in private, so you never know who's ratting on you. All you know is somehow the boss is now treating you differently, with a subtle sense of disgust, or in most cases will actually confront you with proof of your failing. Pointing out someone's failings is fun for a sociopath.

You'll typically find yourself in one of these predicaments when you're in a posi-tion in which you can do nothing to defend yourself. It is when you go on business travel or take personal time off that you'll receive an untimely e-mail or phone call from the sociopathic bully boss, and you're read the riot act for your transgression or failing. Remember cyber-bullying?

Of course, the worst thing you can do is fly off the handle and respond in kind, however tempting that may appear at first. I've found the best thing to do is ignore the situation, suck it up, and never say a word about it to anyone. This has an added benefit. If you don't "screw into the ceiling," which is most often the normal reaction, it'll frost the perpetrator's ass, and the sociopathic boss's ass, and dilute much of their pleasure in watching you squirm.

The only thing you have going for you is that the typical sociopath might suffer from Attention Deficit Disorder (ADD), causing him to make fast decisions lest he forget that he has a problem to solve. This is good because the pain is over quickly as they have moved on to some other poor slob. Remember, sociopaths can attack you one minute and in the next ask you out to lunch. However, don't feel that you're completely off the hook. Most of them have file-cabinet memories, so come review time, they'll pull your file, and your failing(s) will be duly noted and thrown back up to you.

Speaking of ADD, it's probably the single most rampant problem facing American business management today. ADD, coupled with organizational and selective amnesia pose a potent combination all too prevalent in today's management ranks.

In the end, we all know there's always that threat that our employer will go out of business and we'll lose our jobs; after all, most jobs are "at will." In a way, that's manageable, at least, emotionally. However, what's potentially even more dangerous is the threat that your colleagues, jockeying for position at the feet of the sociopaths, will try to throw you under the bus. I've seen it happen and been the target many times, and it's ugly.

Throwing people under the bus is an offshoot of blamestorming, another behavior prevalent in today's workplace setting.

One of the key behavioral traits of sociopaths is that they fashion themselves as infallible. They can't handle any responsibility for a problem because it will tarnish their image. This is why they're so surprise adverse. They don't make mistakes, so in an organization run by them, mistakes and problems are always addressed by castigating someone, anyone. Witch hunts are regular events in these organizations because there's no way in hell that any problem is the direct fault of the sociopathic management. It's called plausible deniability.

While it's one thing to be thrown under the bus by a colleague, it's quite another when it's done by management. The problem is that when most sociopaths are faced with a serious problem, one in which they feel that they might be implicated; they'll find someone to sacrifice on the altar to upper management. Pointing the finger at a subordinate and firing the poor bastard is their way of telling their higher-up boss that they did nothing wrong and are still in control. Their decisiveness is unparalleled. This is why so many "ineffective leaders" stay in power despite how badly the organization performs.

The effect this behavior has on the organization as a whole is high turnover. Sooner or later sane people get tired of the bullshit and leave for a better, saner job. It really does get old having to keep a Pearl Harbor file about everything; however, after the first time this happens to you, you'll be a believer like me and keep copious records.

For the sociopaths, and specifically the bullies, high turnover is a good thing—it allows them to blame a whole new set of scapegoats. Not that it matters much if you've suffered the ultimate fate, but keep in mind, a sociopath will always have select ex-employees to blame. So leaving the organization doesn't let you off the hook. Your reputation can still suffer long after you've moved on.

Our next topic of conversation is the boss and how even he will throw you under the bus. But bosses are supposed to be looking out for their workers' well-being, right? Isn't that what leadership is all about?

CHAPTER 16 THROW ME AN ANVIL

WE ARE ALL SWIMMING AND KICKING AND struggling in a chaotic ocean called the workplace. When hell breaks loose, you must grab any life preserver that's offered before it passes by. Some will throw you an anvil instead so if you can't tell the difference between a life preserver and an anvil, you'll drown.

Many bullies and sociopaths like throwing an anvil to a drowning man, and then get pissed at him for not grabbing on. This chapter is about unsupportive bosses throwing metaphorical anvils to their drowning subordinates. These are the tactics used to undermine the employee's ability to be a success.

They do this by failing to support the employee in accomplishing his work, and then blaming him for not being successful in his job. They do this through the performance review process, but it's not limited to that one-time-a-year ambush. Bosses undermine their subordinates on a day-to-day basis.

It isn't bad enough that your boss may be out to get you but there are also a number of organizational issues and circumstances that can sabotage your performance and productivity:

- Arrogance and ego on the part of management
- Workaholics, or micromanaging bosses
- The Red Queen Effect
- Organizational and selective amnesia
- A fiefdom-rich environment
- Dysfunctional organizational communication
- Negative motivational climate or culture
- Performance appraisals and the focus on negative feedback

- Poorly lived organizational values

- An organization not in touch with reality

- An organization running the relentless race to the bottom

We've learned about most of these behaviors already. When these are the general behaviors and attitudes of the organization, or in particular one's boss, it's a recipe for career disaster. At a personal level, there are many ways that a supervisor or manager can blatantly, actively or inadvertently, sabotage an employee's career:

- Negligence: telling the employee that he/she will do something, yet having no intention of doing it

- Starvation: withholding information necessary for the employee to do his job; failing to provide the employee the necessary manpower, tools, equipment, or budget to accomplish his job

- Ostracizing: subtly, or overtly, excluding an individual from events in which he should be included if he is to be successful

- Discrediting: personal attacks or criticisms used to create doubt about the person's competency or credibility; talking about an employee behind his or her back to the employee's colleagues and peers. Conversely, badmouthing an employee's colleagues and peers to an employee

- Marginalizing: excessive talking and no listening; monopolizing conversations, out-talking the employee either in a meeting or in private

- Obstacles: actively putting obstacles in the employee's path to success

- Diversion: creating a distraction, focusing on the inconsequential, sending someone off on a witch hunt; this is an example of "Pyromania" and the "Stump the Dummy" game

- Workaholism and micromanaging

Organizational dynamics aside, one might think that if you're lucky and survived the obstacle course and you've made the jump to management, you'll be exempt from this (and any other) idiotic behavior. Unfortunately, that's not true. In fact, the stakes become even higher as the bad behaviors become more intense and are played for greater spoils. Behaviors that undermine your personal career are one thing; however, there are games played that will try to dynamite your ability to manage your department or group. The following are some of the actions that a sociopathic boss, intent on torpedoing your career and that of those who work for you, has at his disposal:

- Not providing the tools and resources necessary for your group to effectively and efficiently perform their job duties
- Pedanticism; demanding perfection in everything you do: nothing is ever good enough
- Micromanaging everything you do
- Unconstructive criticism: pointing out problems without any help in solving them
- Artificial restraints on budgets (because the protected fiefdom got all the budget)
- Constant cost-cutting
- Regular RIFs
- Undermining your credibility with your subordinates by going directly to them for information (a "Stump the Dummy" tactic)
- Approving every decision you make including hiring and firing

We learned about the Red Queen Effect and blame-oriented cultures in previous chapters but, needless to say, it's tough to forge a career when your daily modus operandi becomes dodging bullets and fighting a fight with an unloaded gun (the boss wouldn't let you buy the bullets). This is especially true if it's your own boss you're fighting.

Organizational perceptions, amnesia and the unwillingness (or inability) of management to see past the symptoms to the underlying causes and contributors of problems, are what create the daily struggles organizations and employees have in meeting their goals. Harpagon's Syndrome explains many of the behaviors above. When this happens, the organizational atmosphere becomes one of constant pressure for increased performance, which typically results in unrealistic group and personal goals for the employees.

This also leads to the typical belt-tightening synonymous with struggling organizations. This directly affects the resources made available to the employee for use in executing his job function. These are organizations that Seth Godin's says are in "a relentless race to the bottom." All these have the effect of stifling the individuals within the organization.

From an organizational goal perspective, the fact is that dysfunctional organizations typically have profound problems formulating and executing a clear long-term strategy. Most aren't even committed to their own vision or mission statements. This manifests itself in a lack of clear direction to the workforce. The workforce thus has no clue as to what the leaders envision for the organization, let alone where they are and what the roadmap is to get there.

I'm going to focus closely on the effects of bad first-line management (the immediate boss) on the fate of employees. This is characterized by an overall lack of interest in an employee's needs, desires, concerns, or problems.

I believe the biggest factor contributing to the negative, often blasé attitude toward the employees' needs, and one of the biggest weaknesses of management today, is the fixation on negative feedback. There's this inability to give even the smallest of positive feedback no matter what the employee does to please the boss or how well he performs his job. Negative feedback has become the obligatory objective for controlling the employees, and it is what most often dominates the typical performance review process. Positive feedback is rare, and in a dysfunctional organization run by sociopaths it can be nonexistent.

Of course, the worst type of boss is the workaholic or micromanager. He or she assigns way too many tasks to handle, with unclear objectives and impossible deadlines, all the while micromanaging the output. Add pedanticism to that and the situation can be unbearable. When the tasks are done late or the work isn't done to his or her satisfaction du jour, it becomes the employee's fault followed by only negative consequences. This is because sociopaths really have no idea what they want, and their pedantic tendencies mire them down in the details. It's almost impossible to be a success in an atmosphere such as this.

When it comes to their careers, employees must rely heavily on their boss (and management as a whole) for support. This is a big responsibility that's taken way too lightly in today's business environment. According to Nic Patton, in his July 2006 article "Bosses Blocking Worker's Careers," the majority of people (rightfully) blame their boss for the lack of their career progress. In the article Patton cites a study done by UK business consultants *Investors in People*. They found that, "Two-thirds [of employees] said their manager was important to their progression through the company, yet fewer than half believed he or she was doing enough to help them. Even more alarmingly, one in five employees claimed they were miss-sold opportunities for career progression when they joined their organization.

"However, managers questioned about their own development were upbeat about their prospects, with two-thirds claiming to be happy with the progression of their career and almost half seeing no obstacles to further advancement. Whilst happy with the progression of their own careers, many seem to pay lip-service to the development of those around them.

"Keeping employees involved, motivated, and productive is a vital part of any managerial role and crucial to keeping the organization on track. A common problem among employees looking to progress their career appeared to be the lack of new opportunity or role to move into, with more than a third of employees questioned seeing this as the biggest obstacle. Disappointingly, employers were failing to recognize employee concerns and provide a suitable response.

"More than a third of employees claimed their organization let them down when it comes to effective day-to-day management support, setting development goals, and providing regular career reviews to help their progression. These findings should concern employers. By failing to align their people strategy with business goals, employers are undermining the motivation of employees and the development and growth of their organization."[188]

What falls on deaf ears is that employees expect management to actually lead, not just manage. As Seth Godin defines it, "Managers work to get their employees to do what they did yesterday, but a little faster and a little cheaper.

"Leaders, on the other hand, know where they'd like to go, but understand that they can't get there without their tribe, without giving those they lead the tools to make something happen.

"Managers want authority. Leaders take responsibility. We need both. But we have to be careful not to confuse them. And it helps to remember that leaders are scarce and thus more valuable."[189] Remember, you report to a manager, you follow a leader.

There is a difference between leadership and the command and control tyranny common in today's workplace. As we've seen, leadership in most organizations means command, control, and domination. As we've learned these are major cultural biases in today's world; the psychic prisons that become instruments of domination are numerous in today's world of business.

Most people in an average organization have been hired supposedly because of what they bring to the table in ideas, experience, and education, yet once "on the inside" their input is ignored. Isn't this sadly ironic? Why is this? It's because today's management is stuck in the past. They are mired down in both antiquated practices and the need to perpetuate whatever successes they may have had in the past, whether real or perceived.

That's why many bosses will parrot the old line "that's not the way we do things" when confronted with a subordinate's suggestion to improve something. Despite all the rhetoric about hiring the "best of the best" or wanting to be "world-class," they just can't let anything rattle the status quo.

The fact is the "best of the best" won't last long in a sociopathically led workplace and surely not in an environment where the boss actively sabotages their success. For them change is exciting, and to be at their best, management can't get in their way, yet getting in the way is the modus operandi of the sociopathic mentality. However, that scenario unfolds every day in the modern workplace. Remember Marshall Goldsmith's behavior #5: starting with "no" or "but'" or "however" when responding to an employee's suggestion. That's probably the number one demotivational statement that a boss can utter.

Also, if management truly wants the employees to be superior in their jobs, they must allow the employees the ability to make decisions, take risks and sometimes fail without the fear of retribution. The fact that management typically doesn't empower the employee is fundamentally caused by a lack of trust. However, true leaders know that they can't be a success without trusting their subordinates. When these leaders turn around, people are actually following. Management can build trust with the employees by regularly communicating with them in a non-condescending manner and by being open and transparent.

Also because employees must deal with varied pressures and myriad issues that come up unexpectedly and can divert their attention from their jobs, true leaders will make allowances for these personal needs and provide the employees some modicum of respect and flexibility.

Lastly, employees must know where the organization is headed and why. Management must communicate the key vision and be open and honest about the challenges that will be faced by the organization to achieve that vision. As we'll learn later, most often however, management will just publish their vision on posters in the lunchroom and hallways. They are fooled into thinking that this will sufficiently communicate the organization's vision, and everyone will jump on board. This is the worst mistake management can make. That's because most management can only talk the talk, not walk the walk.

Between the organization's performance pressures, the lack of clear communication, the threat of being down-sized at any moment, the lack of clear direction, coupled with the "negative feedback only" mentality, and the outright sabotage performed by the average sycophantic boss, it's a wonder that any organization can hold on to a stable workforce and that anything of value gets done in the modern workplace.

CHAPTER 17 CHICKEN LITTLE

ACCORDING TO RAHM EMANUEL, FORMER CHIEF OF staff for President Barack Obama, "You never want a serious crisis to go to waste; it's an opportunity to do things you could not do before."[190]

The impetus for this quote was the global warming crisis and in particular the prospect of using this scare to promote the green energy movement through President Obama's economic stimulus package of 2008. This chapter is about fabricated crises that are used by the sociopathic element in an organization to execute their brand of command and control.

Everyone has seen the overused Chinese symbol for a crisis, which is written with two letters, with one letter supposedly standing for danger, and the other for opportunity. Despite the fact that this danger–opportunity symbol has been debunked of its meaning, I believe it's still accurate to maintain that in every crisis there's an opportunity to truly make a change or accomplish something that might not have been possible before.

In the case of a true crisis, no more profound words could be spoken; however, just like the global warming scare, too often the crises faced in the workplace are not real. Most of the time, they are fabricated by someone in a high position to provide yet another tool of command, control, and domination (and sport) over the workforce.

Just like with the "Divide and Conquer" game, the lighting of fires around the organization is a favorite tool of the sociopaths in their effort to maintain the chaotic workplace environment in which they thrive best. Everyone has heard the term "fire-fighting," and I'll bet there's not a single person who could truthfully say he hasn't been fire-fighting at one time or the other in his career.

I'm sure you've experienced one of these "sky is falling" doomsayers in the past. Every little issue, problem, misstep, or failing in the organization, whether true or imagined, is blown out of proportion by these nattering nabobs of negativity—the Chicken Littles of the world.

"Chicken Little" is a story for teaching courage. Don't be a chicken little; don't be afraid, the sky is not falling. It's also a symbolic expression of the inner plight of the average worker. This chapter isn't about courage in the face of danger, but of cowardice at the heart of the typical sociopath.

The characters in "Chicken Little" are caught in the middle between the earth and the falling sky, much like you'll find yourself in the typical sociopathic organization. Recall the double bind. The story of "Chicken Little" ends with all the characters dying at the hands of Foxy Loxy. The key to their demise is that they all took Chicken Little literally, and they believed the sociopath Foxy Loxy. Unfortunately, this same type of scenario plays itself out daily in many organizations.

No one wants to work for a "sky is falling" sort of leader. In his March 2007 article, "Are You a Pyromaniac?" Michael Watkins explains, "These are the organizational pyromaniacs; leaders with impulse-control issues who start the fires that waste so much precious time and energy in their organizations. For them, every day is a new crisis to be managed; and they want you to come along for the ride. All it takes is for a few key management people behaving this way and it will drive everyone lower down in the organization into a constant state of hyperactivity."[191]

This behavior tends to be contagious. If a leader demands that his or her sycophantic minions jump to attention and respond to his crisis du jour, they'll have no choice but to salute smartly and go on the perverted safari into no-man's land. And in true "shit runs downhill" fashion, what eventually happens is that the sycophants force their own direct reports into the same Easter egg hunt, and so on down the organizational hierarchy. Before long you have the "student body left" syndrome where everyone is off chasing the latest problem at the expense of doing their regular jobs. When the organization's top leader's behavior gets reflected down through the organization like this, everyone spends their time just jumping from one crisis to another.

This sociopathic behavior is called "pyromania" and I believe this is probably the worst behavior that a sociopath in a management position can practice. But why do they do this?

Watkins explains, "For some, it satisfies a deep need to feel powerful and important. Others find that injecting anxiety in subordinates lessens their own. Some pyros are just suspicious that everyone is slacking off behind their backs. Creating a [fire] can be very satisfying for those who don't trust employees to put in an honest day's work."

I think one reason pyromaniac management may be so prevalent in today's workplace is because of the sociopath's need to judge everyone constantly. Maybe even subconsciously, they use the daily weenie roast as a way to thin out the herd, get rid of those they find weak. Remember the "Selfish Herd Theory." Pyromania becomes the screening process for the sociopaths to identify the targets they'll use when they need a fall guy. Anyone who can't be jerked around by their idiocy becomes useless to them.

This behavior makes your daily routine anything but sane and manageable. You can't plan your day in advance—so much for proactiveness. Every day becomes chaotic and unpredictable. The irony is that, come review time, one of the soft skills you'll be measured on is "effective time management."

Over time, an environment mired down in fire-fighting turns dysfunctional fast. The sane and talented workers depart, leaving an entourage of sycophants who actually enjoy the false urgency of the daily fire drills. It's their chance to shine in the eyes of the sociopaths over which they fawn.

"Most managers struggle to stay focused on advancing their strategic priorities, and to avoid getting trapped in firefighting mode. So the last thing anyone needs is a boss, peer, or even direct reports who make frequent, unnecessary declarations of states of emergency," says Watkins.[192]

We noted in an earlier chapter the advent of the electronic age and the availability of e-mail as a way to speed-up communication. But is it also has its dark side and can be used with ill intent (cyber-bullying). According to Watkins, "These days, pyromaniacs' favorite incendiary devices are BlackBerrys and their [smart phone] cousins. At the same time they have accelerated communications, these devices have dramatically lowered the barriers to lighting fires; now it's just a few key-strokes away."

The problem with e-mail and especially BlackBerrys and other smart-phone devices is that they imply that any message received must be "hot" and must be addressed immediately. This then becomes an immediate distraction for the recipient defer-ring them from what may be more important. As Watkins explains, "Thumb-based communication tends to magnify the firefighting problem because the typical mes-sage is short, so the recipient lacks the context necessary to interpret its true urgency and feels it's safest to respond right away; it interrupts the receiver in the midst of whatever she's doing, so she might as well respond; and is often beamed out to multiple people, and so generates a flurry of back-and-forth requests for elaboration and action." If the recipient is a manager he or she then has to set his or her staff into crises mode in absentia. Let the games begin.

Watkins demonstrates how you can recognize that you're working for a pyroma-niac.[193] He posits that you ask yourself these questions:

- Is your boss prone to demanding immediate responses for information from you, or your direct reports when it's not really necessary?

- The instant you go on business travel or go on vacation, do you receive the hand-grenade e-mail messages asking why something happened in your absence or bringing to light some fire du jour that needs your immediate attention. These e-mails are usually received the minute you touch down from a flight, showing that your boss can think of nothing better to do than try to derail you while you're out of the office and somewhat defenseless.

- Do most of your email messages from your boss have the "important" flag checked?
- Does your boss use the term "sense of urgency" and measure people's performance using this vague yardstick?

"If you answered 'yes' to any these questions, then you are working for a certified pyromaniac and you better always have a fire extinguisher nearby."[194]

The real problem with this behavior is that fire-fighting is only a short-term fixing of symptoms, and is used in lieu of taking the time to fully understand and address the root cause of a problem. Also, "urgent" very seldom means "important."

The pyromaniac, in his sense of urgency style, allows little time for the organization to seek out and correct the root cause of problems, even when they're real. In my experience only a handful of the problems, elevated to crisis mode by the pyromaniac, really have an underlying void in process or procedure that could have caused the problem. Most often the problem is simply that someone has screwed up, plain and simple.

Sociopaths don't cope well with the phenomenon that people make mistakes. They inherently have a need for everything to be running perfectly, albeit by their perverted standards. Unfortunately, that's not how the real world operates, so these worry-warts go through life constantly looking for any problem, however small, to point out and blow out of proportion. This is all part of the overall goal of dominance over everyone around them.

Unfortunately pyromania isn't limited to the executive suite. Pyromaniacs reside in all levels in an organization. These are the organization's knights in shining armor, the heroes who are always saving the day.

There's a rare psychological mental health disorder called "Munchausen by Proxy" that involves exaggeration or fabrication of illnesses or its symptoms. This disorder is named after Baron von Munchausen, an eighteenth-century German dignitary known for telling outlandish stories.

In his November 2007 article of the same name," Nathan Bennett, a Georgia Tech management Professor, coined what he called "Munchausen at Work." Similar to Munchausen by Proxy, he explains it as, "a similar pathology in work when employees create fictitious organizational problems, only to solve them."[195] He describes how this behavior wastes precious management time and resources when they should be concentrating on effectively running the business.

"Munchausen at Work" is when someone exaggerates or even fabricates problems or crises, so they can be praised for being observant and proactive. When these 'problems' are focused on an individual, it's an example of the "thrown under the bus" fate that many people suffer.

The goal of the "Munchausen at Work" game is simple. The perp wants to look good in the eyes of management and believes the way to accomplish that is to go around finding problems, or problem people, to bring to everyone's attention. Woe to the organization whose top management suffers from this malady.

In a way this is pure sycophantic behavior. Many experts believe that it isn't just the attention that's gained that drives this behavior, but also the satisfaction in being able to jerk everyone around, to show how powerful they are.

While real instances of Munchausen by Proxy are rare, I can attest to the fact that "Munchausen at Work" is not. It's alive and well out there in the modern workplace.

These types of employees are in hog heaven if they're lucky enough to land in an organization known for its hero worship culture. One can identify these people by their plaques on the wall that say "Employee of the Month." These hero-worship organizations fan the flames of this behavior.

The bottom line is that most crises are nothing less than a colossal waste of organizational time. Despite that fact, many organizations rush into solving the problem and taking action (any action) before they've had the time to analyze the problem. These are the organizations that typically suffer from the organizational amnesia that we're going to dig into later. In business this type of behavior is inexcusable.

To be in a hurry when it isn't necessary potentially creates more (real) problems than it solves. Giancarlo Livraghi calls this "haste mania," a stupid behavior that, in certain circumstances, leads to a much more damaging practice called "hysterical haste."

Livraghi claims, "Most organizations today 'are in the habit of believing that quick means clever and slow stands for stupid.

"Haste mania is an increasingly dangerous source of stupidity. More so now than at any other time in human history, everybody seems to be always in a rush, though quite often it isn't at all clear where they think they are going, or why.

"Intelligence doesn't have to be fast, or slow. A quick intuition can be refreshing when it works. Sometimes fast action is necessary. But in many situations, we would be less stupid if we didn't jump to conclusions and we spent a little time making sure that we have understood.

"Being in a hurry has become a habit, regardless of any real need for speed. It causes unnecessary tension and anxiety. It's true that some things are happening faster, but not all and not always. Anyhow, even when they do, hysterical haste is not an effective way of coping with change (and even less so with unexpected circumstances).

"This isn't a matter of how long it takes, but of how it's done.

"It can be quite stupid to waste time, to hesitate, to miss an opportunity by dithering when it was the right time to act. But it is just as stupid to rush into doing something before we have had the time to think, to be in a hurry when it isn't necessary, and so to make mistakes that it will take longer to correct, causing a further state of haste, leading into a vicious circle that could have been avoided by getting it right in the beginning."[196]

These collateral damage problems then cause a further state of panic. As Livraghi notes, this can easily lead into a vicious cycle. Seldom, if ever, is one of the fabricated crises a true life-or-death situation for the organization.

Livraghi continues, "There is so much of that going on that we have lost sight of what was the purpose (or the problem) in the first place. So the tail is wagging the dog and the opportunities multiply for the power of stupidity to wipe out any trace of common sense that may be lingering in the mess.

"Haste, when not dictated by a precise need, is nearly always stupid. Not only because it causes mistakes. It also makes us nervous, jumpy, and uncomfortable, rushing ahead with no sense of direction, infecting other people with the same disease, chasing nobody knows what and going nobody knows where.

"In Lewis Carroll's *Through the Looking Glass*, the Red Queen of Chess tells bewildered Alice that "in this place it takes all the running you can do to keep in the same place." This is no longer a little girl's nightmare. It's an effective description of the anxiety-driven haste syndrome," says Livraghi.[197]

When this type behavior exists, the organization can't help but lose sight of what its (business) purpose is in the first place. Every company that I'm familiar with has had this sense of urgency, or haste mania, as a key ingredient in its day-to-day operation, yet I can't think of one that led to any increase in the bottom line or made the customers any happier. Talk about never learning from the past.

It's tough to combat this type of business and cultural model, which is exactly what this behavior quickly becomes. To be effective (not to mention proactive) in your work, it's critical to have a clear sense of what your priorities are, and then stick with them. This is why the organization's vision and values are so important, and when they falter, the organization remains forever in the grip of this crisis mode of operation. It's hard to keep people focused on what's really important in an organization steeped in this behavior.

When dealing with a real or fabrication crises; it's all about response control. Whether at the organizational level or at the individual level, people must resist the temptation to immediately jump on the bandwagon. My advice is to let the sociopaths stew in their own juices for a while, since a pyromaniac finds it great sport to know he has you, or your organization, wound tightly around the axle. Delay the satisfaction, but don't stall too long because then you'll be accused of not having a sense of urgency.

You'll need to resist inadvertently becoming a pyromaniac yourself. The typical pyromaniac is a workaholic, and he will treat you as if you should have his same work ethic and infinite time, capacity, and patience to kowtow to his every whim. Don't ever try reminding him of other priorities that you have and feel are more important, as he will only become agitated and claim that everything is important. You just can't win against this type sociopathic behavior.

In her February 2009 article "Executive's Behaving Badly,"[198] Leslie Ungar details five ways executives use their sociopathic leadership style to create crisis, and how each transgression hinders the organization's ability to move forward toward their true goals. They are:

- The need for constant gratification: The executive who craves constant and immediate gratification can never be satisfied. In its extreme, it's an insatiable need. The more a fire is fed, the more fuel it requires. Everything becomes critical to them. This urgency takes a toll on the entire organization. The team and the company's progress are slowed, because tending to the executive's daily needs becomes the focus rather than the company's long-range vision.

- They need to be the sole point person in the organization: In today's corporate life, executives don't need to know or do everything in their organization. What they do need to be is visionary; to think strategic, yet leave the tactical to the department heads. Organizations always suffer when their executive is taking time from being strategic to be the main go-to person on tactical questions that could/should be answered further down the organizational chart.

- The need to belittle others to look bigger: Playgrounds are not the only place where bullying still takes place. As we've learned, bullies use communication to bully other people lower in the chain of command.

- The need to consistently prove their own value: These sociopathic executives virtually suck up all the oxygen in a room and in the organization. This behavior takes a toll on the executive team and the entire organization.

- The inconsistent leadership style: People want to follow a leader who is balanced, not one who one day praises and the next day criticizes, one-day upbeat, the next day downtrodden.

I believe that management by crisis has become a disease. As we've learned, creating a crisis can be accomplished by the seasoned sociopath in many ways. We've touched on the obvious (theatrical) ways they do this, but there are also some subtle ways that this behavior is carried out.

One way is for them to set much too aggressive schedules or set artificial deadlines. Deadlines are never established based on logical scheduling of larger goals, but instead appear (and are) arbitrary. The sociopath's addiction to the sense of urgency mantra just won't let them give an inch when they make assignments. Yet these are the same organizations that preach the "do it right the first time" creed. However, for the sociopath and his urgency addiction, there's no time to do things the right way.

The most subtle, and perhaps the most sinister, is the practice of many sociopaths to focus on trying to find someone doing something wrong versus finding someone doing something right. We've all heard of this practice. The leadership books expound upon this. "Praise in public, punish in private" is the mantra. Unfortunately, the average sociopath will do the exact opposite. Sociopaths will use their observations as the fuel to create crises. This is a variant of the game of "Stump the Dummy." This bastardized version of "management by walking around" is the favorite game of the sociopathic bully.

What actually drives pyromaniacs to be the way they are? One trait common to this ilk is pedanticism. Pedanticism is a practice by which people are so focused on other's errors that they often end up missing their own errors, especially errors in leadership.

Pedanticism is related to perfectionism in that the individual practicing this form of perfectionism is always experiencing the need to correct faults until there's the illusive absolute perfection. If this person spots an error, he has to correct it, even if it would be deemed unnecessary by any other sane individual.

If your organization has one of these "sky is falling" mentality pyromaniacs, get ready to live in 24–7 crisis mode. It will take a toll on you and everyone else in the workplace. Proof of this mentality is the fact that there seems to be a proliferation of organizations that set up "war rooms" whenever a big problem surfaces. They spend enormous amounts of money on these idiotic mind games. The need for these war rooms and the panic management style they spawn could have been eliminated had the appropriate time been taken to plan on doing the job right.

That being said, one thing I've noticed in my career is that in most organizations there is little fanfare for those who quietly plan, and then meet that plan? I can truly say that in all my years, I've never witnessed someone getting rewarded for that behavior. It's another way the introverts always get the shaft. People who get their job done with no fanfare and no sudden explosion of activity at the eleventh hour and fifty-ninth minute are seldom exalted. That's probably because people who perform their job in a calm, systematic manner are, by far, the minority.

This is why the vast majority of organizations subscribe to the hero worship mentality. Let's face it, heroism is rewarded everywhere, and you can't be a hero if you don't have a crisis. For all the rhetoric that flies around in your typical organization about planning and proactiveness, it amazes me how often organizations will perpetuate this hero worship syndrome and constantly be in that eleventh hour crisis mode of operation.

How do you combat this mentality? If someone sets a fire and pulls you into the firefight, try to first understand its importance (against the overall goals of the organization) before sounding the alarm. If the problem looks legit, then by all means jump right in. But if it looks like the problem is just a figment of someone's immortality project, take a close look at what they're up to, and then do your best to ignore it. However, in a sociopathic organization that's easier said than done.

In the end, we must remember that with this behavior, crisis management has nothing to do with being able to manage a crisis. For a pyromaniac a crisis offers opportunities to experience high drama and get his much-needed adrenalin rush. It also provides a chance to sic his heroes on the problem, the end-game being to find a culprit to victimize and make into a scapegoat.

If your organization suffers from the pyromania syndrome, don't be surprised when the best people flee the sinking ship. You should take the hint and bail yourself, because you don't want to be part of the folks left behind; the poor folks who feel like they have to stay for whatever reason; economic, personal, fear, or comfort. It's this group that forms a target-rich environment for the pyromaniac from which to feed.

So what's the prognosis for an organization populated by pyromaniacs? If you're in one of these organizations, you'll be vindicated in due time. The fate of an organization like this has a name: "The Icarus Paradox."

CHAPTER 17 CHICKEN LITTLE

The term comes from Danny Miller's book *The Icarus Paradox*,[199] published in 1992. It focuses on the phenomenon that many businesses will ultimately fail even after a long history of success. Miller's hypothesis is that businesses bring about their own downfall through over-confidence and complacency. He forgot to mention pyromania because just as Icarus went down in flames, so shall the pyromaniac organization. It becomes a self-fulfilling prophesy. Unfortunately, if you're in one of these organizations, and you stick around too long, your fate will be the unemployment line.

CHAPTER 18 HOWDY DOODY

PHILADELPHIA JOURNALIST FRANKLIN P. JONES ONCE SAID, "Asking for advice is how some people trap you into expressing an opinion they can disagree with."[200]

The Howdy Doody Show was the first TV network kid's show. It started in 1947 and lasted until the end of 1960. As a kid, I remember watching it religiously. The stars of the show included the marionettes Howdy Doody, Heidi Doody (his sister), Mayor Phineas T. Bluster, Dilly Dally, and Flub-a-Dub. The Peanut Gallery was the live audience of kids who sat in the studio during the show. Buffalo Bob Smith (Robert Schmidt) created the show and was the host.

Howdy Doody was a dummy, and someone needed to pull his strings for him to come alive. We all have strings that, when pulled, cause us to react. Sometimes we react positively, but most often negatively.

In the show Buffalo Bob would say, "Say kids, what time is it?" The resounding answer from the peanut gallery was, "Its Howdy Doody Time!" In today's workplace environment, you have Howdy Doody time, but it's more affectionately called "Stump the Dummy" time. This chapter is about the most childish yet sinister of all games played by the sociopaths and bullies.

When you're the target of "Stump the Dummy," you'll find yourself caught in the sociopath's favorite sport. This sport involves attempting to catch someone in a situation for which they're not prepared. The purpose of this game is for the sociopath to reveal you as a dummy and thus demonstrate superiority over you. He wants to catch you off guard and unprepared for his question so that he can say "gotcha!" This is the much-favored vehicle for the pyromaniac to deliver his latest crisis on an unsuspecting target.

When you find yourself in this sick game of sociopathic pleasure, you become the dummy, and the intent is to make you look weak, out of touch with what's happening in the organization, and thus not in control or not doing your job. The fact is if you're the target of this game, you'll no longer be in control of your own fate. Any control you thought you had will be reduced to damage control.

Recall the old saying, "If you want the biggest house in the neighborhood there are two ways of achieving it; you can roll up your sleeves and build it, or you can tear down everyone else's house." In this chapter we'll learn about another game used by the sociopaths to tear your house down, one brick at a time, to make their house appear bigger.

In his February 2008 article, "Psychopaths' Cat and Mouse Game," Steve Becker provides an interesting analogy, "Have you ever seen a cat toy with a stunned, cornered mouse? How it will capture the mouse, dangle it in its mouth for a while, release it momentarily (allowing the mouse the illusion of an escape) only to recapture it, dangle it some more from its mouth, perhaps release it again briefly. Of course, the mouse, increasingly frantic, makes another escape bid, only to be recaptured. The cat will hold the terrorized mouse and dangle it yet some more, in dreadful uncertainty.

"If the mouse could think, it might have thoughts like: what will this cat do with me? How long will it continue to toy with me? Will it kill me, or let me go? Strangely, the cat seems to be deriving a perverse pleasure from my predicament. My helplessness and suffering seems to be entertaining and amusing to this cat. The mouse would think there must be something wrong with this cat."[201]

There is something cold and sadistically wrong about how a cat will play with a captured animal, but this is not unlike how the sociopath will use and exploit any of your vulnerabilities for his or her personal gratification. Welcome to the game of "Stump the Dummy."

Unfortunately, the mouse usually doesn't fare too well when caught in the above game, and neither will you when you're singled out to be a sociopath's next target. He can't literally kill you, but he can, and will, literally kill your career dead in its tracks.

As Becker says, "This is the essence of a sociopath; his joy of the hunt, his contempt for his prey, and his intention to take everything he can, and wants, from his victims.

"When the sociopath takes someone for a ride, that is, when he is victimizing people, it's really not personal. They're simply not enough of a person for it to be personal. In the sociopath's eyes, you are an expedient. When they cross your path [and trust me, they will; you can't avoid them] an experienced sociopath will immediately assess your expediency. Is there something this sucker has, or can do, for me? Is there something I can take from this fool that I want? Something I can take that will make me feel good?"[202]

Remember, they're not looking for anything material; however, in a sense all human beings are mere commodities to them. There's a bright side, though. Once you've exhausted your usefulness, you'll be as useless to them as a book on servant leadership, and they'll move on to the next victim. They treat everyone the same way, so there's some consolation in knowing you weren't singled out. They spread their infectious agony indiscriminately throughout the organization that serves as their playground.

One way the sociopath uses the "Stump the Dummy" game on unsuspecting people is to walk around the workplace and dig up information about a person from their sycophantic staff, unsuspecting middle managers, and most often the person's peers. They'll even occasion the ranks of the proles for here they may get information on a problem that hasn't yet percolated up through the ranks. They especially like going to the lowest level of the organization, because they can intimidate these people into spilling their guts about something that might otherwise be a routine issue. They then blow it out of proportion to make it seem more critical than it really is, and then use this tidbit to become the bearer of bad tidings when they darken the target's doorway.

If pickings are sparse, they resort to hear-say. A sociopath will believe hear-say to always be true; to him everyone is guilty until they prove themselves innocent. In this game, the sociopath asks for opinions and tries to piece together what he thinks might be a problem, even if only a problem to him. He can fabricate a problem out of anything because it's his pedantic way.

It's not beneath a sociopath to even ask a person's peers for personal opinions about them. This becomes fodder for his sadistic game of character assassination that he can use in many different venues, from meetings, to his "Divide and Conquer" agenda, and to playing "Stump the Dummy" and just showing up on your doorstep and dumping a problem in your lap to see how you'll react.

The problem is he never gets the whole picture with this method. It's guaranteed to be just a single side of a story. I don't think sociopaths even have the capability of realizing there are two sides to every story. Thus, they'll usually get just enough information to get a sense of what might be going on. This also means that much of the information might be jaded, because these hallway ambushes on people (who dare not disappoint the boss) will embellish any issue to gain the boss's favor. They feel exalted and important since he has obviously sought them out for advice.

Once armed with some juicy foible, the sociopath will wait for the most inopportune moment to corner you, dump the problem in your lap, and wait for your reaction. The sociopath will most often raise questions that are loosely based in fact, requiring you to find an in-depth answer. God forbid you forget the required sense of urgency and voilà, a crisis is created, but most importantly, he has caused your embarrassment. He has dumped on you an implied action item that now becomes your sole agenda. In many ways the "Stump the Dummy" game may be seen as a perverted conjugal (psychic) prison visit by the boss, because in essence you're getting screwed.

As mentioned, one way the sociopath will get his information will unfortunately be from your trusted colleagues and peers. These sycophants you work with will jump at the chance to throw you under the bus. Be wary if you notice that your colleagues are spending a lot of time in the presence of the Lord. They may not just be the suck-up you know they are; they just might be actively torpedoing your career. This is especially telling when they go out to lunch with the boss on a regular basis. They'll lead the boss to the conclusion that you're mishandling your job or are responsible for any problem that's recently occurred or even some that might occur in the future. They'll remind the boss of any past screw-up of yours so that the boss will now have at the front of his mind how you have a tendency to make mistakes.

The boss will then confront you in perfect "Stump the Dummy" fashion. If your answer is that you don't know and will have to get back to him, he'll exhibit real agitation at your failing but will leave happy knowing that you've just admitted you're not in control. Unfortunately, you've just provided him excellent fodder for your next performance review.

To make things worse, one of your colleagues will probably sympathize with the boss about what a dolt you are for not knowing what was going on. This will further solidify the boss's perception that you're a screw-up. For a sociopath or a sycophant, "There is no sweeter sound than the crumbling of ones fellow man," said Groucho Marx.[203]

There's another even more subtle, but nonetheless despicable, version of this game called "gaslighting." I've seen (and been victim to) this version of "Stump the Dummy" in action. In a nutshell, it's a form of psychological abuse in which false information is given to the victim with the intent of making him doubt his own memory, perception, and even reality.

The term "Gaslighting," and "Gaslight Effect," was coined by Dr. Robin Stern and is derived from the 1944 movie, *Gaslight*, in which a husband attempts to drive his wife insane by manipulating things in their environment, then insisting that she's mistaken when she points out these changes. Since sociopaths are very good liars, this is a perfect game for them.

How do you know you've been the victim of gaslighting? In her May 2009 article "Are you Being Gaslighted?" Dr. Stern suggests you ask yourself these simple questions:[204]

- Are you constantly second-guessing yourself?
- Do you often feel confused?
- Are you always apologizing to the sociopath?
- Do you wonder frequently if you're good enough?
- Do you have trouble making simple decisions?
- Do you think twice before saying anything or offering any opinion?
- Do you feel as though you can't do anything right?

If you answered yes to any number of these, you're probably the victim of this extremely sinister version of "Stump the Dummy."

Unfortunately, there's another level of humiliation you'll experience. This is when the perp ratchets up the abuse another notch by running to your peers and colleagues with the news of how you did something wrong. This is part of the smear campaign an abuser will wage against his victim. He will get to other people first before the shell-shocked victim can pull himself together. His goal is to make himself look like an omnipotent being, and you look like an ignorant nincompoop. This punishment by proxy is typical in a sociopathically run *Lord of the Flies* organization.

"Assassination by proxy" is a favored game of the sycophants who are focused on their constant jockeying for position at the boss's teat. These junior sociopaths take full advantage of any knowledge that they gain about your screw-ups and relish the situation as it supports their goal of tearing down your house.

What's the fallout of being the victim of "Stump the Dummy?" By the time your confronted, and realize that your being targeted, there's already a "kick-me" sign on your back, and you've been labeled as incompetent and witless and, above all, worthy of demotion or eventually firing. At the very least, rest assured you're on the next RIF list.

Rebounding from such an assault can be a long and difficult, if not impossible, process. With sociopaths there's little room for redemption. And even if you could, over time, resurrect your reputation, you better get used to the shitty end of the stick for quite a while.

Don't be tricked into thinking that there's no malice in their actions. You can't do this with a sociopath. Most of them are simply incompetent, certainly in the ways of leadership. This is what's called "Grey's Law," which states, "Any sufficiently advanced incompetence is indistinguishable from malice."[205] Therefore, there's some element of malice in everything they do.

If you're in management, there's a more sinister version of this game that you'll experience at times. Not only will your colleagues and peers play the game at your expense, but if it's truly a *Lord of the Flies* organization, your direct reports will partake in trying to bring you down. This game is even practiced by the proles. Despite how good a leader you might be there will always be someone in your organization plotting to bring you down.

Be particularly cautious of any sycophants you've taken under your wing to coach and mentor. If you're mentoring someone with the sociopathic drive to get to the top fast, you will only appear as a stumbling block in their path. Sooner or later they will decide you must be eliminated from the island.

"Stump the Dummy" tactics are used on groups, in individual relationships, or whenever someone is desperate to establish or maintain authority and status.

These individuals will do nothing but focus their attention on the task of trying to goad you into playing a game in which you're destined to fail. This is another form of the impression management tactics pervasive in today's workplace.

What's been detailed so far is basically the perverse side of the old "management by walking around" practice. I'm not saying that the boss can't or shouldn't walk around and socialize and get updated on issues or hot-off-the press news, but what the boss does with that knowledge, is the issue. I'm a firm believer in "management by walking around" but have a hard time when it's used only to dig up dirt that can be used against someone. True management by walking around is meant to be a way for the boss to catch someone doing something right and thus be able to praise them for it on the spot.

There's another way of describing this basic sadistic side of management by walking around. It's called, "vulture management."

This practice operates much the way a vulture does in hunting for food. They circle the prey, then, at the appropriate time, swoop down for the kill. This management vulture is looking for you to make a mistake that they can capitalize on by attacking you when you're vulnerable. Either way, their intent is to draw the attention to you and to tarnish your credibility.

The vultures use this technique and capitalize on it by diverting the attention of the organization to whatever you may have screwed-up. Remember, screw-ups are an inevitable part of being human, so everyone in the organization is always providing fresh fodder for these birds of prey.

In his article, "Nine Destructive Project Manager Behaviors," Geoff Crane provides us some insight. "Vultures (the actual birds) aren't well liked. We see them when we drive down country roads, perched near the dying, and often have to overcome an urge to throw things at them." The analogy fits well to describe the popularity of your typical sociopath.

"They wait patiently for their victim to die (rather than either offering a helping hand, or a clean kill), and when the victim exhales its last breath, the vulture pulls them apart and eats their remains. They know their prey isn't going anywhere; at least the corpse isn't."[206] This is a metaphor for your career, which most likely will exhale its last breath after you've been victimized a few times by the "Stump the Dummy" game.

Further Crane notes, "One of the most difficult aspects of vultures is they view their own behavior as virtuous. Getting them to break this behavior requires a lot of work. So don't even try. You can't fight them either, because they will mark anyone who challenges them for more abuse. So devoted to this logic are they, that if a vulture is terminated for odious behavior, they will ascribe weakness to the manager who fired them rather than looking forward. They do not have the compunction to look inward. Just like their winged counterparts, vultures aren't particularly introspective.

"What vultures fail to realize is that their success depends not upon the failure of others, but upon the success of others. In a [team] environment, everyone needs to support everyone else. This support shouldn't be at the expense of other work."[207]

It's inevitable that someone in the organization is likely to fall down from time to time, and this opens the cage for the vulture. In this way they have a never-ending supply of prey.

Wouldn't it be nice if this behavior were restricted to the animal kingdom where we wouldn't have to observe it in our day-to-day lives? Unfortunately, it's not the case. Sociopaths behave like this all the time. Back in school they were undoubtedly the class bullies. If you've ever been bullied in school, like I have, you will, for the rest of your life, be reprehensive of this type of behavior. It's unfortunate that for many of us, we couldn't escape these dill weeds in school, and now we find they've moved into management in the company in which we're trying to build our career.

Cartoonist Hugh MacLeod has an interesting anecdote on this behavior. It's what he calls "The Cleopatra Effect." It's based on a scene from the movie *Cleopatra* in which Cleopatra is walking through the palace and is suddenly stopped by the sound of beautiful music being played off in the distance. She follows the sound of the music through the palace, eventually finding one of her courtiers in the garden, playing the harp.

After she compliments the courtier on the beautiful music, she asks if he can teach her to play. The courtier, obviously flattered, agrees. Cleopatra then explains "the deal." If after a month she can't play the harp as good as the courtier, the courtier faces flogging, and if after three months she can't play as well, execution. Cleopatra gives the courtier an evil smirk, then turns and walks off.

Sadistically, this exchange describes exactly the "bait and abate" phenomenon that is carried out every day in today's workplace. I've coined this phrase to capture the essence of the "Stump the Dummy" game. The bait in the game is the question, or accusation, made to you by the sociopath, and the pay-off for him is your abatement—i.e. stumping the dummy.

In the above movie scene, we have Cleopatra baiting this poor slave into committing to teach her how to play the harp. Unfortunately, and much to the horror of the courtier, she sets the terms of the agreement in which no matter the outcome, it means a horrible end for the courtier. Remember the double bind. Thus, the courtier is in a no-win situation much the way people in the workplace find themselves when targeted by a sociopathic bully. No matter your defense, you find that you are indelibly marked by your peers and colleagues and will eventually suffer the rite of degradation—i.e. your abatement.

Through all of this inevitable humiliation that you'll suffer at the hands of the sociopaths and their evil Scaramouche, remember what newscaster David Brinkley said: "A successful man is one who can lay a firm foundation with the bricks others have thrown at him."[208] Unfortunately, that's much easier said than done.

CHAPTER 19 INSANITY

BRITISH INVESTOR SIR JOHN TEMPLETON ONCE SAID, "The four most expensive words in the English language are: this time is different."[209] This is also the most spoken phrase echoing the halls of business.

Remember Santayana's "Law of Repeating Consequences?"[210] It says, "Those who cannot remember the past are doomed to repeat it." This chapter is about just that and its effects on the typical workplace. Another way of describing this comes from the famous quote by Albert Einstein: "The definition of insanity is doing the same thing over again and expecting a different result." There isn't a company that I've ever worked for where I didn't hear either of these sayings bantered about by the management, yet the irony is that all of these organizations repeatedly made the same mistakes.

Companies do have a propensity to collectively forget and repeat the sins of the past. This is largely due to the phenomenon of "organizational amnesia." This chapter is about organization amnesia and its close cousin "selective amnesia."

It's common knowledge, with proof aplenty, that companies repeat their blunders on a regular basis. Studies also found that the management within most organizations has little memory of past problems and how they were solved; either the actions or the rationales, they used. Also, the lessons learned process, which many organizations try, doesn't produce any lasting change that reduces the time and effort needed to solve recurring problems.

From my experience this is a big problem in organizations that are structured with both a project or product development type structure coupled with the typical vertical functional management hierarchy. I've witnessed this over and over; different projects at the same company tend to suffer from the same mistakes. Lessons learned by a project team never funnel back to the functional organizations where action can be taken to remedy any underlying problem. This phenomenon even strikes the same employees who move from one completed project to a new one; they repeat the same mistakes they vowed on the last project to never make again.

It's also a fact that many companies continually reinvent solutions to the same recurring problem, completely ignoring the solutions discovered in past experience. It's generally accepted that there are two basic reasons for organizations to keep repeating their mistakes.

The first is the inability of most organizations to effectively record what they've learned from past experiences. If it's captured at all, it's via tribal knowledge and this can often leave with departing individuals. This leaves the newbies to absorb knowledge by osmosis. This is a recurring fate for an organization that experiences high turnover.

The second reason is the old communication issue, especially the dysfunctional communication that typically exists among parts of fiefdom-rich organizations. We learned about all the roadblocks to communication earlier; however, fiefdoms intensify this organizational flaw. In the organizational example noted above, in which there are both projects performing autonomously and an underlying functional management structure, the effects of the Fiefdom Syndrome on communications and sharing is multiplied. In these organizations, little cross-functional (horizontal) communication happens and this would include the sharing of solutions to problems.

Let's try to understand why this phenomenon exists and seems to be so pervasive in the modern workplace. To do this we need to understand how organizational memory and knowledge works, or in most cases, doesn't work.

Organizational memory is the recorded, or unrecorded, "how" of know-how. It completely defines the characteristics of the organization's ability to perform tasks and in meeting its goals. This is frequently referred to as "tribal knowledge."

Tribal Knowledge is the collective wisdom of the organization. It's the sum of all the "good" knowledge that an organization needs to accomplish each job within the company and achieve its goals, but it also includes all the "bad" knowledge of how to do things wrong. This dark side includes all the information that isn't shared because of the egos or self-interests of insecure people. Every organization has those who feel a need to protect their jobs by not sharing the information needed to do a job. Finally, tribal knowledge also includes the required knowledge for individuals to navigate and survive the culture and the politics within the organization.

In his book *The Tribal Knowledge Paradox: Using the War on Waste to Align Strategy with Process,* [211] management consultant Leonard Bertain asserts that there exists within most organizations what he calls "The Tribal Knowledge Paradox." He defines the paradox as the fact that while an organization believes that its business success is dependent upon the knowledge and skills of the people, its management organization, structure, processes, and actions conflict and inhibit that belief. It is management's caustic rhetoric, games, and dubious actions—not the lack of knowledge and skills—that causes an organization not to succeed. This is the walk-the-walk versus talk-the-talk syndrome.

Thus to fully understand organizational amnesia, it is helpful to better understand what comprises tribal knowledge. Tribal knowledge exists in two forms; explicit (which can be easily recorded and shared), and tacit, which is more intuitive and spreads through the memes of the organization's internal communication channels.

Whereas explicit knowledge is data, tacit knowledge is more the ability of the organization's inhabitants to interpret information i.e., their amazing grasp of the obvious. Tacit knowledge lies in the values, beliefs, and perceptions of the organization and is part and parcel with the organization's culture and politics, and the two are intertwined tightly.

The problem for most organizations is that their explicit knowledge gathering mechanisms are dysfunctional. This typically is the result of the modern business culture of valuing results above the process used to obtain those results. This means that little effort is spent on capturing the knowledge/data of how the organization got to where it is; they only acknowledge the fact that it got there. This is evidenced by the "results" mantra preached in most organizations. Thus, it is no surprise that they can't remember things.

This is particularly interesting in light of the proliferation of metrics gathering that goes on in many organizations. A lot of data are captured; however, it's only superficially reviewed and certainly not with the intent of truly learning anything from it. Remember what Herbert Simon said, "A wealth of information creates a poverty of attention." Most organizations have the needed info; they just choose intentionally (or subconsciously) to not use it, and forget it. Additionally, their tacit knowledge sharing mechanisms are dysfunctional so it's no wonder organizational and selective amnesias run rampant.

It's often more convenient to just discuss a problem again (and again) by going back to square one. This is why we sometimes encounter a sense of déjà vu during meetings. We realize that we've already beaten this dead horse.

To really understand organizational amnesia, we must look at the people factor. This is the real root-cause of why organizations have problems disseminating information, thus learning from the past. As noted above, a big reason organizational amnesia runs rampant in today's workplaces is simply because individuals refuse to share their knowledge. You could categorize that as a communication problem, but it's more than that.

The culture of the organization has everything to do with the company's propensity to suffer organizational amnesia. The typical blame culture that exists in modern organizations is maybe the prime contributor; people won't share information, for fear of being blamed. Also, selective amnesia is the sociopath's defense for conveniently forgetting anything that doesn't support his cause or may show his culpability. This is closely linked to the phenomenon of plausible deniability.

The main characteristic of the personal aspect of organizational amnesia and selective amnesia is that it's mostly one-dimensional. Recalling the previous chapters' behavior pattern, a sociopath has no problem remembering all the things he thinks you did wrong, but undoubtedly selectively forgets his own screw-ups. This propensity to want to forget everything negative, especially your own failings, is a universal human trait and the reason people don't learn from their mistakes. This is The Halo Effect in action.

The typical performance review process is the only place where you'll find photographic memories of every mistake (real or imagined) that has ever been made. In this arena, the sociopaths are like the proverbial elephant that never forgets.

Most organizational amnesia happens at the top of the organization. This is where communication most often breaks down and where most of the games are played. The neck of every bottle is at the top, right?

At the actual working level, the risk of loss of tribal knowledge is minimal unless the organization experiences high turnover or there are knowledge hoarders. Hoarding is especially prevalent in an organization where the threat of lay-off is a constant reminder to the workers that they must somehow develop an edge over their colleagues in order to stay employed. This is The Red Queen Effect in action.

Tribal knowledge at the lowest level in the organization, while painful to lose, can be recreated. However, the knowledge that's lost at the high levels of the organization has more significant effects on both the financial and cultural well-being of the organization. Just as "The Tribal Knowledge Paradox" would predict, this is where I've personally witnessed the most damaging cases of organization amnesia.

Organizational amnesia deeply seated in the executive suite, is what fosters a blaming culture, and the blame always filters its way down the organizational structure to the lowest common denominator. If the proles, or even the sycophants, are blamed for the organization's failure then they will hoard even more information for fear of being blamed for screw-ups.

The good news is that many organizations at least recognize that they're suffering from organizational amnesia and in an attempt to combat it will dabble in the infamous lessons learned process. Do an Internet search on this topic and you'll find many different "lessons learned" processes to choose from. Obviously, businesses aren't wont for guidance on this subject, assuming they choose to actively embrace combating this universal organizational problem.

So how does this "lessons learned" process work? Typically, it involves a multi-step process if you're going to effectively derive benefit from it. The steps vary, but most include collecting, validating, storing, disseminating, and then implementing the information to better the organization's functioning. Another technique that most organizations are familiar with is the simple plan–do–check–act (PDCA) process. This is an iterative four-step management problem-solving process also known as the Deming circle/cycle/wheel. The problem is that many organizations don't/ won't take the time to do all the steps effectively or they do it half-heartedly.

When used appropriately, these techniques can be great in analyzing an organization's past foibles to find root causes, so that changes can be made to eliminate recurrence. However, in all the organizations I've been involved with (that actively administered this process); they still suffered from organizational amnesia despite going through the motions. This is because making a lessons learned program really work is extremely difficult. Most management teams, regardless of what they say, are just not that open kimono when it comes to admitting that their problems just might be their own fault. If you don't admit to your problems, then you can't be blamed. Thus no problems are ever really identified. And if problems aren't identified, root causes can't be found, and thus corrective action can't be taken.

There are many reasons for a "lessons-learned" process to not be effective, but the common thread in all the companies that struggle with this lies with top-level management. The effective implementation of a "lessons-learned" process requires strong leadership, a commitment of resources, and an atmosphere where people are not afraid to admit to mistakes, and in fact, are rewarded for doing so.

Benefiting from the "lessons learned" process means encouraging openness (at all levels) about making mistakes or errors in judgment. However, the typical workplace environment does little to encourage that behavior. Openness means leading by example, and if management is unwilling to admit to and learn from their mistakes, it's unlikely that the rest of the organization will be willing to admit to mistakes. In fact, management must reward people for being open and admitting to making mistakes, bad decisions, or judgment errors, versus what typically happens, which is that mistakes are meticulously documented and thrown-up to the employee come performance review time.

One of the biggest problems in implementing an effective "lesson learned" process is the whole accountability mantra so prevalent in today's workplace environments. In most organizations accountability is just a thinly veiled disguise for blame-storming or finger-pointing. In these type organizations, fear will kill any objective involvement in the "lessons-learned" process. No one wants to go into a "lessons learned" review meeting where they may be identified as part of a problem. Unfortunately, in companies that insist on finding fault, people must protect themselves, and the modus operandi becomes a finger-pointing, interdepartmental blame game.

Seth Godin has an interesting view of organizational amnesia. He calls it "arrogance of willful ignorance." He believes "that if you're doing important work, then you owe it to your [company] or your customers, or your co-workers to learn everything you can. Feel free to ignore what you learn, but at least learn it."[212]

The take-away here is that the only way for organizational amnesia to be eradicated in the modern workplace is for the individual to take the responsibility to learn and apply improvements as he goes about his job. The problem, though, in too many organizations is that the environment forces them to not want to get involved. Just like society at large, even people at work don't want to get involved. They consciously select to become players in the *Eternal Sunshine of the Spotless Mind*, the Jim Carrey movie about erasing the mind.[213]

CHAPTER 20 ZEMBLANITY

IT'S SAID THAT THERE'S A TIME WHEN everyone will experience an instance of serendipity—being at the right place at the right time—or finding something valuable or beautiful when not looking for it. The term is also sometimes used to mean the randomness of fate. Either way, when we experience serendipity it's usually a welcomed surprise. But what if the event or surprise isn't welcomed? Believe it or not, there's a term for that. It is the antonym for serendipity—zemblanity—the inevitable discovery of what we would rather not know.

Everyone is familiar with the old phrase; "If life hands you lemons, make lemonade." That's another of those feel-good sayings that finds its way into everyday life and is supposed to make you feel better when life hands you the inevitable proverbial lemon. It's supposed to help you rise above whatever fate has flung your way.

But stuff happens and surprises get flung your way every day. These are the moments of zemblanity. It's important to understand zemblanity because today's management teams are deathly afraid of surprises or anything that could potentially upset their delicate balancing act or house of cards. You'd be surprised how many businesses are balancing on a precipice and all that's needed is one little problem, let alone an actual crisis, to push them over the edge.

Organizations attempt to battle this and mask their sheer terror of failing through their almost religious addiction to preaching the need to be proactive. As if through this one mantra they will ward off the evil that may befall them that could bring an end to their charade. I can't remember a single organization that didn't preach the proactiveness mantra, yet the management team was the least likely to practice what it preached.

Until now I've used the word "proactive" many times, but always in its true meaning and context. Now I'd to expose that word in the context that it's used most often in business: that of surprise avoidance.

Dictionary.com defines proactive as: serving to prepare for, intervene in, or control an expected occurrence or situation, especially a negative or difficult one. The freedictionary.com provides another definition: acting in advance to deal with an expected difficulty, and: tending to initiate change rather than reacting to events.

However, proactive behavior in the modern workplace usually is an expectation that people will somehow identify potential "un-expected" problems and threats and take preemptive action versus reacting in fire-fight mode after a problem has occurred.

There's an interesting word in the above two dictionary definitions: "expected." This means that, to be proactive, one must actively engage in change as a result of some "expected" event. However, in the context that it's used in the workplace, it usually signifies an expectation by management that if people would only be more proactive, they'd be able to foresee "unexpected" problems before they happen and solve them before they become crises. I find that a bit delusional.

Interestingly, the businessdictionary.com definition doesn't mention the word "expected," but it does include action-oriented behavior instead of one that waits for things to happen and; taking preemptory action against potential problems and threats. This is interesting because at first glance it would appear to support what management is expecting of people when it wants them to be proactive. Thus, proactiveness in the business vernacular means the ability to foresee and address potential problems *before* they happen.

The key point here is that to be proactive, most management expects you to possess the ability to "foresee" potential problems happening. Isn't that the same as "expected?" If problems are foreseen, then in fact, they are expected.

Conversely, let's look at the definition of "surprise." The Google definition is; an unexpected or astonishing event. The freedictionary.com defines it as; to encounter unexpectedly, or take, or catch unawares. The operative word in these definitions is "unexpected." Thus, unexpected is the essence of a surprise.

The question then becomes how someone can be logically expected to be proactive and foresee something that is unexpected. There's a flaw in that logic. Nowhere in any of the definitions does it say one must be able to foretell the unexpected.

So if management really wants the workforce to foretell the unexpected, then what they're really looking for is an army of soothsayers. However, I've never seen that skill listed in a job description or on a performance appraisal form. This is a classic example of what we'll learn in a later chapter, that often what management says is not always what it's expecting or even means.

If people and organizations were truly proactive in their thinking and attitudes, then the fact that the inevitable glitch will happen will be expected, and they would know how to react with calm and poise. What's expected is that there will be things happening unexpectedly.

As Rahm Emanuel noted, we should use a crisis as an opportunity for real change. Recall the third definition: tending to initiate change rather than reacting to events. This then is the true meaning of "proactive." This change component should be the essence of the proactive definition. However, the organizations that preach proactiveness the most are typically the least adaptive, or receptive, to change.

If the whole gist of being proactive is the ability to forecast problems that are yet unknown and take action to circumvent them from happening, then management wouldn't need any other fancy tools to run the business. As a matter of fact, if the employees were so good at foretelling the future, they'd all win the lottery, and quit.

Isn't it a bit naïve to think that you can catch all the potential problems beforehand? Go on using the word "proactive" all you want, but the only way to survive in today's workplace is to understand:

- You must be prepared for the unexpected
- The unexpected will unexpectedly happen

Our decisions and best-laid plans rarely work out the way we expect. However, what often seems to be a surprise catastrophe, if treated correctly, can possibly be an opportunity for change. We've all heard of the immutable Murphy's Law. There's no truer law in the world of business. It's immutable because no matter what proactive bullshit an organization throws around, Murphy's Law—and O'Toole's Corollary of Finagle's Law, which says that the perversity of a universe tends toward the maximum—will always prevail.[214]

The real challenge for management is not being able to forecast problems; it's learning how to react to them without panic. In his book *The Power of Stupidity*, Giancarlo Livraghi shines a new light on Murphy's Law.

"Whatever the origin, or the occasion from which it was born, the fact is that it has become proverbial; if something can go wrong, it will, at the worst possible time. Countless variations on Murphy's Law don't tell us why things go wrong. Often the mess is so malicious that it seems to be the work of some mischievous gremlin. But it's pretty clear that the most frequent origin is human stupidity. It can be our own stupidity, because we have made a mistake, we haven't checked as carefully as we should, or we have failed to consider a variable whose effects come into play when we least expect them.

"Or it can be someone else's stupidity. Someone near to us, who has done something wrong, or is making things unnecessarily complicated.

"Or maybe someone, we may not know who, how, or where, somehow caused us to have wrong or misleading information, or designed a tool that breaks down at the worst possible time. Murphy's Law, if properly understood, is a resource for intelligence.

"The point is that the unexpected is practically unavoidable because we are never able to control all variables, or because some external factors that we can't control come into play when they are least expected.

"There are several ways of coping with this problem so that we are not taken by total surprise. One is to have an effective backup of solutions that can replace the one that suddenly isn't working. Another is flexible planning, that treats the unexpected not as an obstacle, but as a different route to the objective, or maybe the opening of a new opportunity.

"Above all, it's important to know that the unexpected exists and be mentally prepared to face it. Not to be confused or scared, but to be ready to find new solutions, to meet new opportunities, to learn from the stimulating experience of change."[215]

Rick Brenner writes, "It is always amazing to me how important it is for people to not be surprised. Whatever happens in the world is okay as long as it's not a surprise. The manager's fear of surprise is really the desire to always be in control. In spite of the amazing strides of science, in spite of our relentless study of history and our overwhelming compulsion to control our environment, human beings still have a very poor track record of being able to predict the future.

"What does this mean, practically speaking? It means that life is uncertain and things rarely turn out anything like what we expect. Things virtually never turn out exactly as we expect. But something happens to us as we get older. We become not so much risk averse as we become surprise averse. It is not that we don't like to get good news, but it is disconcerting when things don't turn out as we expect, even when they turn out better than we expect, because it spoils our delusion that we are in control of our lives."[216]

The reality of everyday work life forces you to accept that most things are beyond your control. For all the talk that organizations expound about being proactive, the fact is, being reactionary is how you'll spend most of your career.

Brenner explains that, "If you tell people 'I want no surprises,' prepare for disappointment. For the kind of work that most people do, surprises are inevitable. Unfortunately, it's much too broad a message as a day-to-day guide for doing business. Here's a little of what's wrong with a 'no surprises' policy.'

"It's too broad a message; if your policy is 'no surprises,' then you're saying that you don't want any good surprises either. Probably you don't mean that.

"It's an unattainable goal; surprises are inevitable in projects.

"When a surprise does happen, you have a new problem; if your policy is 'no surprises,' and a surprise happens, you have two problems. Not only do you have to deal with the surprise, but you also have a violation of policy. Because policy violations usually require disciplinary action, the policy itself creates a problem.

"There will always be surprises, and here's one: the trick for dealing with surprises is not to avoid them, but to get really good at recovering from them."[217]

That last point is a good one because surprises always lead to a good old healthy, house cleaning, witch-hunt. Witch hunts are just another way that management incites and condones the games of "Divide and Conquer" and "Stump the Dummy" and don't forget pyromania.

In some respects it's not really even their fault that they behave this way. Their behavior can be blamed on the monochronic time system that's in effect in most Western cultures, especially in the United States. Note that I'm not trying to make excuses and justify the surprise adverse sociopathic behavior. I only note this in the interest of being fair; however, it does reveal a major flaw in modern business thinking.

A monochronic time system means that things are typically done serially (one at a time), and all work is segmented and divided into small units, or tasks. Under this system a task (time) is scheduled, statused, and managed, always looking toward the future. The schedule becomes sacred, and getting the job/task done is paramount. I've witnessed this many times in my career; massive schedules are created that extend years into the future, yet are dividing up tasks and scheduling down to the hour. The problem is that because of surprises most of these schedules go off track with days or weeks of their creation. The result is constant re-scheduling to overcome the delay caused by the surprise.

In contrast, a polychronic time system is one in which several things can be done at once, and a more fluid approach is taken to scheduling time. This is how much of Europe operates.

The future-focused and micromanaged orientation of monochronic time contributes to the preoccupation in business with proactiveness, the sense of urgency mentality, and the fear of surprises, or anything that upsets the schedule. The interesting thing is that businesses in the monochronic time system also strive for characteristics of the polychronic system in that the needs to multitask and be proactive are preached so vehemently.

This also reveals itself in how blame is placed within the organization. The monochronic thinking begets the *post hoc ergo propter hoc*–meaning "after this, therefore because of this"–treatment of blame. In practice it means if one event follows another, and that event suffers a problem then the problem must have been caused by the preceding event. Because things are scheduled end-to-end it begets the thinking that the cause of every problem must have been the preceding step, or task that caused it. The take away here is as long as you're in the chain of events, you should expect to get blamed for something sooner or later.

So how does the average organization face the challenge of surprises? Most delude themselves into thinking they're being proactive in their efforts with their risk management plans. They'll try to identify the areas from where they believe the problems will come. They'll perform their "strengths, weaknesses, opportunities and threats" (SWOT) analyses, and they'll dote over these in meeting after meeting and review after review, but most often all that's happening is good old fashioned hand-ringing.

They have elaborate PowerPoint presentations with colorful charts depicting the identified risks they think they'll face. These risk analysis exercises typically use what I call the "rainbow chart" to display the probabilities of problems and issues happening and how the organization thinks it can circumvent them. However, a rainbow chart is just like the real rainbow it's named after. The underlying search for reassurance that all possible risks have been identified and mitigated is as mythical as the proverbial pot-of-gold at the end of the rainbow.

You may have seen one of these charts or even had the dubious honor of making one up. The typical rainbow chart lists the risks that have been identified, or "expected," and attempts to categorize them as to their perceived severity to the organization or the project in question. Supposedly based on an analysis, a color code will be assigned to each risk area. A code of red means that the risk, or threat, is severe; yellow means that the organization must remain cautious (and monitor the risk); and green, or sometimes blue, indicates that there's a mitigation plan needed to be put in place. The fact is that this analysis is little better than the proverbial SWAG: scientific wild-ass guess.

The problem with this approach is that they are only identifying those risks that are apparent. They have an amazing grasp for the obvious. I've never seen a chart that included something like: on Tuesday the production line will grind to a halt because a machine will break unexpectedly. Now that's a surprise.

To compound the problem most organizations schedule so tightly that there's little time for unexpected problems to pop up. When they do, the schedule is immediately in jeopardy. That's the monochronic thinking process at work.

The real risks are the surprises, that can't be identified up front, that create the havoc in the organization. That's why they're surprises. If you can foretell it then it's not a surprise.

What I find most interesting is that while risks, or potential issues, are identified, little is usually ever done to actually mitigate them. If the chart author can identify the problems and risks beforehand, then they are not surprises or true risks, and they should just do something about it, for crying out loud. Why must it be put on a chart? I'll tell you why: it's for everyone to think what a proactive person the author must be.

An example might be the identification of manpower availability as a risk to a project, yet nothing is ever done to hire more people. In fact, at the same time the chart is up on the screen, management is probably planning the latest RIF. This goes back to the idea that withholding resources is one way the boss will torpedo your career. Another might be the acknowledgement that there's a risk that the project may go over budget, yet nothing different is done procedurally to try to circumvent it. Despite what's on the chart surprises will still happen, and the expected will be ignored.

Organizations delude themselves by using risk management to try to circumvent surprise. I'm not trying to knock risk management. It's a good discipline for dealing with the things you know might happen, but it's useless as a soothsaying method. I'm not advocating its abandonment; I just see that too much effort is spent in creating these analyses, yet too little action is taken to solve the identified problems.

In most organizations when the inevitable surprise does happen, there's wailing and gnashing of teeth because nobody foresaw it. The sociopaths look at the poor slob who couldn't foresee the surprise happening as an egregious affront to them and thus will be running around yelling "Off with his head!"

Identifying and managing risk is like a chess game. Who can foresee all the moves that are possible all the way to the end? In the end, events, like chess moves, are serial. *Post hoc ergo propter hoc* implies that surprises happen normally as you progress through whatever you're doing. Things happening as planned will, in fact, create the surprises.

The attempt to foretell surprises is nothing but guesswork at best. Problems are problems. People need to get over them and focus on putting in place a good procedure for crisis management and expect the crises to keep them busy. Just like the guy in jail in the movie *Harold & Kumar Go to White Castle* says, "The universe will tend to unfold as it should."

The key to surviving in the real world, where surprises spring up like a zit on your forehead the morning of a job interview, is to nurture an atmosphere in which problems can be elevated as soon as they appear, not be shuffled under the carpet until they fester and rot into a full-blown catastrophe and someone's running around saying, "I think there's been a dead body in the trunk."

In their book, *TouchPoints: Creating Powerful Leadership Connections in the Smallest of Moments*, Douglas R. Connant and Melle Norgaard define all those day-to-day surprises that happen that can derail even the best-laid plan as "Touchpoints."[218] They claim that these TouchPoints are the best opportunities for management to practice true leadership. Instead of being afraid of these interruptions, or surprises, a true leader will use these interruptions as coaching or mentoring opportunities to bring people together.

Great leaders and good management teams want to hear the problems. However, they also want to hear potential solutions. If all you do is whine about problems, they'll surely label you a drama queen, so to circumvent that stigma, try to suggest a solution. The sociopaths won't adopt it, but at least you can say you tried.

The underlying problem with surprises is that nobody has a crystal ball. Management shouldn't think that its staff or the rest of the workers in the organization are omnipotent. Those who need to be omnipotent are the management. They get paid for that kind of skill.

So if a surprise does happen, don't kill the messenger. Remember #18 on Marshall Goldsmith's list of bad behaviors: Punishing the Messenger. Unfortunately, this is one of the innate traits/skills of a seasoned sociopath.

In her August 2010 article "Help For Abusive Bullies and Targets: Using the Relationship Selling Method for Connecting," Kathleen Schulweis defines four different management styles that I think reflect the underlying management characteristics that can help explain why management is so surprise averse. All management personalities can be categorized into four major styles:[219]

- The Dominant Director: self-contained (not open) but direct. This person is fast/decisive, fears loss of control, will dictate when tense. He values productivity, gains security when in control, wants to be successful, needs you to support his goals, is practical, needs to be in charge, and once he's made a decision, that's it.

- The Cautious Thinker: self-contained (not open) and indirect. This person is systematic, fears embarrassment, will avoid when tense. To gain their trust you must be prepared, credible, supportive, and precise. Cautious thinkers don't like surprises and measure worth through accuracy and productivity.

- The Steady Relater: open but indirect. This person is slow, but easy; fears confrontation, will acquiesce when tense, seeks attention, wants connection, is a conformist, wants to be liked and makes considered decisions.

- The Interactive Socializer: open and direct. This person is spontaneous, relationship oriented, fears loss of prestige, is sarcastic and attacking when tense, seeks recognition and status, wants to be admired and makes spontaneous decisions.

From these descriptions we find that the Dominant Director fears loss of control; the Cautious Thinker fears embarrassment; the Steady Relater fears confrontation, and the Interactive Socializer fears loss of prestige. All these can be the consequences of a surprise for the sociopath, and are why they're so afraid of them. In the end it doesn't matter the management style; everyone seems to react badly to surprises.

There's another underlying problem that's sort of like the elephant in the middle of the room. Most management teams don't know how to really solve problems, so by necessity, they must shy away from any circumstance that presents a problem. They know (deep down inside) they're not good at it, hence the aversion to surprises.

The underlying reason they're not good at problem-solving is because they've never given their organizations the time to actually solve a problem. However, they typically spend a lot of effort on trying to eliminate the symptoms. This is why most problems only rear their ugly heads again later. The biggest reason for this is financial. If monies were spent to really put in place solutions to problems, it would mean management must make an investment that would detract from their monthly/quarterly revenue and profit. This, in turn, might reduce their individual bonuses. So problems become like tin cans and they get kicked down the road.

This is exacerbated by that sense of urgency mentality. This is what drives organizations to never take the time to dig down to the true root causes of problems. When, by chance, they do find an effective cure for a problem, the whole amnesia thing kicks in; hence, they won't remember the secret sauce later when inevitably needed again.

Everyone's experienced those déjà vu moments—the experiences of feeling sure that you've already witnessed or experienced a current situation, even though the exact circumstances of the previous encounter are uncertain and were perhaps imagined. Did you know there is a direct opposite of the déjà vu experience? It's fittingly called *vujà dé*. Maybe the surprise adverse mentality can be explained by *vujà dé*.

The term *vujà dé* (also called "pre-amnesia")[220] describes the experience of feeling that you haven't witnessed or experienced a situation previously. The term was coined by Kurt Kemp in his 2007 book *The Weird Ideas I get*. The term was more notably immortalized by the comedian George Carlin.

The experience of *vujà dé* is usually accompanied by a sense of unfamiliarity, and confusion, or maybe even shock. It can include a feeling of being lost. *Vujà dé* has also been described as "instant Alzheimer's."

Vujà dé explains why some managers develop an ability to see solutions that have gone unnoticed by others. It also explains why others fail to see anything. This is because they stopped looking when they discovered the first symptom, and urgently jumped to a conclusion.

In his February 2010 article "Leadership Caffeine: Its Vujà dé All Over Again," Art Petty offers some insight, "In my experience, too many leaders give up on the power of observation once they've formed initial impressions. They stop looking for opportunities and start managing based on perceptions and all of the inherent biases that go into forming these perceptions. Stop looking too soon and you're liable to miss some remarkable opportunities."[221]

Here's an example of how *vujà dé* can work as a management tool. In World War II, British and United States air forces faced a rising number of their planes being shot down in combat, and the returning planes were badly damaged. A group of scientists were entrusted with the task of analyzing the returned planes to see if there was any pattern to the damage that would provide a clue as to where to place added armor.

The group analyzed the damaged planes and was about to make a recommendation to add armor where there were the most bullet holes, when a young Hungarian mathematician, Abraham Wald (1902–1950), who was part of the group, thought that they were making a grave mistake. Wald analyzed the damaged planes by marking where every bullet hole was on the planes and found that two major sections of the fuselage, one between the wings and the other between the tails, had fewer bullet holes. He recommended putting the armor in those places, where he saw fewer, not more holes. Why? Since the planes he analyzed hadn't been shot down, he postulated that it must be the holes he wasn't seeing (in the planes that weren't returning) that were causing them to be shot down. Thus, he concluded that the extra protection should be placed in those areas where they found no bullet holes. This was exactly the opposite of what the original group was going to recommend.[222]

This is a classic example of finding new ways to look at old things. It also exemplifies the danger of jumping to conclusions and not taking the time to thoroughly analyze a problem before coming up with a solution.

Maybe if management had more *vujà dé* moments they'd be more accepting of surprises; in fact, maybe even welcome them, for as Rahm Emanuel noted, it may provide the crisis needed to truly effect change in their organizations.

CHAPTER 21 ALL HAT, NO CATTLE

COMIC AUTHOR DAVE BARRY OBSERVED, "If you had to identify in one word the reason why the human race has not achieved, and never will achieve, its full potential, that word would be 'meetings.'"[223]

I'm sure some of you may have been to a genuine rodeo. It's a sport that arose out of the working practices of cattle herding in the United States' West and is based on the skills required of the cowboys to effectively control the herd. The term "rodeo" was first used in the early 1800s to refer to a cattle round-up. Today it's a sporting event that tests the skill and speed of the cowboy. The rodeos of today let the most skilled of cowboys show off their roping, riding, and other talents. Being a rodeo cowboy is an exciting occupation, where the strongest are the ones who take home the victory.

Ironically, the term "cowboy" didn't originate in the United States but instead in the hacienda (estate) system of Medieval Spain. The hacienda system was a society of large land-holdings that were managed much like the fiefdoms of the Middle-Ages. And much like the fiefdom system, at the head of each hacienda was the patrón, serving just as the barons did, pledging their oath of fealty to the King. And just like in the fiefdom system, each hacienda's patrón was surrounded by his small circle of elite while at the bottom of society were the down-trodden citizens—the peóns or peasants. Out of this system rose the "vaqueros" who would ultimately be called "cowboys," a term first appearing in the English language around 1725 and a direct English translation of "vaquero," the Spanish word for an individual who managed cattle while mounted on horseback.

In contrast to the haciendas of Spain, where most "vaqueros" emerged from the peóns, in the modern workplace we find the organizational cowboys who can arise from all levels of the organizational hierarchy; the top level sociopaths, the ranks of the sycophants, and even from the ranks of the proles. In this chapter we've going to learn about these organizational cowboys and their propensity to run rough-shod over anyone in their path.

Just like a real cowboy, these organizational cowboys will exhibit their (people) herding and roping skills in the myriad interpersonal events, most notably meetings, which plague the modern workplace landscape. Organizational cowboys turn your everyday meeting into little better than a rodeo. But instead of real riding and roping, they use the many games we've learned about so far to do some metaphorical riding and roping to manipulate a meeting agenda and force their will on the unsuspecting cattle.

The Google definition of cowboy is: a man, typically one on horseback, who herds and tends cattle; a person who is reckless or careless. In the Wild West, cowboys developed a reputation of unruly behavior and lawlessness despite the "cowboy code" that included such directives as:

- The cowboy must never shoot first, hit a smaller man, or take unfair advantage.
- He must never go back on his word, or a trust confided in him.
- He must always tell the truth.

Needless to say, they didn't always subscribe to their own code. In the 1902 edition of *Overland Monthly* an actual cowboy defended his behavior, "We're not near as bad as we're painted. We like to get up a little racket now and then, but it's all in play. Of course, sometimes we fall out amongst ourselves and then there is a corpse."[224]

Most, if not all, rodeo events are performed by a single cowboy, much like most meetings are dominated by a single person. However, there is one event—team roping—that is noteworthy. Team roping, also called "heading and heeling," is where two cowboys capture and restrain a full-grown steer. One horse and rider, the header, lassos a running steer's horns, while the other, the heeler, lassos the steer's two hind legs. Once the animal is captured, the riders face each other and pull the steer so that it loses its balance and lies down.

Meetings also have the equivalent of this team-roping event. Should you be the unlucky target of a sociopathic cowboy in a meeting, you'll feel much like the poor steer, as the cowboy and one of his sycophantic henchmen double team their attack on you.

A meeting cowboy is nothing more than a reckless or irresponsible person, a show-off and when one takes charge of a meeting things might get done, but the result will only be his agenda, and he'll ride roughshod over the participants to accomplish it. He'll get away with it because nobody will challenge him, and certainly nobody can resist. Also, if you've ever been to a meeting run by a cowboy, it's a forgone conclusion that he's already decided the outcome even before the meeting began.

When a sociopathic cowboy is allowed to dominate a meeting, he dominates through the games we've learned about, with "Stump the Dummy" and the "Divide and Conquer" being his favorites, but he's not averse to using the double bind or gas-lighting to quell any opposition. As such, a meeting becomes a typical place in which to find you've, all of a sudden, been thrown under the bus. His aggressive style includes diatribes, criticizing other's opinions (even when they're based in fact) and the most common, interrupting and talking over others.

When he's making a point, he typically uses bullshit; however, some of the more practiced meeting cowboys spew out data and facts to back up their arguments making them, on the surface, look credible. The cowboy generally stifles open discussions, and through his manner prevents any real progress from being made—other than his objective. Meeting cowboys, just like the cowboys of the Old West, are sociopathic in nature, thus you must remember that everyone in the upper levels of management are candidate meeting cowboys.

Cowboys, like all sociopaths, love meetings; it's their equivalent of the rodeo. They especially enjoy the regularly scheduled meetings that have no purpose other than to provide them a bully pulpit. The most common of these meetings is the infamous and dreaded staff meeting. Management cowboys love the staff meeting because it offers them the perfect opportunity to practice their command and control techniques over the sycophants.

From my experience staff meetings—the ultimate goat-rope—are usually held first thing on Monday mornings so as to set the agenda for the work week. However, all it really accomplishes is to remind everyone that they work for a sociopath. It also screws up the whole week by starting it out on the wrong foot.

While these meetings are supposed to serve as an opportunity for the sycophants to get together in the presence of the Lord, to glean information, the typical staff meeting agenda usually only focuses on the Lord pontificating from his laundry list of action items that he then assigns adoringly among his followers. Most often these action items are some pet gripe the boss has with something going on or something that he feels needs to be done, and often they focus on things that will neither help nor promote the business. Unfortunately, most often the action item only gets passed on to some poor bastard down the organizational ladder. I've mentioned the dreaded action item before, and I'm going delve into the details of this sinister command and control technique in a bit.

Of course, the depth and breadth of the meeting phenomenon goes much deeper than the ceremonial staff meeting. Julie Knechtel, in her article "How to Attend a Meeting," notes that there are three basic kinds of meetings:

"[There are] meetings that are held for basically the same reason that Arbor Day is observed, namely, tradition; [second], meetings where there is some alleged purpose, [and finally] meetings where the purpose is to get your input on something."[225]

CHAPTER 21 ALL HAT, NO CATTLE

The best meetings to attend are those with some alleged purpose where you believe you may have a slight chance of accomplishing something and not waste your time. The best meeting is one in which the organizer actually has the courtesy to have a pre-published agenda, so you can be proactive in preparation. Unfortunately, they're rare unless you host the meeting yourself. The thing to remember is that even with a clear agenda, the meeting cowboy will overtake the meeting to promote his own agenda.

I can think of a meeting that may have a purpose, albeit not useful in the grand scheme of things. This is the infamous project status meeting. In some perverted way these meetings can actually be fun. I like people-watching and these status meetings are always good hunting grounds for some amusement. Get to the meeting early so you can watch who positions himself at the right hand of the Lord. Needless to say, this is telling about people and their motivations. It's easy to spot the sycophants if there ever was any doubt in your mind.

In these project meetings, the assembled peanut gallery usually focuses on a lengthy PowerPoint presentation, including the risk charts we covered earlier. The presentation itself is assembled by the project leader, and these project reviews are typically performed for the benefit of the organization's head sociopath and his sycophantic minions. This enables them to micromanage under the guise of communicating with the team.

The meeting is usually somewhat innocuous for most attendees, as the person likely to get all the action items is the presenter (the project leader); however, remember shit runs downhill, so others may get tagged anyway.

This could happen in a couple of ways. The first is when the project lead uses the review as an opportunity to throw anyone (or everyone) under the bus that he or she believes hasn't supported the project. The Lord picks up on this queue and immediately launches a "Stump the Dummy" session with the poor slob who just got ratted on, chastising him or her in the open forum. Remember the old idiom,

"Praise in public, punish in private?" Trust me, it's not practiced in the modern workplace; it's relegated to little better than an old wives' tale. For the unfortunate target, action items are the only things he carries away from the meeting, other than embarrassment and a bit less self-esteem.

The second way you can get targeted is by the head sociopath (the Lord), or meeting cowboy. They'll use any venue to perform their character assassination rituals, and they love the meeting because they have a vast sea of targets assembled for their picking. All eyes will be on their shenanigans, and this feeds their ego.

Another common problem with meetings in general, worth mentioning here, is the "PowerPoint Syndrome." Boring, useless meetings are an organizational disease, and the PowerPoint presentation has universally been the drug prescribed to treat it.

In his November 2003 article "PowerPoint is Evil, Power Corrupts: PowerPoint Corrupts Absolutely," Yale University political science Professor Edward Tufte explains, "Imagine a widely used and expensive prescription drug that promised to make us beautiful but didn't. Instead, the drug had frequent, serious side effects; it induced stupidity, turned everyone into bores, wasted time, and degraded the quality and credibility of communication."[226]

The use of PowerPoint has supplanted the need for anyone to actually be competent in his ability to conduct a useful meeting in which sound data are presented from which important decisions can be made.

Livraghi also has much to say on this subject. "It's easy to imagine a prehistoric painter who had found a quick and easy way of drawing a buffalo, covering cave walls with colorful celebrations of hunting success, regardless of his actual competence in bringing home food for his family or his tribe.

"But most of today's PowerPoint presentations can't be called a work of art or even an example of effective presentation.

"PowerPoint is a competent slide manager and projector. But rather than supplementing a presentation, it has become a substitute for it. Such misuse ignores the most important rule of speaking: respect your audience.

"Visual aids can be used effectively; to focus on key points, to emphasize relevant data, to make things clear. But it's unfortunately easy to do the opposite; to muddle, to confuse, or to deliberately warp facts, issues, and concepts. The abundance of resources for makeup and glitz lead to exaggeration and superficiality. Where appearance prevails on substance, scams and cheats are more easily disguised.

"It seems so easy. An elaborate show can be put together in a few hours. We often see a presenter, imprisoned in a predetermined format, unable to answer a simple question. [This is] because he or she is trained to repeat, without any depth of understanding, [from] a presentation. [T]hey often get lost in the mechanics of form and format, and miss the point of what they were supposed to say.

"The PowerPoint Syndrome isn't just the misuse of technology. It's a cultural disease."[227] Alas, PowerPoint is unfortunately not going away anytime soon.

Let's get back to the meeting itself. The first rule of meeting attendance etiquette is to not speak unless spoken to; however, ultimately someone will surely ask your opinion about something. This is so he can then disagree with you, not because he actually values your opinion. The worst situation to be in is when you're asked something that requires data that you didn't bring because there was no agenda to provide any planning tips. This is how you inadvertently get set up for a round of "Stump the Dummy." Rest assured, the Lord will take note and grill you on the data you forgot, and of course on your lack of proactiveness, sense of urgency, or ability to soothsay.

If there's a question, or action item coming your way, it will undoubtedly be the one for which you don't know the answer or have the time to go witch hunt. In this situation you must learn to practice strategic incompetence; it's your only way out of these sticky situations. Strategic incompetence is the act of either purposely performing a task so poorly as to discourage being assigned this task again, or by telling the enquirer that you're incapable of performing the task. However, eventually you'll get tagged with a useless action item; there's no avoiding it.

Laurence Peter, of Peter Principle fame, actually forecast this method of avoidance in his book, *The Peter Prescription*. I must admit he prescribed it in a slightly different context; he used it in the frame of avoiding a promotion you didn't want, but just as the title suggests, *The Peter Prescription* is a book of suggestions focused on how you can avoid things you don't want to do and the effects of the Peter Principle happening to you.

Strategic incompetence is best done proactively. Remember, being proactive is all about change. You want to change people's minds to the fact that you're incompetent for certain tasks. Thus, when you're on the verge of being tagged with some absurd action item, people will remember that you might not be the best candidate for the task. People will recall your feigned incompetence. Unfortunately, this takes years of practice and until then you'll suffer through many a time-wasting action item before you perfect your game.

Regardless of the type of meeting in which you find yourself cornered, remember the key to successfully surviving is plausible deniability. This is the preferred defense of the Lord or the cowboy, should someone actually be successful in turning the accusatory table on them in a meeting.

Never volunteer for anything, because you don't want to be held accountable. Remember, accountability only means that you are on notice that there will be consequences if you muck something up. Accountability is just another word for blamestorming.

One of the worst types of meeting to attend is the kind where you know going in that someone actually wants your opinion. This is rare, but it can happen. Rest assured however, nobody truly wants anyone else's opinion; it might conflict with theirs. But when it does happen, it's typically because the meeting organizer needs more people to share the blame in case of a wrong action on his part. Many times, though, the real reason it's held is with the hopes of changing your opinion. Cowboys love these types of meetings; in fact, when present, they try to change everyone's opinion to their way of thinking.

What's so abhorrent about going to one of these "change your opinion" meetings? I think it has a lot to do with ego and the need to avoid being seen as wrong. Also, the venue has a lot to do with it.

Seth Godin says, "Conference rooms create precisely the atmosphere where people are uncomfortable flipping positions. A conference room is an arena, and people come armed and ready to support their ideas (and the status quo)."[228]

Regardless of the meeting purpose you should always be mindful of the unspoken communication you're presenting to the crowd—i.e. your expressions, and, of course, your body language.

The best expression is one of raptured interest in the proceedings despite the fact you couldn't give a shit about what's going on. Your body language must also be right. You want to strike a pose that's both non-threatening yet exudes power. However, I've not found one good guide on how to pull off the correct body language for every situation. Most all are geared toward the body language that should be practiced for success, not how to meld into the woodwork to avoid trouble.

About the only common tip I've found is to try to avoid eye contact, especially when action items are being bandied about. The sociopathic narcissist in charge will dominate any meeting he attends, so regardless of the meeting purpose, he needs his ego-fix, so you should look especially fawning and enraptured whenever he speaks.

In his book *You Can't fire Everyone* Hank Gilman has the best advice: "Don't talk when you can nod."[229]

Regardless of the best intentions, most meetings prove meaningless in the grand scheme of things. Nothing is ever truly accomplished in a typical meeting, even with those held to supposedly make a decision. The problem is that people are conflict-avoidant by nature so they don't really want to uncover something that will be painful to solve. That's why meetings typically only focus on the periphery of problems and focus on trivial issues and posturing rather than dealing with reality. By ignoring the real problems facing the company, they fail to accomplish anything of substance. It sounds like the US Congress.

This is what's called Parkinson's Law of Triviality.[230] This "law" contends that in organizations, notably in meetings and group discussions, the time and attention spent on problems or issues is in inverse proportion to its real importance. Parkinson asserted that this effect is an inevitable law or tendency within all organizational behavior, and I can personally attest to its accuracy.

In my career I've attended more meetings than I care to even remember, and one thing I think I can safely say is that in few did any actual good come from them or were any meaningful decisions or actions taken. Most meetings are nothing but pomp and circumstance—a rodeo, if you will. There's a theory that just might explain this.

The inability of any useful decisions or actions to result from a meeting is closely tied to how many people attend. Most meetings are held with the purpose of soliciting consensus; however, most meetings are little more than opinion after painful opinion, being thrown about with the hopes that one will be stumbled upon that all can agree with. Intuitively it should be obvious that that can't work effectively, yet people continue to invite hoards of others in the hopes of reaching consensus and being able to target others who can go down with their ship when it's discovered they made a bad decision.

The theory is simple and can be understood mathematically by the following equation:

$$P_d = 1/2^n$$

In this equation P_d equals the probability of making a decision or accomplishing anything useful, in a meeting. The letter "n" is the variable denoting the number of people in attendance at the meeting. If we crunch some possible values for n, we find that even with one person in the meeting, there's at best a 50/50 chance of anything useful coming from it, let alone a decision being had. So how about if we increase the meeting to just two people? We find with n = 2, the probability of a decision goes down to only 25 percent.

Reflecting on the many meetings that I've been subjected to in my career, there were many in which there was a marching army of attendees. I've been in meetings with twenty people summoned to discuss and decide on an issue or problem. Just for fun, if we plug twenty into the above equation we find the probability of a decision, sound or not, to be astronomically small, at less than .0001 percent. That's ridiculous, you say; you've been in meetings with this number of attendees and have seen decisions made and solutions formulated.

That's because only a handful of attendees actually participate in a meeting, effectively reducing the true number of attendees to something manageable. And even with the odds against it, sometimes they'll stumble to a consensus. Even a blind squirrel finds a nut occasionally.

Another key is that typically only one person emerges as the driving force in having his way; what I call the "Rodeo Syndrome." These are the meetings controlled by the cowboys (the sociopaths) who attempt to cram down your throat their opinions and agenda.

Just like a real rodeo, at any given time, the spotlight is on the cowboy who rides the bull or the bronco to the screams of his adoring crowd. He's surrounded by a multitude of sycophants who are there to support his theatrical performance.

Just like in a real rodeo, these cowboys typically dominate a meeting and end up making everyone else little more than rodeo clowns, or as author Hank Gillman calls them, "monkeys in a circus parade."[231]

There's another reason why meetings typically don't accomplish much; stupidity. Livraghi tells us, "When the stupidity of one person combines with the stupidity of others, the impact grows geometrically, i.e., by multiplication, not addition, of the individual stupidity factors." We discovered earlier that stupidity also is the key stumbling block to effective teamwork.

Just as the number of people attending the meeting affects the probability of anything useful happening, so does the compounding effect of stupidity. Livraghi writes, "It is a generally accepted concept that the sum of a network increases as the square of the number of members, and it seems quite obvious that the same criterion applies to the combination of stupidity factors in individual people. This can help to explain the well-known fact that crowds as a whole are much more stupid than any individual person in the crowd. Stupid behavior and thinking tend to reproduce and multiply so dangerously that the contagion can spread to otherwise intelligent people when they don't realize how they are influenced by collective stupidity."[232]

Another of the big contributors to the fact that nothing useful typically happens in a meeting is the fact that most people don't prepare for the meeting. This is partially due to the fact that most, if not all, meetings are held without a pre-published agenda. Typically the meeting subject gives you a clue; however, most meetings quickly veer off-topic or down a rat-hole.

It's hard to come prepared for all the fun that is unleashed in a typical meeting unless you know the subject. Despite knowing the subject of the latest goat-rope beforehand, you still will most likely find yourself on the defensive at some point during the proceedings.

Another problem with meetings is that many people just don't believe they can make an informed contribution to the meeting so they either don't put much preparation time into it, or they just sit through the meeting without saying anything in hopes of surviving yet another face-to-face with the devil. They provide the cowboy the exact conditions he needs to affect a takeover.

In his book, *Death by Meeting*, Patrick Lencioni[233] reveals that the conduct and way meetings are managed actually mirror the organization's leadership and management skills, competencies, and its culture, including where it's likely headed. He asserts that just by observing a typical executive meeting, you'll see a visible snapshot of the organizations mediocrity, disenchantment, and complacency.

Do meetings at your company generally feel like a waste of time? Are they dominated by workplace bullies and cowboys using it as a forum to rant, rave and manipulate? Are people intimidated into silence? Do meetings at your company have vague objectives and no pre-published agendas? Are there action items galore, issued with arbitrary deadlines? If you answered yes, then you're in an organization with dysfunctional management. In an environment like that, when there are no clear objectives, it can be tough to determine what's important and what isn't. The pyromaniacs love it, though.

In his book *Claw your Way to the Top*, Dave Barry[234] tells us that the modern corporate meeting can be compared to a funeral, in the sense that you have "a gathering of people who are wearing uncomfortable clothing and would rather be somewhere else. The major differences are that most funerals have a definite purpose and reach a definite conclusion, whereas meetings generally drone on until the legs of the highest-ranking person present fall asleep. Also, nothing is ever really buried in a meeting. An idea may look dead, but it will always reappear at another meeting later on."

Psychologists call this last phenomenon "perseverating," which means to repeat or prolong an action, thought, or utterance after the stimulus that prompted it has ceased. Have you ever been in a meeting in which issues, which seem to have been long since solved, rear their ugly head again and dominate a meeting? Even if an issue has been fully explored and discussed ad nauseam to a point of resolution (and exhaustion), it's not uncommon for something to trigger the re-investigation of the matter.

Another element absent from most meetings is simply the truth. Most meetings become a battle of wits, half-baked opinions, and bullshit, and we all know the quote from the movie *Dirty Harry*: "opinions are like assholes; everybody's got one and they all stink."[235] In fact, some of the idiotic battles I've witnessed in meetings have reminded me of the war between Lilliput and Blefuscu in *Gulliver's Travels*. Lilliput and Blefuscu battled over which end is proper to break a soft-boiled egg.[236]

In the workplace, people manipulate and bullshit the truth to sell their agenda and/or cover up for their screw-ups, and the meeting is the favorite venue for this game of blamestorming. No wonder the US Congress works the way it does.

Another euphemism used to mask the negative connotation that the meeting evokes is to call the get-together a "committee meeting." Remember Quality Circles? As journalist Richard Harkness says, "What is a committee? It's a group of the unwilling, picked from the unfit, to do the unnecessary."[237]

The committee is a veiled attempt to try to convince those invited that this time will be different and that this meeting is really teamwork in action. However, as Dwight Schrute noted in the TV show *The Office*, "These are no more a team than people staying at the same hotel are a team."[238]

My personal least favorite type of meeting is the infamous off-site meeting. Recall the "rites of renewal." These off-site meetings are a management retreat, typically held at an upscale hotel, supposedly to discuss work-related issues such as team-building, or improving the morale of the workforce, or to create a strategy, or gin up another set of organizational values (because the last set didn't seem to stick).

Most of these off-site discussions develop into a war of wits and egos, and syco-phants jockeying for position and trying to impress the head sociopath. Just like your average run-of-the-mill meeting, they accomplish little except everyone comes away with a shit-load of action items, and is five pounds heavier from all the food and booze bought with monies that could have been put to better use.

Action items are another paralyzing problem for business. The propensity to have to assign action items as a result of every meeting or conversation, no matter how meaningless the subject matter, is a typical ploy of the micromanaging sociopath in charge. This is his way of exercising his command and control superiority over every-one because he has the power to make the student body veer left or right at his whim.

When faced with an action item, you must ask yourself this: Does this action do any-thing to build the business? If not, then it's probably firefighting or worse, it's just a plain old ineffective use of time that can be better spent. Time is the most valuable asset for any organization, yet most waste it with things that don't do anything to build the business or enhance customer satisfaction Also, when an action isn't clearly defined (and most aren't), it can only lead to a mediocre job of executing it.

Action items are a derivative of the "sky is falling" mentality found in sociopathic management, because they're not happy unless the organization is mired down in chasing fabricated issues or problems.

However, don't miss the action item due date, because if you do, you obviously don't have a sense of urgency. I actually know of an executive who instructed his executive assistant to track action item completion dates versus target due dates for those on his staff. I'm not sure whether there was any thought given to the substance of the responses, but all that seemed to matter was that as long as the action item was com-pleted on time, then (in his mind) people were being held accountable.

The executive who's fixated on the action item truly believes that this management style is contributing to making the organization more efficient. However, efficiency shouldn't be the prime directive. Effectiveness is the key to organizational success and action items should be screened for their effectiveness in contributing to the bottom line. Sociopaths mistake their ready-fire-aim approach as being efficient, when in fact they should be trying to be effective. Unfortunately, none truly grasp the difference between efficiency and effectiveness.

Your only hope is that every meeting ends as does the one below.[239]

As George Bernard Shaw once said, "I learned long ago, never to wrestle with a pig. You get dirty, and besides, the pig likes it."[240]

CHAPTER 22 WHAT, ME WORRY?

ALFRED E. NEUMAN IS THE FICTIONAL MASCOT and iconic cover boy of *MAD* magazine. Neuman's likeness, with his ears that make him look like a taxi with both doors open, a missing front tooth, and one eye lower than the other, has graced the cover of *MAD* since its inception. As a kid I religiously read *MAD*.

MAD editor Harvey Kurtzman described Neuman as "a face that didn't have a care in the world, except mischief."

Neuman's famous motto is "What, Me Worry?" It means I don't have to worry about anything. Neuman is the absurd personification for a state of denial, and a state of denial is the world in which most of today's business management operates on a daily basis.

In the business world, this state of denial is called "plausible deniability." We're going to investigate this phenomenon and why it runs rampant in today's management ranks. When you've mastered plausible deniability, you truly have nothing to worry about.

Plausible deniability refers to the denial of blame for acts in which someone has clear culpability yet somehow manages to leave no trail leading back to him or her. You typically see it practiced by upper management where the upper rungs of the organization apply the blame for failures to the lower organizational rungs.

I find this practice quite comical because the typical sociopath likes to promote the image of being hands-on, in touch, fully aware of what's going on throughout his domain, yet he'll cry "nobody told me" when the shit hits the fan. The latest high-profile leader to plead this is Rupert Murdoch.

For plausible deniability to work, the person denying culpability has to have someone who can be blamed other than himself. It doesn't matter much to say "I didn't know," and it's much better to say, "I didn't know, but I know who did." Without a scapegoat, plausible deniability is neutered. To just say you didn't have any knowledge of something doesn't get you off the hook quite like being able to point out the real culprit. Remember, it's not a fun game without a winner, and someone (typically a sacrificial sycophant) to serve as the loser.

Another interesting phenomenon is at work here, that is that in the typical workplace, blame is always one-directional. When someone in the lower echelon of the organization tries to reveal the screw-up, or flaws, of his or her boss or, worse yet, the sociopath in charge, he'll typically be accused of being a whiner or a drama queen, or worse yet removed from the organization. Whistle blowers aren't treated very well anywhere you go. Pointing out the flaws of management just doesn't work and isn't healthy for your career. The plausible deniability behavior always focuses the blame (or the wrath), either directly back at you or onto some other unsuspecting sucker.

There's an irony to being labeled a drama queen by the sociopaths; it's sort of like the pot calling the kettle black. I'll explain why.

Wisegeek.com defines a drama queen as someone who tends to; react to every situation in an overdramatic or exaggerated manner, or someone with a; demanding or overbearing personality who overreacts to seemingly minor incidents or whenever order is disrupted sometimes resulting in explosive emotional outbursts. Colloquially drama queens are often described as being self-centered or self-absorbed, often viewing others as only existing to serve their personal needs. This sounds like the average sociopath.

Therein is the dichotomy. The same people who are quick to call a whistle blower a drama queen are the same ones who most exhibit the drama queen behaviors.

I'm sure you've heard the statement, "It's about the process, not the people." This implies that the scrutiny will be placed on what process may have failed, not on the person to blame. This is the sociopath's way of trying to make his witch hunts palatable to the rest of the organization, but all it does is mask the true intent.

However, people execute process, so if something has failed, there's undoubtedly a person who's responsible. When you finally get to the root-cause, most often it's simply that someone screwed up, and contrary to the "process versus people" rhetoric, most organizations can't function without someone's head on the chopping block. Thus, the outcome of the witch hunt (or lessons-learned goat-rope) is always that someone gets blamed. This is what the sociopath's call "accountability." However, calling it process driven lets the sociopaths sleep at night.

Passing along blame is contagious, and the problem is particularly rampant in today's workplace. Has your company caught the blame contagion?

Nearly everyone has played the blame game at one point or another. The problem with this behavior is that when someone gets blamed for a mistake, it only pushes him or her to practice the same approach. Blame spreads like a contagious infection. We've learned how people, trapped in the same organizational soap opera, begin to emulate each other. As the Red Queen Effect would predict, merely watching the blame game in action greatly increases the chances that you'll do the same thing to protect your reputation at a later date.

Blame-setting and its close cousin—hiding mistakes—is typically built right into the organization's culture because of three built-in dynamics: politics, games, and the performance review process. Politics and games become the modus operandi when people become overly concerned with what people think of them, or they want to better their advantage over their peers. Remember, politics is just another name for impression management. Also, the desire for a great, or even just a good, performance review causes people to cover up anything negative that can be thrown up at them come performance review time. Since we're rewarded or punished based on what's in the review, we all have a need to hide our mistakes.

However, if we created a blameless work environment, what a wonderful place that would be in which to work. In this utopia, people would be encouraged to admit to their failures, rather than hide them for fear of being punished. They could face their mistakes and failures and learn how to make changes in their behavior or in whatever skills are holding them back from contributing to the organization's goals. They wouldn't find themselves under the bus or on stage having their strings pulled.

Ironically, that's exactly the (stated) goal of the typical performance review process; however, the typical performance review process used in today's workplace is focused on measuring individuals against an arbitrary standard, identifying their shortcomings and failings, punishing them by withholding raises, and then tasking the individual to change without any guidance on how to accomplish that change. Remember unconstructive criticism?

In an organization that practices finger-pointing, employees start actually believing that they can't make mistakes because they have perfected the game of plausible deniability and shifting blame to others. Passing the blame also leads to the attitude that as long as it was not me under the bus, why should I care? When a problem occurs, employees become more concerned with avoiding blame and framing someone else rather than solving the problem. Once again this means problems are never really solved.

As we'll see when we investigate the performance review process, when the blame game is the organizational norm, those who have been singled out for blame during the year will be remembered more for their mistakes than any positive contributions they've made to the organization. In this type culture, the quicker one makes it known that a failure was the fault of a co-worker who wasn't on the ball, the less likely that person will be the one to get fired. Of course, that just perpetuates the game, as most people believe that blaming others is unavoidable because, after all, they'd do the same thing to you.

The blame game stands in sharp contrast to constructive criticism, which you'll find copiously missing in the typical sociopathically-driven organization. That said I do believe that constructive criticism exists in the modern workplace, because I agree with Scott Adams, "The only constructive criticism is the kind you do behind people's backs."[241] As we've learned, ratting on your co-workers can be constructive to your own career and that's all that counts.

It's easy to get blindsided by a sociopath or bully playing the blame game. A victim of workplace scapegoating often doesn't realize what's happening until he's called into the boss's office for a tense discussion about a problem. In such situations, the victim is caught off guard, and any attempt at defense comes off as making excuses and not taking responsibility, or accepting accountability. Anyway, plausible deniability doesn't work *on* a sociopath because it's reserved only for them to practice.

So what should you do if you find out you're targeted by plausible deniability (or any other blamestorm) and find yourself under the bus? Remember, mounting a defense isn't easy because you're automatically presumed guilty. Unfortunately, your best defense is to try to avoid being in a position to be made a scapegoat in the first place. To do this you need to tune your radar to people who might have a reason or motivation to try to throw you under the bus. You need to be proactive. Take a look around the organization and know the sociopaths, bullies, and back-stabbers, the people you've heard bad-mouthing others, and realize that they could and will direct their ire at you someday. Then try to stay as far away from them as you can.

Be especially wary of your so-called friends. It is so common for people to not want to be blamed that even people who are your friends will feel justified in blaming you, when they feel their career is in jeopardy. The best policy is to consider no one at work a friend.

In a blame-oriented organization, telling HR or management that you've witnessed, or been the target of, scapegoating or back-stabbing, won't get you anywhere.

I'm convinced they actually like that atmosphere, because they know it churns out the necessary data they need to put in everyone's dossier. We'll learn why when we tackle the performance review process.

As we've learned, blame is typically focused vertically down the hierarchy, as failures that occur at the top levels of an organization are denied and passed down to those who have received delegated duties or can be blamed without repercussions.

This is the essence of plausible deniability. It's called the kick-the-dog effect, where someone high in the hierarchy makes a mistake and blames the person below him for the mistake, and that person blames the person below him, and so on. My only advice if you find yourself in this situation is to, "Never let your face show how hard your ass is being kicked," a wise statement from Senator Arlen Specter.[242] Don't give them the satisfaction.

In his July 2009 article, "Blame Storming – One of the Signs of Weak Management," Mark McDonald describes blame-storming as, "where people admire problem[s], describe how things got that way and where to place blame and responsibility. Weak managers flock to blame storming. It provides them with a way to retain responsibility while shifting accountability to others."[243]

CHAPTER 23 DRINKIN' THE KOOL AID

IN LEWIS CARROLL'S *ALICE'S ADVENTURES IN WONDERLAND,* Alice asks, "Cheshire pus, would you tell me, please, which way I ought to go from here?"

"That depends a good deal on where you want to get to," said the cat.

"I don't much care where," said Alice.

"Then it doesn't matter which way you go," said the cat."[244]

In *Animal Farm,* when the animals first revolted and took over the farm, they developed seven commandments for how they were to run their society. They were:

1. Whatever goes upon two legs is an enemy
2. Whatever goes upon four legs, or has wings, is a friend
3. No animal shall wear clothes
4. No animal shall sleep in a bed
5. No animal shall drink alcohol
6. No animal shall kill another animal
7. All animals are equal

The commandments the animals developed are much like those that are developed in the modern workplace. The parallel here is that just like in *Animal Farm;* they all start out virtuous, but over the course of time become forgotten, ignored, or worse, simply bastardized.

We've learned that all organizations, however democratic they start out, evolve into an autocracy. By the same token, at the end of *Animal Farm,* the pigs had become nothing more than dictators and the seven commandments were all ignored or violated. As the animal's hypocrisy toward their commandments unfolds they are dropped one by one until, in the end, they all were reduced to a single phrase: "All animals are equal, but some animals are more equal than others."[245]

We're going to look at the equivalent of an organization's commandments—its vision and values. All organizations develop these with the best of intent; however, over the course of time, just as in *Animal Farm*, they become compromised.

What are vision and values? Vision is often referred to as the corporate mission. The vision statement is meant to be a description of the state and function of the organization once it has implemented its strategic plan or achieved its goals.

Unfortunately, for most organizations, the vision statement has morphed into something that management tries to use as a motivational tool instead of a road-map to greatness. Why? Because they cut themselves short. Most organizations pick goals that they can't realistically achieve, or they limit their vision to the products and services they currently offer and don't realize that they may, in fact, be part of something much larger. For example, an airline might frame its vision in terms of customer service or on-time departures when, in fact, its business is bringing people together.

A good vision statement should be short, to the point, and include descriptions of the organization as it effectively carries out its operations. Like everything in business there is a spectrum of good to bad mission statements floating around out there. An excellent example can be seen in Duke Energy Corporation's mission statement:[246]

"Our purpose is to create superior value for our customers, employees, communities and investors through the production, conversion, delivery and sale of energy and energy services."

I'm not going to show an example of a bad vision statement in order to protect the guilty, but trust me, you can find plenty, you don't have to look too far, how about your own company's vision statement?

An organization's vision should be an inspiring statement of what it intends to become when it figuratively grows up. Further, it should be stated in terms that are broad and forward-thinking and should provide an invitation to expand the business's reach into the market. It should not go so far as to start detailing the tactical plans for achieving those goals. An effective vision statement is meant to be a strategic statement, not a calculated tactical plan.

A good vision should provide an enthusiastic rallying cry for the organization; however, most often they turn into an edict typically seen posted in the lunchroom or delivered in a PowerPoint presentation by the head sociopath at an all-hands meeting. It's this one-time approach that typically sets them up for failure. Vision and values, and leadership, are tightly coupled. For them to be effective, the leadership must repeatedly communicate the vision (and values) in a simple and consistent manner; the operative word being repeatedly.

It's really more important for the organization's leadership to create a "sense" of mission or vision than to just publish it and walk away. By sense, I mean something that's seemly built right into the very fabric of the culture. Thus, the more compelling the vision that management can articulate the more it pulls everyone in.

The big problem is that for most organizations the vision statement changes nothing in how they conduct their business. The exercise of crafting them is a complete waste of time and talent if vision statements are used for nothing but an exercise at an off-site management goat-rope.

The primary reason the vision (and more importantly, the values) statements of most organizations fail to change anything is management's naiveté. They forget that success isn't achieved by edict—that simply stating and publishing the vision and values statements don't guarantee they will come to pass. A more profound reason is that management flat out doesn't practice them, or just as bad, practices them in a cyclical manner. Management begins every quarter preaching teamwork, good communication, growing the business, building strong relationships among employees, but by the end of the quarter, when their financial targets are missed, Harpagon's Syndrome sets in, and they're back to the "command and control," micromanaging, workaholic rhetoric.

This is why the vision statement forms the first half of what's called the "motivation delusion." The delusion being that if management can write and publish a good vision statement, then everyone will be miraculously motivated to make it happen. In reality, nothing is farther from the truth.

The other half of the motivation delusion, the values statement, typically details the moral, ethical and behavioral qualities that the organization considers worthwhile–their highest behavioral priorities and deeply held principles. Values statements should be affirmations of how the people in the organization want to value customers, suppliers, and most importantly how they want to interact with each other. The values that an organization demonstrates are most important and are what drive an organization to be either functional or dysfunctional and why, when they are not practiced, they become so demotivational.

The typical values statement includes some combination of the following goals that all organizations say they're striving for:

- Customer service
- Professional image
- Performance, results
- Healthy work environment
- Integrity
- Commitment to quality
- Loyalty
- Trust
- Work ethic

- Team play
- Efficiency
- Accountability
- Respect for the individual
- Work-life balance

They all boil down to examples of ethical behavior, and the problem in today's business environment is that ethics just may be a thing of the past. However, if an organization's values are realistic and practiced by all, especially at the very top, they provide a sense of organizational identity and unity. They will build trust, teamwork and a sense of common purpose, thus molding a fundamentally ethical culture within the organization. This then becomes the essence of determining an organization's functionality versus dysfunctionality. That's a tall order for a simple wish list, and for most organizations, that's all these statements ever really are.

So why do values statements, so often, fail? In his June 2010 article "A Primer on Corporate Values," Oliver Serrat, explains it simply. "Most often corporate values backfire when management or personnel fail to live up to these self-proclaimed messages."[247] That seems simple enough. Management thinks that by publishing the values they'll somehow miraculously come to pass. Overnight the workplace will become the utopia the values describe.

This management belief is what Marshall Goldsmith calls "checking the box."[248] He explains it as the "disconnect between understanding and doing." By publishing the values statement, management checked the box and went on its way, assuming everyone read them and understood them. However, if the workforce doesn't understand them and buy into them they can't/won't implement them.

Another problem with values implementation is that different people value different things from their employer, depending on where they are in their lives and career. For example, one of the common values floating around most organizations is the pledge to promote "work-life balance." That may be a prized thing for some but a twenty-something probably couldn't care less.

Management needs to understand the dynamic at work here. Goldsmith says, "In their twenties employees are out to learn. In their thirties they want to advance, and when in their forties, they want to run the place."[249] There's a big difference in what each of those groups holds dear.

Another reason values become hard to implement lies in the fundamental way that businesses run. Serrat explains, "This [lack of living the values] becomes a sure-fire recipe for disenchantment or cynicism among customers, management, and the personnel itself. In most such cases, the cause of tension is that organizational goals, which are always couched in financial terms, do not jibe with the corporate values propounded and the underlying organizational culture from which such values are supposed to spring."[250]

I've personally witnessed bullies in the top management position being quite outspoken in preaching the company values, thinking they can pressure everyone into modifying their behavior despite evidence, known to all, that the bully (and his followers) consistently violates those values. For example, the bullies don't realize that when they stand on their bully pulpit and preach the virtues of work-life balance, everyone in the crowd is rolling their eyes because they know their workaholic micromanaging tendencies fly in the face of a healthy work-life balance.

Serrat provides another example, "One of the old standards that have been used in scores of companies is very simply: 'We treat our employees with respect and dignity.' Your employees will naturally buy into the value and hope that it is true, but with every conflict they encounter that resolves against them, they will grow increasingly cynical." And every time one of the games we've learned about is inflicted on some poor unsuspecting person, it's easy to understand why values statements don't stick.

Serrat explains further, "The stakes are raised for the leaders' behavior even more by the magnifying effect as you move down the organizational hierarchy. If the leaders have only small gaps between their behavior and values, the level immediately below them will have a larger gap; two levels below there is an even larger gap; etc. In the level below that, the conflict becomes more intense, and for each level below the problem expands. Thus, the magnifying effect in the organization means that the leaders must address [even] the small details or the values will not become a reality in the organization."[251]

The management hypocrisy regarding values is a condition called "the Smart Talk Trap." The phrase was coined by Robert Sutton, in his book *The No Asshole Rule*, and as he describes it, "Empty talk doesn't just happen at bad companies. Even the best managers sometimes forget that, to inspire action, they need to do more than simply spout platitudes. Writing, displaying, and repeating words about treating people with respect, but allowing or encouraging the opposite behavior, is worse than useless.

"Leaders in most organizations not only get paid more than others, they also enjoy constant deference and false flattery. A huge body of research, hundreds of studies, shows that when people are put in positions of power, they start talking more and taking what they want for themselves, ignoring what other people say or want, ignoring how less powerful people react to their behavior, acting more greedy, and generally treating any situation or person as a means for satisfying their own needs—and that being put in positions of power blinds them to the fact that they are acting like jerks."[252]

Management in these types of organizations routinely overcompensate for their inability to hold true to their values by having all-hands meetings, in which the employees are reminded of the values statement. The thinking is that if the values are flashed before the troops often enough, this will persuade everyone to adopt them, just as they believe that having seminars on communication and team building will lead to better communication and teamwork. These are all just examples of "checking the box." Organizations do this despite the fact that there's sufficient data out there proving that the retention and action rates of people attending these types of events is measured in weeks, if not days. After that, they'll revert to their old habits. The same holds true for published values statements.

Another favorite simple value like "respect for others" can be seen in many organizations' value statements. Personally, I believe it shouldn't be on the list at all. Respect for others is a fundamental behavior that everyone should bring to the table as a societal norm. The fact that it finds its way to the list just shows that my predictions about where society is headed are correct. If we, as a society, have resorted to the point where people need to be commanded and reminded to treat each other nicely, then this reinforces my premise that rudeness and incivility have become epidemic.

But, these statements do make their way into most companies values, because publishing the commandments is needed to remind the management that those who "talk-the-talk" should try "walking-the-walk." For most dysfunctional organizations, writing a values statement is, as Scott Adams says, "like writing a first-hand account of the experience of the Donner party based on the fact that you've eaten beef jerky."[253] They have no clue how to implement them and live them; therefore, they have no right to write them.

In his book *Flawless Consulting*, Peter Block has an interesting take on what he calls the myth of vision statements. He asserts that most organizations conduct what he calls "leadership by lamination." Block explains, "The myth is that if we just get the message sufficiently clear and compelling, if we can describe the burning platform with enough urgency, and a bright tomorrow with enough zeal, change will occur. This leads to great emphasis on communicating the vision and the business case for change.

"[These vision statements are] compelling and are 'laminated' in wallet-sized versions so [everyone] could have them with [them.] Many [are] hung on office walls and reception rooms, many signed by the management team. All had a common theme: building a lasting organization required the top to have a vision.

"The problem is two-fold. First, we affirmed, at the moment of lamination, that top management's vision was the one that counted. We all wanted to know what top management was seeking. Once we knew, we could all align ourselves and proceed to live it out.

"The second consequence of lamination was that management's vision could now withstand the ravages of wind, and rain, and dark of night. Nothing would keep them from their appointed duty.

"We believe that the top should decide the culture that the middle and the bottom [should] live by. This is the mind-set that takes the power out of vision [and values], even though the middle and the bottom want to hear what the top has in mind. The fact that everyone wants to know the vision [and values] of the top doesn't make it meaningful. Most frequently when the organization hears the vision of the top, they are vaguely disappointed."[254]

I've seen this "leadership by lamination" technique used first-hand for both the vision and values statements. The reasons I've detailed explain why, in most organizations, the vision and values statements typically fall on deaf ears, and why they are so tough to make stick. Block's description of how the vision statement is accepted holds true for the values statement as well, which I believe has an even more damaging effect on the organization when it's not practiced by management.

Most of the corporate values statements' failure can be traced to a simple behavior, or mindset, that's lacking in most organizations: trust among the players in the organization. Shared values are supposed to build trust, and trust is the glue that holds the organization together. Everyone must trust each other that they will carry out their job function. When they repeatedly don't, trust is absent. Remember the old saying, "Teamwork is really nothing more than completing your job on time so someone else can complete theirs."

An organization that experiences a breakdown of its shared values will have a lack of trust. An organization that practices the behaviors and games we've seen in this book—promotes a blame culture, focuses on problems rather than opportunities, where failures and mistakes are not tolerated—is one in which the people quickly lose confidence that management can effectively guide the organization.

The W. Edwards Deming Center for Quality Management has shown that organizations waste up to 50 percent of productive time through lack of trust. Trust is an intangible that organizational values can certainly promote if they were actually followed. Every values statement I've ever seen has had the trust component yet, not surprisingly, every one of those organizations was at some level trust bankrupt.

It's not surprising hypocrisy is the most prevalent and most damaging ethical lapse in the workplace and a dysfunctional workplace always includes hypocrisy at the top. This is what promotes disrespect and distrust among the workers. In these organizations the executives refuse to fess-up to the problems plaguing their company, and more fundamentally, they can't "walk-the-walk" in regard to their espoused values. As with any fantasy based culture, management attempts to promote the illusion that the organization is healthy and that all is under control and they have a plan for the business; however, the average worker sees through this pretty quickly.

In these organizations, the workers suffer from a condition called "anomie." a personal feeling of a lack of social norms, or normlessness. Simply stated, it's the breakdown of social values. Anomie arises when the actions of the top management are directly opposed to what the employees hold as their own personal values. It's common in dysfunctional organizations, run by sociopaths, with too much command and control and no individual empowerment.

I have a novel approach to the whole values debate. I guarantee management would get everyone's attention if it made just one simple statement: "We vow to change our behavior." What do I mean by that? Recall Marshall Goldsmith's twenty bad behaviors[255] that he discovered all successful people usually fall prey to? He describes them as the barriers to moving to the next level in their careers. I'll repeat them here:

1. Wanting to "win" too much
2. Adding too much value
3. Passing judgment
4. Making destructive comments
5. Starting with "no," "but," or "however"
6. Telling the world how smart you are
7. Speaking when angry
8. Negativity
9. Withholding information
10. Failing to give proper recognition
11. Claiming credit that we don't deserve
12. Making excuses
13. Clinging to the past
14. Playing favorites
15. Refusing to express regret
16. Not listening
17. Failing to express gratitude
18. Punishing the messenger
19. Passing the buck

20. An excessive need to be "me"

It's the above behaviors that should be laminated and kept in every manager's pocket as a reminder how not to act, not the platitudes you usually see in values statements. These are the behaviors that need to change before any workplace can become a great place to work. If management worked, with even just a little effort, changing these behaviors, the employees would notice. Only then can management truly "walk-the-walk" instead of just "talking-the-talk."

I want to highly recommend Marshall Goldsmith's book *What Got You Here Won't Get You There: How Successful People Become Even More Successful*. I believe that it should be mandatory reading for anyone who's currently in management or anyone aspiring for a management role in the future. For the first group, it can serve as a reminder of the behaviors, some of which they're undoubtedly guilty of, that need changing if they want to be true leaders. For the second group, it can be their checklist of behaviors they shouldn't cultivate as they rise through the ranks. Maybe if more up-and-comers adopted that perspective, there wouldn't be a need for values statements at all.

As Mahatma Gandhi once said, "Your beliefs become your thoughts. Your thoughts become your words. Your words become your actions. Your actions become your habits. Your habits become your values. Your values become your destiny."[256]

CHAPTER 24 LAKE WOBEGON

THE LAST CHAPTER WAS A GREAT SEGUE into what's coming up next. This whole chapter will prove the truism, voiced by Johns Hopkins University Professor Michael Mendelbaum: "People do not change when you tell them they should; they change when they tell themselves they must."[257]

The focus of this chapter is the futile performance appraisal process in place in most of corporate America. I've saved the best for last.

Todd:	Rajiv, Jerry wants us to do employee evaluations.
Rajiv:	Wonderful, sir. I'll bring the tissues for the tears that will follow our reviews.
Todd:	No one will be crying.
Rajiv:	Well, not if you do it right.
Todd:	You know, I think I'm just going to do it myself.
Rajiv:	Just remember, sir, fear is the best motivator. Sometimes I think shame, but mostly fear.
Todd:	If they ever build another death star, there's a captain's chair with your name on it.
Rajiv:	Is that a management position?

The exchange above between characters on the NBC sitcom *Outsourced*[258] is an eerily accurate description of the performance appraisal process in most modern organizations.

As we seen, there are some pretty good reasons why we find dysfunctional work-places out there in the real world. However, if you're still a non-believer, then I'll prove my point through the exposure of the performance review process adminis-tered in most modern organizations. This is the *coup de grace*, so to speak.

I think it almost goes without saying that the annual performance review process is the single most abhorred event in corporate America. It probably beats out even meetings. In this chapter we're going to find out why.

First, the annual performance review process creates a high level of stress for eve-ryone involved–the workers, the bosses stuck filling out the endless forms, and the HR staff stuck administering the process. Additionally, the entire workforce gets mired down in this process, which can take weeks from start to finish, tying up val-uable time that should be used to run the business. This makes everyone involved less effective at their jobs. It's also a highly subjective process. It's entirely based on the worker's relationship with his or her boss, and we all know it's tough to have a lasting relationship with a practiced sociopath. The performance review process also does nothing to better that relationship.

Second, and probably the most profound problem with the performance review process is the fact that it simply doesn't work for the intended purpose. This is what no one in corporate America seems to want to admit.

Remember the definition of insanity: doing the same thing over again and expecting a different result. Companies carry out this perverted ritual year in and year out, deluding themselves that this process will make the workplace better for all and that it will actually help them achieve their goals. In effect, they're blowin' smoke up their own skirts because the effect is the exact oppo-site. In fact, it may be one of the single most hypocritical things that manage-ment can do, thus making the workers believe that the values rhetoric is, in fact, just hollow words.

The scary aspect, in my humble opinion, is that there are many managers and bosses out there who actually relish the performance review process and its associated pomp and circumstance. It's a way to establish and maintain command and control over the workers, which is the typical management mindset prevalent in the workplace today. These polemicists actually thrive on the terror they instill in their unsuspecting minions.

I can personally attest to the fact that the performance review process is the number one contributor to employee stress. It certainly was for me, whether on the giving or receiving end. You can actually see and feel the climate of the workplace change as this dreaded event draws near: the angst ratchets up a few notches for both the employees and the management team. The atmosphere around review time can best be described as Kafkaesque—time marked by a senseless, disorienting, often menacing complexity, surreal distortion, and a sense of impending danger.

Maybe the performance review is so hated because it's conducted as just a single yearly event, like a drive-by gang shooting in which innocent people become the victims. I joke, but in reality that just may be the biggest contributor to why the performance appraisal process doesn't work and it may lead us to a solution to this idiocy.

The performance appraisal process is like a self-licking ice cream cone; a self-perpetuating system that has little value except to sustain itself. This is evidenced by the fact that within the organizational Sophist community—the human resources world—there's a whole cottage industry in place just to support this annual goat-rope.

In his October 2008 *Wall Street Journal* article, "Get Rid of the Performance Review," UCLA management Professor Dr. Samuel Culbert explains, "Even the mere knowledge that such an event will take place damages daily communications and teamwork. The alleged primary purpose of performance reviews is to enlighten subordinates about what they should be doing better or differently. But I see the primary purpose quite differently. I see it as intimidation aimed at preserving the boss's authority and power advantage. Such intimidation is unnecessary, though. The boss has the power with or without the performance review."[259]

In his book, *Get rid of the Performance Review! How Companies Can Stop Intimidating, Start Managing and Focus on What Really Matters*," Dr. Culbert adds, "Then there are second-order problems. A subordinate who objects to a characterization of faults runs the risk of adding another negative trait to the boss's list; 'defensiveness and resistance to critique.' And bosses who get their minds turned around by a subordinate's convincing argument run the risk of having a bigger boss, who knows the going-in assessments and compensation guidelines, thinking they 'wimped out' by failing to hold the line on what was budgeted for the work unit."[260]

For most employees and bosses there's no happy ending come performance review time.

Too often an employee who receives a bad performance review is placed on a performance improvement plan that's supposed to serve as a remedial rehabilitation program. Typically these plans are little more than a dictate to the employee to change, to meet some arbitrary performance goal that, in the reviewer's opinion, wasn't met by the employee during the review period. In essence, the employee is being fitted to the organizations Procrustean bed, which could be just another term for "performance review." To be fitted for the Procrustean bed means you're being compared to some arbitrary standard in which conformity is forced.

In Greek mythology Procrustes, or the stretcher, was a blacksmith who physically attacked people, stretching them, or cutting off their legs to make them fit his iron bed's size. The Myth has it that he would invite a person to spend the night, then he'd set to work on him, to stretch him to fit, or amputate the excess length. That's the performance improvement plan process in a nutshell and more over the goal of the whole performance appraisal process.

These improvement plans are typically geared toward setting a timeframe—such as three months or six months—for the employee to improve his performance or change his behavior, thus meeting the goal of the plan. If the employee meets the goal, the plan is closed. If not, the implication is that he will be terminated. Because of the implied threat of termination, these plans do nothing but elicit more defensiveness and anxiety in the employee, as he naturally has doubts about whether or not he can improve. They do not motivate the person to change at all, as few, if any, offer concrete steps on which the employee can focus. This "unconstructive criticism" leaves the employee feeling hopeless to meet the new goals.

In the book, *Primal Leadership: Realizing the Power of Emotional Intelligence*, Daniel Goleman, et al. tells us that when these same performance improvement plans are geared toward what's called a "learning agenda,"[261] the results prove much more successful. In simple terms, a "learning agenda" is a set of questions that is broad in scope that directly relate to the employee's work. It encourages individuals and teams to reflect on and learn from their experience and from that of others. This may be the answer to organizational amnesia.

An effective learning agenda focuses on setting goals that actually resonate with the employee's ability to work better and are more aligned with his personal goals and dreams. And as we've seen, most management is not in tune with the personal goals and dreams of the employees. Further, the learning agenda sets meaningful standards of performance rather than some arbitrary standard of perfection. It does not concentrate on conformance to the arbitrary soft skills that are harped on in the typical performance review process.

Another problem with the performance review process is that it tends to focus attention only on the differences in people when compared to some mythical standard of behavior. On a typical performance review, more than 90 percent of the form is geared toward rating the employee's ability in the "soft skills" and very little is focused on how the employee actually performed the job he was hired to do.

This can create subconscious frustration, undermining the person's sense of identity and purpose, which negatively affects his performance and teamwork. This mindset becomes counter-productive and unrelated to the person's daily tasks at hand.

Within most organizations, the performance review process could be viewed as a self-defeating prophesy. We learned earlier about the self-fulfilling prophesy, but the difference here is that the prediction itself actually prevents what is predicted from happening. This is also known as the "prophet's dilemma."

Given the universally known problems with the performance review process, why is it perpetuated? The official reason you'll hear is that it's meant to enhance and improve the organization's overall performance by raising all the employees to a higher level of performance—i.e. make them more efficient and effective. However, because of all the negative effects the process has on everyone involved, the opposite typically becomes true. Also, I'll reveal later that, despite the rhetoric, performance improvement isn't the real reason organizations are so addicted to this process.

As I note, the performance review's purpose is supposed to help elevate the employee to a higher level of performance—one that the organization believes is needed for it to be a success. Yet subconsciously most organizations don't view themselves as operating at high performance. We see evidence of this when we examine how organizations typically advertise themselves to prospective employees. Have you ever heard a company HR person describe his company to a prospective recruit?

I've worked in many organizations in which HR flaunted that they offered "competitive wages and benefits" and a "professional environment." It sounds like a great place to work, right? However, in his book *The Gifted Boss: How to Find, Create and Keep Great Employees*, Dale Dauten dispels this as nothing more than self-defeating. "When you say 'competitive wages' what you're saying is 'ordinary, average, about like everyone else's.' And when you say a 'professional environment,' you are saying the same thing. 'Professional' means that it's typical of the profession, which is another way of saying that it's what's common or standard. So you have, in effect, told me that your policy is to offer average rewards in an average environment. In other words, you are trumpeting your mediocrity."[262]

The really humorous part of this is that these same organizations also say they're looking for "the best of the best" when recruiting. There's something wrong with this picture. No wonder many companies are always on the quest to upgrade their organization. They hire average people and offer average salaries, because that's what they advertised for, and (as we'll see) they use the performance review process to browbeat these new hires into becoming something they're not. Industrialist J. Paul Getty put it perfectly when he noted, "The employer generally gets the employees he deserves."[263]

Most organizations, even if they manage to hire the best, don't really know what to do with good talent once they have it in hand because they treat employees like tools and nothing more than a means to an end.

In his April 2011 *Financial Times* article "Look to Your Players, Not to the Rulebook," Ravi Mattu explains, "Big organizations, in spite of their heavy investment in talent management processes and expensive campaigns broadcasting their excellence to attract the best recruits in the first place, can still do a poor job of getting the best out of their people. In spite of their rhetoric, they are not usually designed to get the best out of individuals, but rather geared to maximizing efficiency through strict processes, systems, and structures. Organizational culture triumphs over the logic of nurturing employees as a means of adding value to the business."[264]

Have you ever really thought about what personal traits companies claim to be after in a prospective employee? The following is a sample of the types of skills that I've seen in job descriptions:

- Good verbal and written communication skills
- Strong work ethic

- Teamwork
- Dependability
- Good decision-making skills
- Initiative
- Self-starter
- Creative

Peruse a typical job description, and you'll find that most companies advertise these "soft skills" or some derivation thereof, as being critical for success in the position they're looking to fill. The problem is these skills are virtually unverifiable at the time of hire, and as we'll find, they're not really measurable anyway, except subjectively. Yet through an employee's entire career, he will always be judged against these vague skills.

Organizations can't verify from previous employers that the candidate possessed these skills. The previous company is not at liberty to divulge this type of information, and they don't know anyway because they, too, were incapable of accurately measuring the past employee's soft skills. Besides, in today's litigious society, asking a third party for a personal reference may be useless, as many won't offer them (good or bad) for fear of being sued. In the end, the organization must take the candidate's word that he or she possesses these skills.

That's why we all know the only way to get a job is to play up to these elusive skills by referring to them somewhere in our résumé and thus flaunting our overall good work ethic. Everyone does it because they know these are the "catch-phrases" that the recruiters and hiring managers are looking for. Many companies even use automated systems that screen résumés for key words or phrases such as these and bounce those that don't reflect the supposedly critical differentiators to the job in question. Résumé writing thus becomes a game of trying to second-guess the critical key words necessary, pick them from the job description, and then fold them seamlessly into your résumé.

In this manner we actually contribute to perpetuating this myth that we can judge, and be judged, by these feel-good skills. This myth is further perpetuated by the performance appraisal process whereby every year companies try to judge the employee on these same criteria.

While I'm on the subject of recruiting, another common requirement, especially for candidates coming right from college, is the pedigree of the school one attended and the GPA acquired. Google has done studies relating to this, and according to Stacy Sullivan, head of Google's HR department, (in commenting on Sergey Brin and Larry Page's preoccupation with a candidate's GPA), "We know there's no correlation between [performance and] where you went to school and your GPA, because we've done correlation studies."[265]

These soft-skills, and the overpowering need of the organization for its employees to possess them, coupled with the inability to analytically measure them, is one of the fundamental reasons the modern performance appraisal process fails to accomplish much of anything useful. Along with the myth of attaching pay as a function of the review results, we have a system that deludes both the employee and the company administering it.

Comic author Scott Adams has an interesting view of why the performance review exists. As he notes, "The real objectives of the performance review are:[266]

- Make you work like a Roman orchard slave
- Obtain a signed confession of your crimes against productivity
- Justify your low salary"

Those last two reasons are the key and we'll find out why later.

While the whole performance review process is typically conducted under the guise of improving the organization's overall performance, I could find no supporting data or studies that correlate that annual pay and performance reviews will lead to corporate improvement, yet the performance review process has been done in every organization in which I've ever worked.

Now that's a metric that would be interesting, but I've never seen one in any organization I'm familiar with. Why? Because the truth that the performance review process doesn't correlate to organizational improvement is too hard to face.

So, why carry out this abhorrent process year after year? Why waste the manager's time filling out the forms and the employee's time listening to the rhetoric, not to mention the motivation-killing atmosphere that surrounds the process.

The truth is that the documentation they provide is needed in case they have to eliminate, or fire, an employee. That is the heart of the matter and Scott Adams hit the nail on the head.

The mindset from the beginning is a negative one in that the appraisal is a tool for documenting the employee's short-comings so that it will support a later firing, or layoff, decision. The parties to the action can sleep at night because they've deluded themselves into thinking the review process will better the organization. The fact is they're building the cases they may later need to remove the "bad" employees from the ranks–i.e. when they start cutting heads when times get rough.

If you find yourself in the top 10 percent of the organization (based on your performance review), relish it while you can, because with sociopaths good reviews are short lived. Sooner or later you'll fall from grace and be discarded, and the performance review will be the tool used to seal your fate. Just as for Caesar, your Ides of March will come. The sociopaths will hide behind the performance appraisal form to feel justified in the action to get rid of you.

Motivational speaker and business expert Tom Peters notes that in today's business environment lay-offs and right-sizing are common occurrences. This is because most companies don't have a clue how to cut costs without cutting heads. They all try to "shrink their way to greatness."[267]

If there's anything that's truly proactive in today's typical workplace, its management's use of the performance review process to always have a ranked list of employees such that picking from the bottom makes the next "reduction in force" (RIF) a quick and easy event. I've worked in organizations where the RIF had become at least yearly events, if not, quarterly massacres. And as a manager, I was required to always have an up-to-date ranking of everyone in my organization.

As we all know, the typical employee's biggest fear is probably that of being fired. No matter where you look, this possibility hangs in the air like the Sword of Damocles, and at this writing the economic forecast for the future doesn't help. As we've learned, most organizations have in their values statement that they are "employee- first." It baffles me, as it does Kip Tindell, CEO of The Container Store, why they can't understand, "You can't go around calling yourself an employee-first culture and then lay people off."[268]

Now that we know the stated purpose of the performance review process and its real purpose, let's expose the blatant failings in how the typical performance review process works, because I seriously doubt the performance review practice will go away any time soon.

Most companies say they "pay for performance," and thus the modern performance appraisal systems are flaunted as setting pay as a function of the words being written in a performance review. However, that usually is not true, because the pay adjustment is usually determined before the review is even written, making pay for performance a farce.

The traditional model for performance review standards and the associated compensation starts way before the yearly goat-rope begins with the organization setting pay for each of its job descriptions. This is the amount the organization believes each job function is worth to them. This salary data typically are specified by the min, mid, and max pay that each position is worth to the organization.

Here comes the first myth of pay-for-performance. Most companies that I'm familiar with try to hold an individual's compensation to the nth percentile of that title-linked salary range. That nth percentile, of course, varies from company to company, but most I've seen target the 75th percentile. So once an employee reaches that threshold, the company will do anything and everything it can to limit further pay raises, regardless of the employee's level of performance. The performance review then becomes the tool of choice to justify this practice.

Further, the system is focused not so much on how the employee performed his job but how the employee stacks up to the mythical "perfect employee." As we'll see later, the criteria for rating the employee is usually a one-to-five rating system. Each of the soft skills is rated using this system and they are then averaged to give a composite score of the employee's overall "performance." A "five" is the mythical perfect employee thus, in this system; a "one" is what an employee would be rated if you wanted him to leave, and a "five" becomes the employee who regularly walks on water–i.e. your sycophants or the organizational heroes.

In this system, everyone is striving to be rated a five, yet like I noted above, only the sycophants and heroes ever see this rating. It's been my experience that if I tried to give one of my workers a five, I'd be told by human resources that I can't because then the employee won't have anything to strive for. The irony is that let's say an organization were to be successful in hiring the best-of-the-best–wouldn't they all be 5s?

Now that we know the measuring standard, let's take a look at the actual mechanics at play in the typical performance appraisal process. As noted, the system requires the one-to-five scale, with the rater considering various personality traits (soft skills) such as creativity, problem-solving ability, motivation, teamwork, and so forth. The problem is that most of the traits are not at all objective. Further, little, if any, training is ever provided to the reviewer to teach him or her how to evaluate these traits. Bosses typically aren't psychologists, and that, in my opinion, is the only profession even remotely qualified to assess people against these traits. Also, this "one size fits all" method ignores the fact that some jobs just don't need all these traits and skills for the person to do a good job.

I've seen performance review forms that attempt to remove some of the mathematical coldness by having the reviewer score the employee with just the ratings of excellent, good, fair, or poor. Again, it's totally up to the rater to make this determination, and there are no objective criteria available to do this consistently.

Fairness and accuracy in these systems is highly suspect, since they're completely subjective and, as we'll find out later, the review is just a means for the reviewer to justify the wage action that was determined long before pen went to paper. Thus, the review becomes the method for the reviewer to make him or herself feel justified in the pittance of a raise that will be given.

In addition to the skills rating, most performance review forms have an area for the reviewer to list goals for the employee that are to be the key discriminators of his or her performance for the next review time. Equitable systems would call for the employee and the reviewer to mutually agree and document these during the actual review presentation; however, these are typically unilaterally determined by the reviewer prior to the employee ever being brought into the process.

Additionally, any goal should be measurable and attached to some aspect of the job that the employee can actually affect; however, many times they're couched in terms that are virtually meaningless. A goal like "increase production output by x percent" might actually be something the employee could attain; however, a goal such as; "increase profit margin by x percent" is virtually useless as an individual goal. Many times I've witnessed goals that are purely reflective of the want by management to continue the molding of the employee into the uniform behavioral drones that they're looking for. This would be evidenced by a goal such as "be more contributive at meetings" or "be more assertive." These are not easy for an introvert to score big on.

From my perspective the problem is that most organizations make the mistake of giving the employee too many goals, and as such none are ever really realized to their fullest extent. I think a better approach can be found in the OKR (Objectives and Key Results) methodology. Here only one objective is set with the key to success being that there are also three key measurable results that are then used to measure whether the goal was achieved.

I think that Scott Adams nailed the real process of goal setting in the following dialog Dilbert has with the boss:[269]

Let's take a look at the practice of ranking the employees because it's the corner stone of the whole process. Many companies actually flaunt the fact that they rank employees such that they have a means to remove the so-called deadwood if and when they need to. Jack Welsh immortalized this ranking system by revealing that his goal was to be able to get rid of the bottom 10 percent of employees every year. For organizations that are convinced that there's a need to constantly upgrade the organization, this becomes their modus operandi.

Ranking the employees might not seem to be such a bad thing; after all, people do follow the bell-curve distribution, so there will naturally be good employees and bad employees. The problem is the ulterior motive behind the practice and the fact that the ranking is usually performed subjectively in advance of the actual performance review process, not as an objective *result* of the performance review process. The ranking process has nothing to do with the employee's ability to do his or her job or actual worth to the organization, but instead on how the employee and boss get along. The employees whom the boss "likes" will always score at the top of the rating. These are his or her sycophants and they must be protected.

Let's take a closer look at the "Welsh" ranking process. It's also known as the 20/70/10 rule. In this system, the organization partitions (ranks) its employees into the top 20 percent, the middle 70 percent, and the bottom 10 percent. The top gets a good review, the middle a mediocre review, and the bottom a "needs improvement" type review. The poor 10 percent at the bottom become nothing more than the employees you keep in your hip pocket, so to speak, in case you're faced with the need to cut staff during hard times, or at a moment's notice. For some organizations, that's a frequent event. This practice lends credence to the fact that the whole process is solely for the goal of having legal back-up in case a disgruntled ex-employee decides to sue.

Despite the identified three tiers, in practice there are really only two groups, just like the competitions in *Big Brother* where the house guests are divided into either the "haves" or the "have-nots" depending on their performance in competition. The winners—the "haves,"—receive perks, like freedom to eat anything they want, while the "have-nots" have to eat the prescribed "slop" for the week. This is not unlike the business environment where if you find yourself in the favor of the sociopaths you'll be treated well, while those out of favor will be taking the proverbial cold shower, waiting out their time until the next RIF catches up to them.

Most people might think the next step in the performance appraisal model would then dictate that if someone received a good performance review over the past year they would earn good raise. Herein we find another fallacy which is at the heart of the myth of pay for performance.

What actually happens is that the raise pool (of dollars) is set long before the performance appraisal process begins. The manager, provided with this information, is then faced with the task of making sure all the suggested pay adjustments for his subordinates are, in total, at or below the raise pool budget. This pool is usually dictated by the corporation as the target percent that's the average rate increase for the average employee–i.e. those supposedly in that mid 70 percent group. The goal is that the whole work force, in total, on average, will receive this x percent increase in compensation. In this way, the corporation can limit the yearly impact on its labor costs. Good budgeting technique; bad motivational technique.

Using the pre-determined ranking, the boss then assigns pay raises to each employee, with the goal of rewarding his/her stars or heroes and punishing those he dislikes, putting them on notice that their performance needs improvement. Theoretically, the middle 70 percent (remember they're average) should get the average percent raise and the top 20 percent should get more. But to give the top group more money (the kind of money the best-of-the-best expect), it has to come at the expense of those in the bottom 10 percent, and to a large extent those in the middle; otherwise the boss would never balance his pay raise budget.

So some of those average employees will, in fact, get stiffed with below-average raises despite being the core group that keeps the organization humming along. You must accept that in business there's the 1 percent that get the good reviews and raises and the 99 percent who will in some way be stiffed. Starting your own "Occupy HR" movement won't do a thing to change this fact.

Actual fairness in compensation could work by normalizing people to their true market value, as it's unlikely that the current methodology reflects the true external market value of the employee. The only way you have a chance at receiving market value is when you first hire in to an organization, and even in that case the hiring company will want to know your previous pay so it can hopefully limit your raise. These are the only data about an employee that will be typically given out by a past employer as part of the reference process; they all conspire together to help each other hold down wages.

In my experience, the new employer will limit the pay raise it gives the prospective new employee. They'll offer, say, 10 percent over the past pay, claiming that's a fair raise, when in fact the market may demand that the person get much more. The prospective employee is then left with a dilemma. If he really wants out of the hell-hole he's presently in, he'll take it for fear of losing his chance to exit his undoubtedly crappy current job.

This practice can also be explained somewhat by 19th century philosopher and activist Ferdinand Lassalle's "Iron Law of Wages,"[270] which asserts that "real wages always tend, in the long run, toward the minimum wage necessary to sustain the life of the worker." In other words, companies will pay the minimum wage that they think the market will bear. You're sure to get the "best of the best" with a system like that.

Without indexing to market value, over time, employees can get materially under-, or over-paid, relative to the market. When under-paid, employees are in perpetual job-hopping mode to take advantage of a chance of receiving a good raise. When over-paid, employees are trapped in their current job. Thus a consistent market-based pay system would be a much better model.

Ralph Waldo Emerson, in his 1841 essay, "Compensation,"[271] wrote that each person is "compensated in like manner for that which he or she has contributed." Thus Emerson's "Law of Compensation" says that you'll always be compensated for your efforts and for your contribution, whatever it is. This is the mantra that most organizations subscribe to and continue to tell the employees. However, this is unadulterated bunk; business will always try to pay however little they can get away with.

Emerson's Law of Compensation is also described as "pay for performance;" however, a true pay for performance system would require that the employee first be assessed of his or her performance, then receive a pay raise that's appropriate for that contribution. In the real world, however, the review will always support the pay action because the pay was set first; this is the myth of "pay for performance."

The biggest glaring problem with the whole performance appraisal and raise process is the performance appraisal process itself.

The Google definition of appraisal is; an act of assessing something, or an expert estimate of the value of something. The key word is "expert." Not every boss doing an appraisal is an expert. He may be qualified to assess whether the employee performs the job he was hired for, but he is not qualified, or even remotely an expert, when it comes to assessing the soft skills. How on earth can you expect a sociopath to assess someone's leadership skill? That's almost oxymoronic.

In reality, the performance appraisal is only an expression of the evaluator's self-interests, not the subordinate's performance or capabilities. Thus the relationship between the reviewer and reviewed is what's key. This drives the result of the appraisal more than anything.

In a performance review, employees are supposed to be measured along some predetermined checklist of skills or competencies that some expert has assumed that competent people have. The fact is none of this is relevant to the performance review process. Just like when being hired into an organization, the performance review is all a matter of the impressions made by the employee during the year and the perceptions the boss has toward that person. The boss either likes you or not, and that will affect whether you get hired and how you're treated from there on out in the performance reviews you'll receive.

In her November 2010 *Financial Times* article "Next Time Don't Give Hiring a Moment's Notice," Lucy Kellaway sums it up best, "[The] corporate world has developed a raft of complex promotion systems, all based on merit. We compile long lists of 'competencies' and draw matrices and give people scores. We have industries of HR people and headhunters to agonize about 'skillsets' and 'cultural fits.' But even with the best will in the world, we often don't know what sort of merit we are looking for or recognize it when we see it. In hiring; 'we compare [the candidates] to ourselves and either hire people just like us, or under extreme duress [from HR], we hire people because they are not like us at all."[272]

Let's take a look at the soft skills that make the performance review process such a farce. Here's a much more comprehensive list of the typical performance review soft skill sets:

- Communication skills (written/verbal/listening)
- Planning
- Teamwork
- Proactiveness
- Cooperation, teamwork, coordination
- Time management
- Decision making ability
- Problem solving skills (analytical/conceptual abilities)
- Involvement/willingness to take responsibility (willingness to take the blame)
- Initiative
- Creativity (thinking and application)
- Responsiveness (sense of urgency)
- Resilience (the ability to cope with pressure)

- Adaptability (ability to cope with change)

And if you're already in a management position, you'll be measured by some additional parameters such as:

- Leadership

- Ability to influence

- Team management

- Delegating

- Appraising

- Presenting

- Coaching and mentoring

- Motivating

The above are all highly subjective in nature, yet, they all will be attempted to be measured on that objective one-to-five scale. Some are personality traits, and not one is an objective measure of whether you accomplished your job during the review period. Introverts or extroverts, all are measured by the same criteria.

As an aside, I've found that there's now a new skill that the employees will have to worry about come review time. It's called "Emotional Intelligence." While I haven't personally seen this attribute included in a performance review form, I'm sure it's just a matter of time before this is included in the list of skills that the untrained boss will be asked to evaluate his or her employees against.

A national survey was conducted by Harris Interactive® on behalf of CareerBuilder, questioning 2,662 hiring managers asking them about Emotional Intelligence (EI).[273] According to the survey:

- 34 percent of hiring managers said they're placing greater emphasis on Emotional Intelligence when hiring and promoting employees.

- 71 percent said they value Emotional Intelligence in an employee more than IQ.

- 59 percent of employers wouldn't hire someone who has a high IQ but low EI.

- 75 percent said they're more likely to promote the high EI worker.

When asked why Emotional Intelligence is more important than high IQ, employers said (in order of importance):

- Employees [with high EI] are more likely to stay calm under pressure.

- Employees know how to resolve conflict effectively.

- Employees are empathetic to their team members and react accordingly.

- Employees lead by example.

- Employees tend to make more thoughtful business decisions.

In other words, the sociopaths are looking for the exact traits in their subordinates that they, themselves do not have.

So what is this new psychological attribute that's so cherished? In their influential article "Emotional Intelligence," Peter Salovey and John D. Mayer defined Emotional Intelligence as "the subset of social intelligence that involves the ability to monitor one's own and others' feelings and emotions, to discriminate among them and to use this information to guide one's thinking and actions."[274]

Salovey and Mayer have been the leading researchers on Emotional Intelligence since their article was first published at the University of New Hampshire in 1990. In fact, the current professional measure of Emotional Intelligence is the Mayer-Salovey-Caruso Emotional Intelligence Test (MSCEIT), which is a series of emotion-based problem-solving questions. It's the only accurate and reliable way to measure EI. Since the MSCEIT is an abilities test, unlike standard IQ tests, its questions don't have objectively correct responses. Therefore, it requires evaluation by a trained professional.

An organization's management doesn't constitute trained psychological professionals, so now we have potentially yet another subjectively measured behavior administered by incompetents used to evaluate employee performance.

Don't misunderstand, I agree wholeheartedly with the concept of Emotional Intelligence and its importance. After having had many people, in both professional and non-professional roles, work for me during my career, I have to admit I'd much rather have people displaying those attributes versus just having a high IQ. However, I do not claim the ability to accurately evaluate someone for them. At best it's just a feeling I have about someone.

From my perspective, those EI traits detailed above all seem familiar. In fact, they're all the traits of a good servant leader. This leads me to the disturbing concern that by adding this new attribute to the measure of an employee's worth, the very people who are saying they value these attributes, and are evaluating the employee against them, are the same people who themselves most often don't practice these servant leadership fundamentals. Sociopath's just don't believe in servant leadership.

So that leaves us with the question of how exactly might a sociopath measure an employee for his or her Emotional Intelligence?

Again, according to the above noted survey, HR managers and hiring managers assess their candidates' and employees' EI by supposedly "observing" a variety of behaviors and qualities. These are the top responses:[275]

- They admit and learn from their mistakes.
- They can keep emotions in check and have thoughtful discussions on tough issues.
- They listen as much or more than they talk.

- They take criticism well.
- They show grace under pressure.

Ironically, these sound like all the behaviors expected of an employee as they're forced to suffer through a performance review. They are expected to listen to their mistakes (and how they are not "responsive" or exhibit a lack of "initiative"); keep their reactions in check and show grace under the pressure; listen to the "expert" reviewer and don't talk back; and take their medicine and learn from it so they can change. Ironically, these are all the behaviors that the sociopaths are not good at, so if we ever see EI become part of the performance review process we'll have a real dose of hypocrisy in action.

Also, show me one boss who spends the appropriate amount of time calmly observing his inmates to be able to reasonably assess those traits. In most instances the only one-on-one observation the boss has of an employee is when the performance review is administered. And how long does that last—a half hour at best?

My fear is that EI could become yet another vehicle for the boss to rate his employees on a very subjective trait providing yet more ammunition for negative feedback during the performance review.

And if being rated on a 1 to 5 scale isn't enough, in the performance review forms that I'm familiar with, there is also an area for the reviewer to write (essay style) some justifying words to support the particular score given for each of the soft skills being measured. This is where bullshit enters the picture and reigns supreme.

Samuel Culbert helps us understand this by providing us some typical narrative comments given in actual performance reviews:[276]

- There's clearly impatience about her that people can detect.
- Can be a bit pushy
- Struggles with people who have a divergent leadership style

- Often will spend too much time on things that really aren't important
- Not a good people manager
- Self-centered versus team-centered
- Will micromanage
- Can be overwhelming in the sense of urgency to get things done immediately

Don't these traits all sound familiar? They almost come right from the playbook of sociopathic behavior. Isn't it interesting how a typical sociopath can blast a subordinate for certain behavior that he himself displays? We're back to that values thing again.

In the end the real danger is placing too much emphasis on soft-skills that are so clearly only personality traits. If these interpersonal skills really can affect how the employee does his job, then okay, but the fact is they typically don't. What they become is a tool for the reviewer to earmark those who are different, and thus support the ranking and the low pay raise that will follow.

A good example is communication skills. Considering that people have different styles, if the person being reviewed isn't an extrovert as the reviewer probably is, does that mean he can't communicate? What if the job is as an individual contributor and the job can be accomplished autonomously? Why would communication skills necessarily be an issue?

The most idiotic part of the performance review is the "ethical behavior" checkbox. I've seen this on many performance review forms. They sprung up as a result of the 2002 Sarbanes-Oxley Act.

For this measure, the reviewer must check a box indicating whether the employee has, or has not, acted ethically during the review period. In all the reviews I've ever done, there wasn't a single time I've had to check the "no" box. If you have an employee who's not acting ethically—of course this completely is determined by the organization's definition of ethical—he or she shouldn't have survived until review time. Come to think of it, that would mean that senior management should have been fired, but we all know unethical behavior in the upper ranks is a given.

Unfortunately, the employee is forced to contribute to the performance review charade; because the typical review process begins with the employee self-assessment—a worthless exercise in futility.

Of all the self-assessments I've read in my career, I've never come across one in which the employee was truly introspective and critical of himself. Most employees use it as a means to remind the reviewer of the good things he or she has done through the year, assuming that the reviewer may not be aware or has forgot them. Personally, I've avoided filling them out for myself whenever I could. I can't believe someone would consciously divulge his or her shortcomings when there's a chance the reviewer might not be aware of them. All you're doing is opening a potential can of worms. As Dr. Culbert points out, "You don't want to hand someone a club so they can turn around and beat you with it."[277]

This, coupled with the natural tendency for us to over-estimate our abilities and achievements, particularly in comparison with other people, is what makes these self-assessments worthless. This latter phenomenon is what's called the "Lake Wobegon Effect."

Lake Wobegon is a fictional location where "all the women are strong, all the men are good looking, and all the children are above average," and has been used to describe a real and pervasive human tendency to overestimate one's achievements and capabilities in relation to others. It also describes the goal of many organizations to want to have only the "best of the best" in their employ.

On his radio show "The Prairie Home Companion," Garrison Keillor says the town's name comes from a fictional old Indian word meaning "the place where we waited all day in the rain." That's exactly how you'll feel after your annual performance review.

The "Lake Wobegon Effect" has its basis in what's called "illusory superiority;"—a cognitive bias that causes people to overestimate their positive qualities and abilities and to underestimate their negative qualities. This is evident in a variety of areas, including intelligence, performance on tasks and the possession of desirable characteristics or personality traits. It's one of many illusions we all have relating to our own capabilities.

This phenomenon has also been explained as the "Dunning-Kruger Effect,[278] which helps better describe illusory superiority. The Dunning-Kruger Effect occurs when a person is incompetent, but his incompetence denies him the ability to realize this. Thus incompetent people tend to rate themselves above average. On the other hand competent people tend to underrate themselves. According to David Dunning and Justin Kruger, this is because incompetent people possess an erroneous view of their own capabilities, and in how they compare themselves to others.

It is illusory superiority that can wreak havoc with the performance review process, as those that rate their own ability as above average will always be disappointed by the performance review process. We'll see exactly why in a minute.

Dunning and Kruger proposed that, for a given skill level, people will:

- Overestimate their level of skill
- Fail to recognize the full scope of their inadequacy
- Fail to acknowledge genuine skill in others

This phenomenon has at its origin the fact that most of us like to consider ourselves above average when we compare ourselves to others. Most of us consider ourselves to be in the top few percent of the workforce. This happens largely because we derive our sense of self-worth in contrast with other people. Because of the Halo Effect and our impression management regime, most of us consider ourselves better than our peers.

However, the typical boss (the reviewer) has a tendency for the flip side, or what's called the "negativity bias." That's the last point on the Dunning-Kruger list above. Bosses will pay more attention and give more weight to negative attributes when assessing others.

This means that if the employee's tendency is to rate himself in a positive way and the reviewer's tendency is to rate the employee in a negative way; we have the makings of a standoff of opinions and the resulting unhappiness or possibly even confrontation. These phenomena seem to be reason enough to shit-can the performance review process. How can we expect people to come away from the performance review process in any way motivated?

And that's exactly the crux of the performance review process; we have this need to always rate people as good or bad, positive or negative. As Marshall Goldsmith says, "We have to stop couching all our behavior in terms of positive or negative. Some of it is simply neutral. Neither good nor bad."[279]

The negativity bias has also been defined as part of "The Reverse Halo Effect." We examined the Halo Effect in the first chapter on organizational perceptions versus reality. It's the cognitive bias whereby the perception of one trait (i.e., a characteristic of a person or object) is influenced by the perception of another trait (or several traits) of that person or object.

"The Reverse Halo Effect" is exactly what it would seem: the tendency for individuals judged to have a single undesirable trait to be subsequently judged to have many poor traits. It's when we allow a single weak point or negative trait to influence our perception of another person. The best example is how overweight people are always judged to have little discipline. This "judging" happens more than any of us realize or would like to admit.

Because the "Lake Wobegon Effect" and the negativity bias are unfortunately diametrically opposed, it naturally pits the employee's perception of himself against the boss's perception of the employee. The process is doomed, yet this review process has career life-or-death consequences for the employee.

Given the typical organization's "one size fits all" performance review process, you'd think the goal of many organizations would be to create a fungible[280] workforce of Oompa-Loompas, all with the same skills and abilities. Sadly, there's a lot of truth to that statement. While you may think this is conspiracy-theory thinking, consider this: the benefit of a fungible workforce is that it provides the sociopaths a long list of workers whose jobs can be out-sourced and off-shored to cut costs when their backs are against the wall. It also provides them moral justification for their belief that they must constantly crusade to upgrade the organization.

In his 2005 book, *The World Is Flat: a Brief History of the Twenty-First Century*, Thomas Friedman discusses the fungible jobs that can be outsourced to other countries. His guidance to all of us trying to prosper in the modern world of out-sourcing and off-shoring is that we need to take control of our own careers and do whatever needs to be done (training, schooling, etc.) to give us the flexibility to change careers when we find ourselves on the latest RIF list. In other words, you do not want a fungible job in the twenty-first century. I think every employee understands this, even if only subconsciously. It explains the information hoarding we talked about in the chapter on dysfunctional communication. The more information one keeps to oneself regarding how to perform his job the more job security he believes he has and the less likely his job will be eliminated.

Also, that upgrading process and the search for the "best of the best" mentality might lead you to believe that most organizations seem to want only the "stars" on staff. Unfortunately, as much as they would probably like to, they can't have a staff completely filled with stars. How would you ever be able to have a meaningful employee ranking? Also, no company will give you the budget needed to do it. The typical business budgeting process has no room for everyone to be a star and command top dollar wages. The whole process is management doubletalk. Even if you did have an unlimited budget, you still wouldn't want to have an all-star staff because the glare from all those egos would be blinding. Plus, somebody needs to do the fungible shit jobs—until they're sent offshore.

Why is the process of rating people on soft-skills so difficult? This is because it's typically geared toward rating people on extroverted criteria. Remember, the appraisal criteria were developed by the sociopaths, whom we all know are extremely extroverted. While an introvert may well be very good in all those skills on the review form he won't usually score very well. This is because it's impossible for an extrovert to rate an introvert fairly.

In her October 2009 article "Introverts v. Extroverts in the Workplace," Trina Isakson tells us that there are studies that show that about half the general population is extroverted, "and reward systems and job recognition are generally set up to value extroverts. Extroverts get rewarded because their work is apparent. They talk openly and often about what they're working on and how busy they are. With extroverts, often what you see is what you get.

"Introverts, however:

- Like working in quiet spaces
- Enjoy working independently
- Are reluctant to delegate, but when they do, provide little information
- Work well without supervision
- Think and reflect before taking action
- Sometimes share ideas only when prompted
- Listen well
- Appear calm under pressure
- Have good depth of knowledge

"Unfortunately, these introvert characteristics can come off in a negative light. Introverts can appear to not be team players. They may seem aloof, slow, serious, secretive, or lacking ideas. They seem not busy, not productive, or not outwardly stressed enough given the pressured circumstances."[281]

Introverts can bring certain other qualities to the organization, including but not limited to:

- Reliability
- Initiative
- Persistence
- Depth of knowledge
- Prudence
- Precision and accuracy
- Independence (requiring little supervision)

In his 2003 article "The Tyranny of the Extroverts" Allen Downey has an interesting take on the "introvert versus extrovert" dilemma. He explains, "I think there is a danger in placing too much emphasis on skills that are so tightly linked with personality traits.

"If "interpersonal skills" really means skills, then I can't object, but I'm afraid that in the wrong hands it means something more like "interpersonal style", and in particular it means the style of extroverts. I have the same concern about "communication skills." People have different styles; if my style isn't the same as yours, does that mean I lack skills?

"As for teamwork, well, I'm sure there are some problems that are best solved with collaborative, active learning, but I am equally sure that there are problems you can't solve with your mouth open.

"I shouldn't have to say this, but there is a place in the world for introverts. Show me the ten most innovative minds of the twentieth century, and I will show you ten introverts. From Albert Einstein to Charles Darwin to Sir Isaac Newton, not one of them could carry a conversation if you put handles on it. I wouldn't want to eat dinner with any of them, but I'm grateful they lived and died before the performance appraisal had the chance to fix them.

"If these people exist [and who are we kidding that they don't?], then the question is what are we going to do with them? Instead of changing the more introverted people to make them fit into the world of extroverts, maybe we should be looking for ways to take advantage of the particular styles and abilities of introverts. And instead of trying to fix them, maybe we should be making sure that smart, interesting people who happen to be introverts get the same respect and recognition as their extroverted counterparts."[282]

In his November 2010 article "Leadership Is Not Just for Extroverts," Philip Delves Broughton offers another viewpoint. "One way academics have sought to categorize traits required to succeed has been [through this process of] dividing us into extroverts and introverts, and much research has found that it is the extroverts who do best. Decent people [introverts] who might actually make better leaders seem to have a harder time scrambling upwards. They may have exactly what it takes to lead, but lack what it takes to get the chance.

"Extroverts like to be the center of attention, seek status and approval, and talk a lot in social settings. So what hope is there for introverts? Are they simply to bask in the sun of the extroverts or can they lead, too?

"One key variable has been underestimated in the argument over which character-type does best in business: the degree to which a manager's employees are proactive. If employees are passive, an extrovert thrives by giving a clear lead. If employees are more proactive, the introvert does better because he actually listens and incorporates advice into his decision-making.

"What is novel here is that, up to now, the advice for introverts in business has generally been to be more extroverted."[283]

The irony here is that the mantra of proactiveness has been one of the key performance criteria used by virtually all organizations in their performance review process. Introverts typically are very proactive, yet I bet the negativity bias insures they are typically rated low in this category.

And when leadership potential is brought into the mix, Broughton makes an excellent point. "Far better to have an introverted leader ready to absorb a lot of input in order to discover the best processes or business models. To get to be leaders, introverts must still prove themselves terrific individual contributors. But once in a leadership or managerial position, they no longer need to worry about loosening up at parties and becoming more extroverted.

"They can succeed by surrounding themselves with proactive employees, and giving them the autonomy and responsibility they require to perform at their best."[284]

I believe there's a bad set of cultural behaviors that are reinforced by the performance review process; however, there is at least one expert who believes that performance reviews should not be abolished. Dr. Robert Sutton, a Stanford University management Professor and author of *The No Asshole Rule*, says they can actually be valuable if properly executed. But he adds, "In the typical case, it's done so badly its better not to do it at all."[285]

Dr. Gary Namie, director of the Workplace Bullying Institute in Bellingham, WA, and author of *The Bully at Work: What You Can Do to Stop the Hurt and Reclaim Your Dignity on the Job* sums up the verdict on the performance review process. "They are a very biased, error-prone and abuse-prone system. It should be replaced by daily ongoing contact with managers who know the work and who can become coaches. People confuse the review with who they are; if they get a review saying, 'You're not effective at work,' they would hear, 'You're not effective as a person.' It isn't, 'How are we going to work together as a team?' It's, 'How are you performing for me?' It's not joint performance that's at issue. It's always the employee's performance that's a problem."[286]

So what's the answer to this problem called the performance review? The alternative to one-side-accountable, boss-administered performance reviews is a two-sided, reciprocally accountable, event that Samuel Culbert calls the "performance preview." In this system the boss's assignment is to guide, coach, tutor, provide oversight, and generally do whatever is required to assist a subordinate to perform successfully–i.e. practice servant leadership.

These previews are problem-solving, not problem-creating, discussions about how the boss and employee, as teammates, are going to work together even more effectively and efficiently than they've done in the past. Thus the preview becomes a coaching session focused on the next year versus taking cheap shots at the employee in the performance review at the end of the year drive-by.

Intuitively this would tend to bring out the best, versus the worst, in the employee. The best part of this process is it forces management to act as a coach, not a critic. For more detail on this process, I suggest reading Dr. Culbert's book, *Get Rid of the Performance Review! How Companies Can Stop Intimidating, Start Managing and Focus on What Really Matters*.

Unfortunately, most bosses think they accomplish this "coaching" through their open-door policy. The illusion is that any employee, even the one who would skip a management tier by doing so, can come any time and talk with the boss, supposedly about any subject. What a farce this truly is in most organizations. Scott Adams hits the nail on the head in this discussion between the intern Asok and the pointy-haired boss:[287]

As noted earlier, the stated purpose of the performance review is both to better the organization and provide the employee feedback on how he can better himself. However, even when done right, most people automatically equate feedback with the delivery of bad news and criticism of their performance, because that's exactly what many organizations are fixated on.

I'll bet if the majority of managers were to come clean about their biases during review time, they'd have to admit they focus on what is bad about their employees rather than on what is good. This is proven by the fact that the most overheard phrase in the workplace is "I only hear from my boss when I screw up." That's the vulture management style in action.

The negativity tilt that most performance appraisal systems dwell on results in a passive-defensive workplace culture where employees avoid responsibility so they can't be blamed for anything. It's a vicious circle that contributes to the blame game.

There is one useful thing the performance serves; in a "hero worship" or "sky is falling" type of organization, the performance review becomes the key tool used to document the heroic antics of the sycophants that always step up and save the day.

These organizations routinely applaud eleventh-hour hero performances and snub folks who get their job done in eight hours. The interesting thing about this is that one of the soft-skills people are typically graded on is "time management," yet most organizations frown on people who are, in fact, good time managers and can get their work done in eight hours. Talk about irreconcilable differences.

Companies may not realize it yet, but the performance review process, as it's currently carried out across business today, will pose an ever growing problem as the workforce starts to transition to the next generation of worker.

In his June 2009 article "Generation Y is Poised to Dominate the Workplace," Ray Williams explains, "There are seventy-six million members of Generation Y (born 1981-1999) or millennials, as they're called, coming into the workforce. A yawning generation gap among American workers, particularly in their ideas of work-life balance, has arrived. Generation Y assumes [people] at work are on their side. They were raised by parents who often acted more like friends and mentors [than parents]. So Gen Y comes to the negotiating table with unprecedented confidence about what kind of workplace they want.

"In the coming years, Gen Y will replace the Baby Boomers in the workplace. Smart companies are reacting to the new workforce conditions dictated by Gen Y. And while Gen Y likes the 24/7 social networking connection and dislikes long working hours, they are fundamentally conservative in their lifestyle, with a dislike of ambiguity and risk. Old assumptions about what employee's value in the workplace doesn't always apply with Gen Y. Gen Y are not workaholics, and understand the relationship between a balanced life [they put family and friends before work and career] and productivity." [288]

I've also read where they are freer with their opinions and don't take orders, criticism, or direction well. That is definitely going to be a problem in the modern autocratic workplace. This appears to be a disaster waiting to happen. If companies continue to manage and measure the performance of this new generation with the same old laundry list of talents and skills and "command and control" style, few will be getting any raises, as none will live up to the antiquated standards.

I think there's a way to capture this generation, and those from previous generations who are out there in the workplace now. That's simply that companies must create trust throughout their organizations. I believe the key to a healthy organizational culture is *trust* between employees and management. This can only happen when there's open and truthful dialogue.

The organizational pyramid must be turned upside-down, and the lowest on the organization's hierarchy must be treated as if they're equally important to the organization's success as the highest executive. This, in essence, makes management accountable to the frontline workers and is a first building block of servant leadership.

What the whole performance review system fails to recognize is what writer Lucy Kellaway observes. "By the law of averages, most of us are deeply average." The review process can't change that regardless of management wishing it could. So when an average person gets a review rating him below average, what's a person to do?

In her November 2010 *Financial Times* article "Better to Save face than Take a Long look in the Mirror," Lucy Kellaway asks the question, "Which is better: telling yourself soothing stories that may not chime with the facts, or staring at the truth in all its harshness?

"We've all been taught that if you've been accused of being an underperformer the worst thing you can do is blame other people to try to save face. Instead we're told we must acknowledge our failures and recognize what has gone wrong. We must never be defensive. We must ask ourselves, and others, if we have the right skills and capabilities. However, there is only one problem with this great advice: it's wrong. It is based on a commonly held, yet fantastical view of human nature; that we are willing or able to change, and that we are rational about ourselves. Both points are false, especially the second.

"When it comes to our own poor work, we are constitutionally incapable of occupying a neutral ground. We either refuse to acknowledge it at all, or we wallow in it, preferring words like useless, failure, and screw-up. This is when things go really awry. Thinking you're crap always makes you much more so. It isn't the first step to improving. It's the first step to being unable to get off the sofa all day.

"It is therefore infinitely better to tell yourself a pack of self-serving half-truths. Face-saving stories are absolutely vital to survival." [289]

Personally, I believe the whole performance review process could actually prove to be a viable tool to increase performance if management were to understand and utilize "The Pygmalion Effect" to its benefit. g The name comes from the 1912 play *Pygmalion: A Romance in Five Acts*, by George Bernard Shaw. In the play Professor Henry Higgins makes a bet that he can train a flower girl, Eliza Doolittle, to pass for a duchess by teaching her to assume a veneer of respectability, the key being impeccable speech.

Also known as the "Rosenthal Effect," it refers to the phenomenon in which the greater the expectation placed upon people, the better they perform. The Rosenthal Effect is named after the American psychologist Robert Rosenthal, who conducted extensive research on the influence that beliefs, biases, and expectations can have on people. His work provides proof that people can act in accordance with motives and expectations of others.

The Pygmalion, or Rosenthal, effect can, if used properly, be a form of self-fulfilling prophecy. This is how this would work; employees believed to be poor performers would be reviewed and graded as better than average. If the Pygmalion Effect is real, then these employees will rise to the occasion and become better employees accordingly. It's not such a leap when we consider most organizations are already living in a world where perception is more important than fact.

The key is that reality can be influenced by the expectations of others. For the individual, this influence can be beneficial or detrimental. The Pygmalion Effect, if used properly could result in a beneficial effect. What have we got to lose by trying—we already know the typical performance review does exactly the opposite. Hence, we have the whole problem with today's approach to performance reviews: focusing on the negative begets a negative response, whereas focusing on the desired behavior—i.e. the positive—maybe will encourage the employee to step up to the challenge without even knowing it. Hence why I noted at the beginning of this chapter, "People do not change when you tell them they should; they change when they tell themselves they must."

This observer-expectancy effect has been tested in real-life situations. According to Rosenthal's research, a person's expectancies for himself can affect his reality and create self-fulfilling prophecies. In other words, you get what you expect.

I firmly believe that when the performance review process zeroes in on employee deficits rather than strengths, it results in everyone in the workforce spending most of their time trying to fix what's wrong instead of identifying and focusing on making a few things (as Seth Godin would say) "remarkable."

Another replacement for the performance review process that must be mentioned is called "The Hawthorne Effect," and like The Rosenthal effect, it might prove to be a good tool for motivating employees instead of demotivating them with the performance review process.

The Hawthorne Effect is when someone improves, or modifies, an aspect of his behavior or performance simply in response to the fact that there has been a change made in his workplace, or personal situation.

The term was coined in 1950 by Henry A. Landsberger, who discovered this effect by analyzing older experiments performed between 1924 and 1932, by Elton Mayo of Harvard, at the Hawthorne Works, a Western Electric factory outside Chicago.

Hawthorne Works had commissioned a study to see if its workers would become more productive in higher or lower levels of light. The result was that the workers' productivity seemed to improve when higher levels of light were introduced and when light level was reduced, productivity slumped.

Unfortunately, the productivity gain was short-lived. Be that as it may, maybe there's more to this Hawthorne Effect than meets the eye. Maybe, if management where to show more interest and attention in creating the right environment, throughout the year, for the workers, the motivational effect might be lasting.

Thus, I believe the whole performance review process could be scuttled if companies would just understand the simple reality that if management creates the right environment for the employees they, in turn, give their best. People will do much better in their careers and love their work if they work in an organization founded on trust, not one motivated through fear. It's also one in which servant leadership would be at the forefront of employee relations.

Also, if companies were to spend more time training managers, and potential leaders, good coaching skills rather than how to fill out the performance review form, there might not be a need for the classical performance review process at all.

Daniel Goleman et al. tell us, "Coaches help people identify their unique strengths and weaknesses, tying those to their personal career aspirations. Only by getting to know employees on a deeper, personal level can leaders begin to make that link a reality. A good coach communicates a belief in people's potentials and an expectation that they can do their best. [However], when executed poorly, the coaching approach looks more like micromanaging or excessive control of an employee.

"[Unfortunately most managers are required to] concentrate solely on short-term goals, such as sales figures. That solution-oriented bent keeps [managers] from discovering employees' long-term aspirations, and employees, in turn, can believe that the leader sees them as mere tools for accomplishing a task, which makes them feel underappreciated rather than motivated."[290]

If your company still thinks the performance review is the way to go, here's a final thought. For the performance review process to truly work toward improving the organization performance it should be only task- and results- oriented versus focusing on the person's skills or personality. After all, results are what most organizations preach incessantly. We all can attest that when we receive positive feedback that's both constructive and focused on outcomes, rather than on our character, we accept it more openly, and we get less defensive.

I'm not advocating that management should ever tolerate poor performance. What I am against is when they don't tolerate mistakes. Taking action against poor performers is a sign of true leadership and you don't need a performance review to accomplish that. However, when management does not tolerate mistakes, it's indicative of the "command and control" management mentality.

Companies need to stop trying to manage employees and instead lead them. They need to find a way to inspire them. Google stands out as a prime example of an organization that realizes that little perks can make a big impact on the employees' general state of mind and thus inspire their performance. Even Clever Hans, the horse, got a treat when he answered a question correctly.

Steven Levy, in his excellent book *In the Plex: How Google Thinks, Works, and Shapes Our Lives*, comments on just this question. "This raise[s] the question of whether even a cash-strapped corporation might do better by budgeting money to make its employees happier and more productive. Was it possible that such a workforce might be more likely to turn around a troubled company? If you were a highly sought after recruit, how could such a contrast not affect you? If you were an employee who saw evidence, every single day, that your company valued your presence, would you not be more loyal?"[291] That's some food for thought.

Still not convinced that the performance review process should be scuttled? Then I whole-heartedly suggest you read Dr. Culbert's book *Get Rid of the Performance Review! How Companies Can Stop Intimidating, Start Managing—and Focus on What Really Matters*. It certainly helped make me a believer.

Remember what newspaper columnist Robert Benchley once said, "This is a test. It's only a test. Had it been an actual job, you would have received raises, promotions, and other signs of appreciation."[292]

EPILOGUE

PRESIDENT LYNDON B. JOHNSON REPORTEDLY ONCE SAID, "It's better to have your enemies inside the tent pissing out, then outside pissing in."[293]

Robert Sutton also has some advice for us, "There are times when the best thing for your mental health is not to give a damn about your job, company, and especially all those nasty people."[294]

There's a saying, however, trite, "If you're not having fun at your job then you're doing the wrong thing." The behaviors that I've described in this book explain why people get to the point in their careers where they're so unhappy that they think about this statement, and then subsequently rationalize their damaged careers by believing Nietzsche's famous quote, "Whatever doesn't kill you, makes you stronger."[295]

What does it mean to have fun at work? We all strive for that, right? In their August 2010 article "Workplace Fun and Its Correlates: A Conceptual Inquiry," Mildred Pryor, et al. provides some insight. "[First], workplace fun is not an oxymoron. Fun is enjoyment, pleasure. Fun is the pleasure you experience while you are involved in some action such as doing something, seeing something, or even relaxing. There's no reason why 'fun at work' can't be a legitimate goal. Fun at work is not an 'all or nothing' situation—i.e. [we have] no fun or a hundred percent fun. Instead, fun at work is experienced along a continuum that implies one can experience less or more fun at work and that there are factors that can decrease or increase the pleasure that one experiences at work."[296]

So why is it so hard to have fun at work? Pryor offers more detail. "There are factors that could decrease fun, or contribute to limited fun, in the workplace, such as negative culture and work environment, management inadequacies and failures, non-management inadequacies and failures, and systems and structure inadequacies." And then there are all the games we've learned about.

"Workplace fun can be dramatically decreased by a negative work culture and dysfunctional work environment. Such negative cultures and environments often do not tolerate creativity and suggestions for improvement [instead]; they allow gossip, harassment, and violence; and/or they are rife with distrust and fear."[297]

Unfortunately, for all who strive to have fun at work, Larry Niven provides a warning you should remember, "Mother Nature doesn't care if you're having fun."[298] The way that should read is, "Human nature doesn't care if you have fun," because human nature after all, is what runs organizations and ultimately can make the workplace a living hell.

The majority of us try to start our careers by focusing on what we'd like to do with our lives and hope that along the way we find a job in which we can also have some fun. We might, and probably will, however, get detoured along the way, but it's safe to say we don't start our careers with the intent of being unhappy with what we do for a living. So what happens?

As we've seen, today's average workplace can help ruin the dream of a happy, fulfilling career for many people. I know it's been said ad nauseam that the only path to true career happiness is to be your own boss, but realistically that's not in the cards for the vast majority of us. Most of us must fend for ourselves in the corporate world, battling to keep any sense of our dignity and integrity. However, we do have options.

Probably the easiest option is for you to elect to become one of them (the sociopaths) and thus rise to the top of the heap. I'm not sure that will ultimately be any fun, though, or that you'll be happy because, to get there, you'll have to not only endure the abusive antics we've learned about, but you'll also have to adopt them yourself. You must fight fire with fire, right? So if you have any shred of self-respect, morals, integrity or ethics that's not the road to take.

The other option is the proverbial high road. That's the road of becoming a true leader, in spite of all you see around you, by following the advice I'll offer a bit later.

To start, you have to ask yourself what you want for your legacy. Do you want to be remembered as the sociopathic bully, or a respected leader? Both of these can offer a path to success (in the business sense). The choice is yours.

If the first option is your calling, then this book has hopefully formed a primer for how to behave badly and get ahead in business. If you're leaning toward taking the high road, then there is another path to the top that's much less traveled.

As we've seen, success isn't necessarily guaranteed by having a depth of technical expertise. However, you do need the technical talents and capabilities to perform your job before you can even think that you'll rise to the top. Effective leadership isn't about technical job skills or skills that you learn in college. Remember, it doesn't matter if you're the best musician in the band on the Titanic.

Unfortunately as we've discovered, the typical model for behavior in the workplace is the battlefield, right? Take the popular TV show *The Apprentice*, where men and women try to slaughter each other to win the praise of Donald Trump. It's a leadership model that transcends a militaristic tone and could be called downright gladiatorial. It reminds me of the Starz network series, *Spartacus*, in which all the gladiators vie for the top spot, the undefeated champion and the praise of their doctore.

That's really not unlike the challenges we face in our careers, although for the gladiator, each fight is literally life or death. Similarly, your career will be filled with symbolic "life or death" struggles. You'll spend every day trying to please the boss (your doctore) in the hopes that you'll fare well in the next performance review (you're time in the arena).

I believe shows like *The Apprentice* (and *Big Brother*) do little to help the workplace situation. While they're interesting to watch, I think they do more damage than good as they glamorize dysfunctional sociopathic, bullying behavior. The worst part is they reinforce in the sociopaths and bullies that their behavior is acceptable and justified. I think they're popular because it reminds the viewer of their struggles at work and they can dream of being the person who comes out on top.

Despite which path to the top you elect the question still remains: How can we address trying to change the workplace for the better? The simple answer to our evil workplace dilemma is wrapped up in the concept of *equity*. For employees to be loyal to an organization and perform their jobs day-in and day-out, investing their life and energy, then the least an organization can provide is some equity. I'm not talking about equity of pay and certainly not equity of power, although the pay would be nice. An equitable workplace means that everyone is held to the same high standard of behavior, including top management, and everyone practices mutual courtesy and exhibits genuine caring for each other. In other words they act out their values. Management teams must create an environment where everyone feels they're part of an organization that respects them and their opinions, while recognizing their personal goals, needs, and problems. That's a tall order, I know.

But alas, the sociopaths rule, and "equity" is the most foreign word to them. While the odds are overwhelmingly against it, if more people begin their careers with the mindset that they won't tolerate sociopathic behavior, then maybe there could be hope for the modern workplace after all. If more people turn the bullies in to HR and pressure for something to be done about them, maybe there'll be change and some equity will be created. If we let the sociopaths get away with their behavior, we're in effect condoning it and we get what we pay for, as they say.

So if the high road is your elected path, then you need some guidance. There are some alternatives if you're looking for help on how to be both a good leader and be successful without resorting to becoming a sociopathic bully. Being a leader is not that hard, actually. Leading versus just managing is not something to be feared.

First, know that you don't have to be in management to lead and change the workplace around you; the best way to affect a decent equable workplace is through your ability to influence others and the example you set. Being a good example is the essence of true leadership.

In their book *Primal Leadership: Learning to Lead with Emotional Intelligence*, Daniel Goleman, et al. have researched what it takes to be a successful leader in today's business environment. They have boiled down their findings to a core behavior that they call "primal leadership."

They write, "The fundamental task of leaders is to prime good feelings in those they lead. This occurs when a leader creates resonance, a reservoir of positivity that frees the best in people. At its root, then, the primal job of leadership is emotional. When leaders drive emotions positively, they bring out everyone's best. We call this effect resonance. When they drive emotions negatively, leaders spawn dissonance,[299] undermining the emotional foundations that let people shine.

"Intellect and clear thinking are largely the characteristics that get someone in the leadership door. However, intellect alone will not make a leader; leaders execute a vision by motivating, guiding, inspiring, listening, persuading—and most crucially through creating resonance. [The right] moods are especially important when it comes to teams. The ability of the leader to pitch a group into an enthusiastic, cooperative mood can determine its success. On the other hand, whenever emotional conflicts in a group bleed attention and energy from their shared tasks, a group's performance will suffer."[300]

This is because when people are thrust together for any length of time, they begin to attune their emotions to whoever has the strongest emotional presence, whether positive or negative. This phenomenon is called "mirroring." So to be a good leader, you must fully understand this phenomenon and use it as a tool to set the mood for the entire organization. In this manner, you'll be leading with Emotional Intelligence. It's also simply called setting a good example.

In his April 2011 *Financial Times* article "The Workplace is Like a Cold Bed: The Warmth Will Spread–How to Cultivate the Right Attitude," Rhymer Rigby tells us, "One of the manager's key responsibilities is how they affect a team's attitude and how they enable people to have a positive attitude. The workplace is like a cold bed; the warmth will spread."[301]

So how exactly does one lead with emotional intelligence? From my experience in leadership roles, I'm convinced the best practice, and what's worked quite well for me, is *servant leadership*.

Servant leadership is the philosophy and practice of leadership, coined and defined by management extraordinaire Robert Greenleaf. However, the most recognized work on servant leadership may be by Ken Blanchard.

Servant leaders achieve results for their organizations by giving priority attention not only to the needs of their colleagues but, most importantly, those they serve. In servant leadership, the ones served are the people who work with you and for you, not necessarily those above you, in the organization. The problem is that most management has no idea what it means to be a true servant leader. In this culture of "me, me, me," people want to be served, not to serve. Today's management practices only imitate society as a whole.

Servant leadership serves as a good complement to leading with Emotional Intelligence. Servant leadership works because the key to (your) success is the people who work for you. Not you, your boss, your colleagues, or peers will have as profound an effect on your career as the people who perform their daily jobs successfully for you. They'll do this because they respect and admire you, because you are willing to care about them and give something of yourself back to them.

However, the typical management style prevalent today is the fear and loathing, "command and control" approach in which self-described leaders believe the only way to get people to be at their beck and call is by intimidation and threats of reprisal. There's also the misguided belief that, to lead a group of people, you must be an expert in the particular field. This explains why people who are typically the most knowledgeable in a field are promoted into management. The problem is they're never provided any management, let alone or leadership, training and thus they have to wing it, most often creating irreparable damage as they train on-the-job.

As famous management consultant Peter Drucker once said, "The [true] test of organization is not genius. It is its capacity to make common people achieve uncommon performance."[302] Servant leadership has proven time and again that it can make that a reality.

Author William Arthur Ward said it perfectly: "We must be silent before we can listen. We must listen before we can learn. We must learn before we can prepare. We must prepare before we can serve. We must serve before we can lead."[303]

What specifically are the habits or traits of a servant leader that make it such a successful technique and those who practice it so successful? There are basically eight traits:

- Patience: showing self-control
- Kindness: is an act of love
- Humility: displaying an absence of pride
- Respect: treating people like they're important
- Selflessness: meeting the needs of others
- Forgiveness: letting go when someone fails
- Honesty: being free from deception
- Commitment: sticking to your choices and decisions

I think the most important is forgiveness (or letting go) as it's the trait that enables the servant leader to empower those who work with him. Unless people are forgiven for their failings, they'll never feel empowered.

This leads to the second tenant of my leadership mantra: empowerment.

According to Webster's Dictionary, empowerment it is to confer power upon, or to authorize. Empowerment is probably the most prized condition in the modern workplace and yet the most elusive. Organizations say they strive for empowerment, but most cannot shed the "command and control" approach to managing so that it can take hold.

Mildred Golden Pryor et al. offers some insight into how to empower people. "Employees can be empowered in their work [by] allowing them to participate in decision-making, goal-setting, and ownership in organizational outcomes." Decision-making is tough enough but, as we learned, in the absence of practiced values, it completely neutralizes empowerment and teamwork becomes non-existent. Both of these are necessary before decision-making can make its way to the rank and file.

She continues, "The underlying premise of empowerment is simple: choice gives people a sense of personal control, which in turn enhances their intrinsic motivation toward their work. The results include increased employee morale, higher creativity and innovation, better performance, greater organizational commitment, and lower turnover.

"When a man perceives his behavior is stemming from his own choice, he will cherish that behavior and its results. However, when he perceives his behavior as stemming from the dictates of external forces, that behavior, and its results, although identical in other respects to the behavior of his own choosing, will be devalued."[304] Fear is a great motivator in the short-term but fails miserably over the long haul.

In most workplaces management only provides its employees with what's called "Hobson's Choice,"[305] the take-it-or-leave-it mentality that rules the average workplace. As we've learned, nowhere does that mentality become more visible than in the performance appraisal process, which is the antithesis of empowerment.

A good leader emphasizes empowerment as a cornerstone for his or her success. For empowerment to work, the employees must be aware of the leaders' and the organization's mission or vision, values, and policies. More importantly, they must believe them. For the employees to do that, the leaders must live those values in their everyday behaviors.

Needless to say, for empowerment to work, the empowered must have the ability, knowledge, and technical skills needed to do their jobs. But the onus must still be on management who must take an active role in ensuring the employees have the training and resources needed to excel in their jobs. Once this foundation is in place, management's purpose is to serve as coaches. Having a good coach along with the necessary training and resources paves the way for empowerment and thus the ability for people to effectively and efficiently perform their jobs. That's exactly how a sports team becomes a winner and the parallel can work for business.

An empowered workplace can easily be recognized by the atmosphere of mutual trust and caring. In an empowered workplace the employees have bought into the ownership of the organization's success. The employees have begun to think only from their customer's (both internal and external) viewpoint. This is a key element of successful organizations; *they focus on their customers and their satisfaction as the prime metric to success*. This is the only bandwagon worthy to jump on.

When empowered, the employees are allowed to work out problems and be responsible for their own performance. Management must be willing to let go and let their people do their jobs in the best way they see fit, for empowerment to work. And the hardest part of empowerment for most management is to let go when the employees make mistakes.

How do you change an organization from a "command and control" mentality to one that's empowered? While extremely difficult, organizational change can occur if the leadership is committed to change. The methods are quite simple: *trust and truth*.

We all intuitively know that fear and conflict can only change things for the worse, yet it's the typical modus operandi in the workplace today. All this creates is a more combative work environment, one that actually encourages the behaviors and games that we've discovered in this book.

However, I believe that *values-based leadership* can help change the workplace. This is a way of making authentic decisions that builds the trust and commitment of employees and customers.

In his article "What is Values-Based Leadership," Vadim Kotelnikov tells us, "Leadership is not limited to just a singular measure of effectiveness; it is a multi-dimensional phenomenon. Values-based leadership is different from [other leadership models] in that it includes only three factors:[306]

- Effectiveness: measuring the achievement of the organizational objectives and goals
- Morality: measuring how change affects concerned parties
- Time: measuring the desirability of any goal over the long term [versus the typical short term corporate mentality]"

These are the true metrics that an organization should be measuring (along with customer satisfaction), not the ones that every other organization is chasing. Here's where management can begin to do something truly remarkable.

Leadership is not just about financial goals: thus the time component can be most important, as the typical short-term financial focus stifles an organization from thinking beyond one to two years, most often only a quarter.

Kotelnikov continues, "Values-based leadership is not simply about management style, how-to, following some recipe, or even mastering the vision thing. Instead, it is about ideas and values. It is about understanding the different and conflicting needs of followers, energizing followers to pursue a goal that they had never thought possible."

In practical business terms, it's about creating conditions under which all followers can perform independently and effectively toward a single objective. Remember, if you think you're leading and you turn around and find that nobody is following, then all you're doing is taking a walk.

Kotelnikov continues, "Why values based leadership? Values-based leadership is a must in modern flat organizations characterized by transparency and easy availability of information.

"A vibrant, living set of values provides the basis for forming and regenerating community. Values provide a context that facilitates and enables local, independent action. In today's fast pace workplace effective self-management and opportunism creates a competitive advantage."[307]

Also, there's another aspect of servant leadership that I think is important to mention. Don't be afraid to be self-effacing, especially in situations in which you don't have all the answers. This is a critical part of making servant leadership work. It's a powerful tool that gets its strength from highlighting your own weaknesses, often in a humorous way.

In my career I've received a lot of push-back and criticism from my superiors on using this approach. Sociopaths see this as a sign of weakness. I disagree and think people who practice self-deprecation can be perceived as strong, secure, confident, and likable. It helps to portray you in a more genuine and authentic manner.

I believe this to be a key characteristic of a successful leader. So never fear telling folks you don't have all the answers. In his November 2005 article "Public Speaking:

Self-Effacing Humor," Tom Antion explains why self-deprecation works, "weak people feel the need to inflate themselves and powerful people don't."[308]

Loyalty is another key trait that will help you become a successful leader. You must be loyal to those working for you, even in a sociopathic, fiefdom-rich environment. Loyalty is a key aspect of true leadership, and servant leadership teaches you this. I know this will be difficult to do, as the sociopaths will demand allegiance to them even to the point of requiring you to sacrifice your staff. Remember the plausible deniability routine.

Fiefdom-rich environments offer a distinct challenge to this guideline, because these environments are typically ridden with conflict, finger-pointing (especially among competing groups), and scapegoating at the personal level. You'll constantly be at risk of being thrown under the bus, as will your group as a whole. As we've learned, the sociopaths always side with an accuser, so you're constantly defending both yourself and your subordinates. I know this from first-hand experience. I've been told in no uncertain terms that it was expected that I be loyal to my peers and colleagues, over my staff. This pushes you into practicing the sociopath's plausible deniability mentality and adopting "command and control" tactics. This is their plan because you'll scare them with the whole servant leadership thing.

The single best advice to remember is Hank Gillman's "Small Roles Theory,"[309] which says that employees will measure you on both the big things and the small things that you do. Don't be above doing the small things. It shows you're not an egotistical pooterhead.

Here are a few other miscellaneous pearls of wisdom that can help you survive the everyday jungle and be a good leader:

On your path to the top you must always keep a "Pearl Harbor File,"[310] especially if you find yourself in a sociopathic organization. This is a file maintained to show your innocence after an anticipated or inevitable disaster takes place or when the blame may come home to roost on your head. Remember the "search for the guilty," and "punish of the innocent" behavior.

Also, don't ever jeopardize your commitment to your own personal values. Don't let the bastards get their way and make you circumvent them, even a little. For the sociopaths, once they get their foot in the door and get you to turn to the dark side, you'll be one of their unethical stooges forever.

Since it's common for most organizations to favor candidates with an MBA degree for management positions and speaking of ethics, I came across this August 2010 *Wall Street Journal* article "Promises aren't Enough: Business Schools Need to do a Better Job Teaching Students Values," by Rodrigo Canales, that I find apropos.

Canales tells us, "It is the sign of the times that hundreds of Harvard Business School graduates took the MBA Oath. These students promised to serve the greater good, act ethically, and refrain from pursuing greed at others' expense. We [should be] inspired that students who will soon be in positions of leadership vow to reject the temptations their predecessors could not.

"Like a chastity vow, the MBA Oath has an unstated assumption that those who have gone before are somehow different. They had weaker wills, less resolve, looser morals. The Oath is meant to signal a stronger commitment to values. The danger is the false sense of moral inoculation such oaths engender.

"Analytics [and technical knowledge] are not a substitute for values. Indeed, an overreliance on analytics leaves managers poorly prepared to lead in moments when statistics obscure the human dimensions of a choice.

"MBAs who take an ethics oath without enough supporting leadership education are likely more vulnerable to ethical breaches.

"It isn't that MBA programs haven't taught leadership and ethics. They have. But most do it poorly.

"Leadership courses tend to emphasize such things as social influence and public speaking, while ethics courses often focus on legal aspects. This leaves the connection between values, leadership, and action underdeveloped. Leadership entails thinking beyond the day's crises to focus on the longer term, grasping the impact of decisions on broader constituencies and sensing a responsibility that goes far beyond the immediate result of a decision.

"MBAs are too often unaware of this. For example, in a workshop at a leading business school, students were asked to list the qualities that a successful business leader should possess. While vision and business acumen were invariably among the first qualities listed, honesty and responsibility for others emerged only after considerable discussions. Meanwhile, when asked about the characteristics they most value in human beings, compassion, integrity, and responsibility appear at the top of the list.

"Taking an oath of ethical leadership is not enough to bridge this gap, and recusing ourselves from teaching leadership makes it worse."[311]

In her October 2010 *Financial Times* article, "Power Posing and Flattery Beat and MBA Any Day," Lucy Kellaway tells us maybe there's an alternative to that MBA anyway?

"[There's] a new scientific theory that states that by assuming a powerful position you become more powerful. To sit legs up does not merely make you more impressive in the eyes of the world; it makes you more impressive in your own eyes, too.

"According to research done at Harvard Business School, striking a power pose raises testosterone levels by an average of 20 percent, and lowers cortisol (the stress hormone) by an equal amount." This just might be that missing ingredient we were looking for earlier when we were searching of the perfect posture for a meeting.

She continues, "Strutting your stuff is now proven to make you more powerful. Here is a dead easy way of being more successful that doesn't involve putting you career on hold for a year while you spend $100,000 on an MBA. To make it, you simply have to fake it!"[312]

You're going to be disappointed with the caliber of people who actually get to the top. We've looked at the bad behaviors that permeate the top management levels in today's businesses and in most cases they had MBAs, by the way.

By this point some may believe that I'm exaggerating or being overly theatrical in my description of what goes on in the modern workplace. However, the very leaders whom I lampoon would readily admit to the behaviors detailed in this book. In fact, many actually pride themselves on them. Apparently, these behaviors have worked for them; they're successful.

In her March 2010 *Financial Times* article, "Chief Executives are Even Worse than They Think," Lucy Kellaway talks about how executives—a.k.a. management—view their faults. "For the past year and a half, the *Financial Times* has asked business leaders twenty questions including; 'What are your three worst features?' I've amassed a treasure trove of data that overwhelmingly support a long-held pet theory of mine. The worse traits of chief executives are a lack of self-knowledge, and a quite extraordinary willingness to give themselves the benefit of the doubt. When it comes to describing their dark sides, fifty-eight out of sixty felt bound by the same rule: 'any weakness is perfectly admissible, so long as it is really strength.' One, when asked of his flaws replied, 'I must not have any or I couldn't have become CEO, right?'"

From all the responses, Kellaway compiled a list of the seven most common deadly management sins:

- They're control freaks
- They're vain
- They're ditherers
- They don't listen

- They're bullies
- They're afraid of conflict
- They can't do small talk

Kellaway continues, "[However] the real problem is worse; they don't know what their faults are. A decade of psychobabble, coaching, and 360-degree feedback has made no difference."[313] Thus, they don't recognize the above behaviors as faults.

In her September 2010 *Financial Times* article, "The Real Reason CEOs Cry All the Way to the Bank,"[314] Kellaway asserts that the best CEOs [management] exhibit the same traits as a toddler.

She tells us, "Until last week, I had always thought it was the worst CEOs who had so much in common with two-year-olds. Both groups tend to swagger round with a wide-legged gait. Both say 'mine' a lot and are exceedingly bad at sharing. Both have short attention spans. Both lack common sense and have issues with listening. CEOs and toddlers are also hazy about the existence of other human beings, tending to view them as objects. They both inspire fear in the hearts of handlers. And anyone who has observed how toddlers behave on aircraft will realize why it is a good idea for CEOs to travel in private jets."

Kellaway goes on to show how there are also toddler traits that equate to a great CEO. They are:

- Toddlers are full of energy and enthusiasm
- Toddlers are natural risk takers
- Toddlers are persistent
- Toddlers are inquisitive
- Toddlers are creative
- Toddlers have great interpersonal skills

She continues, "There is one final way in which the toddler is a great role model for the CEO [management]: language. Toddlers say what they mean and say it simply. They never feel tempted to dwell on paradigm shifts or value stacks or synergies. I suspect the reason management thinkers have avoided the parallels with toddlers is it upsets their faith in the idea that leadership is an endless journey of improvement or lifelong learning."

You'd think that emulating a two year old wouldn't get you far in the corporate world; however, the way I see it, this may just a matter of going back to the basics. If more business leaders exhibited these good toddler traits maybe more true leadership would shine through and the workplace would be a more bearable place.

Speaking of paradigm shifts and synergies; one of my pet peeves with what goes on in the modern workplace is all the popular and repulsive management catch-phrases, or buzzwords, that float around like the smell of a dead body in the trunk.

Here's a list of those that I've personally been subjected to in my career. Sit through any meeting and you'll probably hear many of them:

- Think "outside the box"
- Crisp
- Synergies
- Core competency
- Paradigm
- Metrics
- Take it offline
- Down-sizing, right-sizing
- Upgrade the organization
- Best of the best
- On the Runway

- Leverage
- Win-win
- Exit strategy
- Low-hanging fruit
- Learning curve
- Value-add
- Accountability
- Multi-tasking
- Bandwidth

I liken the whole buzzword mentality in business today to "duckspeak," an Orwellian term that was part of the "goodthink" language called "newspeak" that he created for his totalitarian state Oceania in his novel *1984*.

Orwell described "newspeak" as an impoverished language promoted by the state, with the aim of making any disruptive thinking unacceptable and a crime. He called this "crimethink." As many words as possible with negative meanings were removed from the Oceania language, with the ultimate aim being that "newspeak" would reduce everything to a single word that was a "yes" of some sort—an obedient word everyone used to answer anything that was asked of them by the state.

"Duckspeak" meant literally to quack like a duck or to speak without thinking. Orwell foresaw this happening when he described how language of his time was becoming full of metaphors, rhetoric, and meaningless words, all of which he thought contributed to fuzzy ideas and a lack of logical thinking.

My advice is to try not to get sucked into business "duckspeak." If more people ignore the buzzwords and just use plain old English, maybe these moronic terms will die the ignominious death they deserve.

###

In the end, your career is truly in your own hands, and the course you take is your decision, but if you use the insight laid out here, you just might be much happier than most people. At least you'll be able to look at the events around you with rose-colored glasses. That might make you a little happier. It also just might be the only survival tactic available.

For the rest of you, however, you'll get stuck playing this game we call "business" and wait for the time until you can find another job—the chance to trade your current job for what's behind door #2 and start the whole sordid process over again.

You're probably telling yourself that there's no way you're going to fall for the games being played and certainly not the games targeting you. You're wiser and more astute than your colleagues. It's human nature to believe we can see through the façade that's perpetrated by others. This phenomenon is called the "illusion of asymmetric insight." It's the condition in which we believe we know everyone else far better than they know us. And not only that, but we know them better than they know themselves. This happens despite the fact that we know that everyone around us is showing a side of themselves they want us to see and not their real self—i.e. we subconsciously acknowledge that impression management is at work. The problem is that we also seem to believe that we're wise to that game, that they're not fooling us.

Conversely, we also believe that others can't see through our mask, that they are not onto our games—our impression management—and that somehow our personas are impenetrable.

You need to shed this self-delusional thinking that you somehow have insight into others and that they in turn don't have the same insight in you. It's not true. Everyone in the modern workplace believes this, so reach out and be different. If you really need to have a "brand" this is one to have; start by just believing in you, by practicing the following simple disciplines:

- Act professionally: live your values, even if no one else is, especially in the midst of the absurdity you see around you.

- Believe in yourself: face and accept the truth about yourself, even if you don't like what you see. Acknowledge your weaknesses—be self-effacing.

- Be genuine: we talked about this in the second chapter; try to be different than everyone else; don't subscribe to the herd mentality.

- Remain fearless: live without irrational fears, like fear of failure, rejection, and of losing your job, and most importantly, fear of change.

- Be courageous: always stand up for yourself.

The first thing the sociopaths will want to destroy will be your courage. With courage and the other four disciplines, you'll be a threat to them. Courage and a mastering of these disciplines will help you cope with the modern workplace and come out ahead in the end.

The goal of this book has been to equip you with the knowledge you'll need to navigate the modern workplace and to survive. I hope I've accomplished that. We've learned of the types of characters who populate the workplace, their behaviors, games, and the personal agendas that they'll attempt to force and inflict upon you.

You must stay vigilant, lest you either become one of them or you suffer both physical and emotional damage at their hands. Make no mistake, without some miracle; the modern workplace won't change for the better. Getting frustrated by what goes on will only give you an ulcer. For as Benjamin, the donkey in *Animal Farm* says, "Life will go on as it always has—that is, badly."[315]

I want to end with some further insight and tools I've found on how to spot an evil organization so that you can immediately start making new career plans. In his February 2009 *CareerBuilder* article "15 Signs Your Workplace Is Dysfunctional,"[316] Dr. Albert Bernstein compiled a useful guide for observing the behaviors in your workplace so that you can recognize trouble as its happening. He has graciously given me permission to reprint them for you. We've covered all of these in copious detail, so the following can serve as a recap. You may want to hang these on your cubicle (or office) wall in a conspicuous place so that the sociopaths and bullies can see them and will know you're onto them.

Sign No. 1: Conspicuously posted vision or value statements filled with vague, but important-sounding words like "excellence" and "quality" [and the most hypocritical of all: "respect for the individual."] These words are seldom defined, and the concepts they allude to are never measured, and worse they're not practiced.

Sign No. 2: Bringing up a problem is considered more as evidence of a personality defect rather than as an actual observation of reality. In a dysfunctional company, what it looks like is not only more important than what it is, it is what it is.

Sign No. 3: If by chance there are problems, the usual solution is a motivational seminar. In a dysfunctional organization, there's an elephant in the middle of the room, but no one ever mentions him. To stay sane, you have to pretend that the elephant is invisible, and that drives you crazy. The emperor may be naked, but if you have a good attitude [and are a good team player], you won't mention it.

Sign No. 4: Double-meaning messages are delivered with a straight face. Quality and quantity are both job one. You can do it both cheaper and better, just don't ask how—management brags about, "When we were at [company name inserted] we cut costs by x [some astronomically high percentage]." The implication, why can't you? Interestingly, when pressed, they can't tell you how they did it or the steps taken to achieve it. Their purpose is to lay down this elusive gauntlet for you to ponder and stress over. Remember, nothing is impossible, only highly improbable.

Sign No. 5: History is regularly edited to make executive decisions more correct, and correct decisions more executive than they actually were. History is regularly reviewed [lessons learned sessions], but they never change future events or actions. The organization continues to make the same mistakes over and over.

Sign No. 6: People are discouraged from putting things in writing because you can never tell when you might need a little deniability. What is written is done only from the "Pearl Harbor file" perspective.

Sign No. 7: Directions are ambiguous and often vaguely threatening. Before you respond to a vague threat, remember this: Virtually every corporate scandal begins with someone saying, "Do it; I don't care how." However, that person is seldom the one who gets indicted.

Sign No. 8: Internal competition is encouraged and rewarded. The word "teamwork" may be batted around like a softball at a company picnic, but in a dysfunctional company the star players [the heroes] are the only ones who get recognition and big bucks.

Sign No. 9: Decisions are made at the highest level possible. Regardless of what it is, and what your position, you have to check with your boss before doing it.

Sign No. 10: Delegating means telling somebody to do something, not giving him the power to do it. According to Webster's Dictionary, you delegate authority, not tasks. In dysfunctional companies, you may have responsibility, but the authority lives in the office upstairs.

Sign No. 11: Management approaches, gleaned from the latest bestseller, are regularly misunderstood to mean what's being done already is right on the mark. The management sociopath quotes from the latest management bestseller and is convinced he or she is leading by example. *The Goal, Seven Habits of Highly Effective People*, *Good to Great* and *Who Moved My Cheese* are bantered about in an attempt to create the illusion that they reflect the leadership's abilities.

Sign No. 12: Resources are tightly controlled. Your department may need tools, people, etc. but there's always a spending freeze or because the boss is a sociopath and wants you to fail, he withholds approval.

Sign No. 13: You are expected to feel lucky to have a job and know you could lose it if you don't toe-the-line. Dysfunctional companies maintain control using the threat of punishment. Most will maintain that they also use positive rewards; however, in reality the reward is only your regular paycheck.

Sign No. 14: Rules are enforced based on who you are rather than what you do. Fiefdoms and favoritism run rampant. In a dysfunctional company, there are clearly insiders and outsiders, and everyone knows who belongs in each group.

Sign No. 15: The Company fails the "Dilbert test." Dysfunctional organizations have no sense of humor. People who post unflattering cartoons risk joining the ranks of the disappeared. When an organization loses the ability to laugh at itself, it's headed for big trouble. If you get in trouble for printing this list and posting it on the bulletin board at work, maybe it's time to look for another job before this one drives you crazy.

I'd like to add my own #16 to this accurate and thorough checklist: the overused threat of accountability. And it typically is used as a threat versus a gift. Merriam-Webster defines accountability as: the quality or state of being accountable, especially: an obligation or willingness to accept responsibility or to account for one's actions. It's the last definition that shows how accountability is typically practiced in today's workplace. However, true accountability is more than that and even more than the other definitions.

As noted above, accountability is the acknowledgment and assumption of responsibility for actions and being answerable for resulting consequences. However, true accountability is not this one-sided. What the dictionary definition lacks is that accountability is really a relationship between two individuals—in our case, the boss and subordinate. That adds a whole new perspective.

Most management teams don't have a clue what holding someone accountable really means. That's because true effective accountability is a tricky thing to pull off. In most organizations accountability is just a sugar-coated term that means punishment will follow any screw-up. Ironically with today's management mantra being accountability, what most of today's management doesn't understand is that accountability cannot happen without empowerment. It's the precursor. They go hand-in-hand.

Also, for empowerment to work, the empowered must accept and believe that they are empowered. They must feel they have some power in shaping outcomes. In a "command and control" environment, this cannot happen, so empowerment can never gain a foothold.

True accountability is the sharing of the responsibility for something by both the leader and the subordinate. Thus, to be held accountable is to share in the outcome, good or bad. The problem is that in a sociopathic "command and control" environment, where the tenets of servant leadership are foreign concepts, any leader who tries to foster empowerment or true accountability will probably be accused of abdicating his or her responsibility. This is because servant leadership and true empowerment are threats to a sociopathic management style, so when you practice them you'll face the accusation that you're abdicating your authority. This is their defense mechanism.

To truly abdicate one must pass off his or her responsibility for an outcome and then blame the "empowered" when the outcome isn't reached, or the person makes a mistake. Thus, abdication is the complete relinquishment of responsibility to the subordinate. That's not what true accountability is all about and the sociopaths miss that point.

The funny thing is any management that would accuse a servant leader of abdicating, is exactly the one that practices its own brand of abdication by holding subordinates completely responsible for screw-ups, while it hides behind plausible deniability.

To empower, and hold accountable, you first must believe people have good intentions and want to do a good job. Sociopaths can't accept that. They believe everyone is out to screw them out of their power and prestige, so they do anything they can to keep the threatening herd at bay. The modern performance appraisal system is the proof.

Sign no. 15 also is of great importance, as I believe that a sense of humor is an important quality in both individuals and in the corporate personality. As noted above, dysfunctional organizations have no sense of humor, so my advice is to keep your sense of humor, despite the idiocy you may see surrounding you. Personally, I feel this may be the most important quality that a leader can have, as I've always felt people with a sense of humor are more genuine and self-aware.

Since democracy stops at the front door in most organizations, so does simple common sense. Things never are as they seem. Our perceptions, while being more important than fact, usually have some level of truth buried within. If you ignore your perceptions, however painful, about the place where you work, you'll end up spending your career hiding in a fantasy world. For as Hugh McLeod so humorously points out, "Business life is just like ordinary porn, or real estate porn, except instead of it being about the women we wished we could sleep with or the houses we wish we owned, it's about all those cool, lucrative, exciting jobs that we wish we had, instead of the normal, tedious, schleppy crap most of us end up doing to pay the bills."[317]

Unfortunately, in his November 2010 *Wall Street Journal* article "The Perfect Stimulus: Bad Management," Scott Adams bursts our bubble about finding a fun job. He tells us, "The last thing this world needs is a bunch of dopey-happy workers who can't stop humming and grinning. Our system requires a continuous supply of highly capable people who are so disgruntled with their jobs that they are willing to chew off their own arms to escape their bosses. The economy needs hamster-brained sociopaths in management to drive down the opportunity cost of entrepreneurship. Luckily, we're blessed with an ample supply.

"To put it in plainer terms: The primary purpose of management is to kill any hope that staying in your current job will work out for you. That sort of hope is like gravel in the engine of progress. The economy needs workers who are fed up, desperate, and willing to quit their jobs for something better. Remember, only quitters can be winners, because you can't do something great until first you quit doing something that isn't."[318]

In her January 2011 *Financial Times* article "My Measure of a Good Employer is Better Than Botox," Lucy Kellaway writes, "We all know what distinguishes a good employer from a bad one. A good one provides four basic things. First, it makes sure that everyone has a proper job to do. Second, it pays them fairly. Third, it makes employees feel that their efforts are recognized. And fourth, it gives them nice people to work with. That's all: there is nothing else."[319]

Alas, wake up and smell the bullshit; the typical workplace is not like that at all. What you'll find is management fixated on that relentless race to the bottom, managing in the only way they know how, as witnessed by the conversation below between the Dilbert crew and the pointy-haired boss.[320]

Such is the fate of many modern organizations run by sociopaths. This is a classic example of Seth Godin's "relentless race to the bottom."

Many outstanding organizations follow such paths of deadly downward trajectories that lead them to falling sales, plummeting profits, and eventually bankruptcy. Remember "The Icarus Paradox." What do these companies have in common? They suffer from the Halo Effect; they tend to continue doing the things to which they credit their success, even if that success came about by pure dumb luck.

Recall we learned that the sociopathic mentality allows the leaders to confuse the tactics that helped them gain power with the tactics that are best for leading a team or organization. As the sociopath goes, so do the organizations that they will ultimately lead to extinction.

Don't be disillusioned by this though, because this is good news. In the end, all organizations led in the manner in which we've discovered and investigated in this book shall meet their demise, their ozymandias.[321] Ozymandias is Percy Bysshe Shelley's sonnet about the eventual downfall of all leaders.

I'd like to end the book with some words of wisdom to be found in the tribal lore of the Dakota Indians, which says that, "When you discover that you are riding a dead horse, the best strategy is to dismount." Quit that evil job and find your own "evil plan," as I have.

As the square in *Flatland* writes from his prison cell, "Yet I exist in the hope that these memoirs in some manner, I know not how, may find their way to the minds of humanity in some dimension, and may stir up a race of rebels who refuse to be confined to limited dimensionality."[322]

Throughout your read of this book, you're probably been asking yourself what the title of this book has to do with anything you're reading. Let me answer that by first pointing out that most people and organizations spend their time "baptizing a billy goat,"[323] or wasting time on inconsequential things, chasing the latest management fad, never taking true risks or doing anything significantly different. They make few lasting improvements or significant changes in their lives or their organizations, as they plod along mired down in the status quo and their own brand of hopeless mediocrity. Wanting to change things even when the going is smooth takes fearless-ness—the true act of being proactive.

On the other hand, "puttin' cologne on the rickshaw" is all about taking action, doing something risky, something out of the ordinary, something never tried before, something that will make a change in your life and effect progress. It's about doing something different, however crazy it may seem at first. Author Dale Dauten put it best: "Different isn't always better, but better is always different. You can't get to better without going through different." [324]

So if you work in an organization that trumpets its mediocrity and is devoted to doing things the same way it's always done, be a rebel and become an advocate for change.

EPILOGUE

And certainly if you find yourself in an institution displaying any of the behaviors described in this book, you definitely need to do something that will make a change in your career and your life. In both cases maybe it's time you put some cologne on the rickshaw.

Visit me at my blog puttincologneontherickshaw.com, at Twitter @ colognerickshaw or on Facebook @ puttin' cologne on the rickshaw and share your own workplace horror stories and let me know whether you liked the book.

NOTES

1   Hugh MacLeod, *Evil Plans: Having Fun on the Road to World Domination*, ©2010, quoted with permission from Penguin Group Publishers

2   Shari Springer Berman and Robert Pulcini, *American Splendor*, 2003, quoted courtesy of Home Box Office, Inc. A Time Warner Entertainment Company

3   *Network*, 1976, courtesy of MGM Entertainment and Paddy Chayefsky's estate

4   Tom Peters

5   Pooterish; taking oneself far too seriously; believing that one's importance or influence is far greater than it really is–i.e. being thoroughly convinced of one's own importance. The term comes from Charles Pooter, the fictional leading character of George and Weedon Grossmith's 1888 comic novel *Diary of a Nobody*

6   Shannon Bell, "Time: Are We Becoming An Uncivil Society?", January 17, 2011, quoted with permission from www.pohdiaries.com

7   Giancarlo Livraghi, *The Power of Stupidity*, ©2009, quoted with permission

8   Richard J. Herrnstein and Charles Murray, *The Bell Curve: Intelligence and Class Structure in American Life*, ©1994

9   Dennis Wholey

10   Marshall Goldsmith, *What Got You Here Won't Get You There: How Successful People Become Even More Successful*, ©2007, quoted with permission

11   Dr. Nassir Ghaemi, "Depression in Command," July 2011, quoted with permission of the *Wall Street Journal* Copyright ©2011 Dow Jones & Company, Inc. All Rights Reserved Worldwide. License number 2719510636119

12   *Death of a Salesman* is a 1949 play written by American playwright Arthur Miller

13   Ben Carlsen, "Save Yourself from Workplace Violence," September 7, 2010, quoted with permission

14   Daniel B. Rathbone, Ph.D. and Jorg C. Huckabee, MSCE, "Controlling Road Rage," June 9, 1999, quoted with permission from AAA Foundation for Traffic Safety www.aaafoundation.org

15   The act of mistreating a peer, or family member, out of frustration because a superior (whom you can't argue with) has treated you poorly

16   2007 Workplace Bullying Institute, Waitt Institute for Violence Prevention (the margin of error in the study was ± 1.1%). www.workplacebullying.org

17   Rachel Silverman, "Hey You! Rude People Earn More, Study Finds," August 2011, quoted by permission of the *Wall Street Journal*, Copyright ©2011 Dow Jones & Company, Inc. All Rights Reserved Worldwide. License number 2730420800382

18   Robert I. Sutton, Ph.D., *The No Asshole Rule*, copyright ©2007 by permission of Grand Central Publishing, All rights reserved.

19   Pryor, Mildred Golden, Singleton, Lisa Pryor, Taneja, Sonia, Humphreys, John H, "Workplace Fun and its Correlates: A Conceptual Inquiry," August 20, 2010, quoted with permission

20   Gary Namie, PhD Research Director , 2010 Workplace Bullying Institute Survey–conducted by Zogby International, May 5, 2011,

21   Robert I. Sutton, Ph.D., *The No Asshole Rule*, copyright ©2007 By permission of Grand Central Publishing, All rights reserved.

22   Gareth Morgan, *Images of Organization*, copyright ©1998 Quoted with permission of the publisher Berrett-Koehler Publishers, Inc., San Francisco, CA. All rights reserved.

23   Francis Fukuyama, "Trump Bid Reveals the Myth of the CEO President," *Financial Times*, April, 27 2010, quoted with permission

24   Simon Kuper, "Superman: the Survival of the Personality Cult," April 29, 2011, quoted with permission from the *Financial Times*

25   Felix Dennis, *How to Get Rich*, ©2006, published by Ebury Press, quoted with permission

26   Eric Hoffer 1902–1983

27   David Brooks, "The Modesty Manifesto," March 2011, The New York Times

NOTES

28   Gareth Morgan, *Images of Organization*, copyright ©1998 quoted with permission from the publisher Berrett-Koehler Publishers, Inc., San Francisco, CA. All rights reserved.

29   Gareth Morgan, Images of Organization, copyright ©1998 quoted with permission from the publisher Berrett-Koehler Publishers, Inc., San Francisco, CA. All rights reserved.

30   Gary Small and Gigi Vorgan, "Is the Internet Killing Empathy?," March 4, 2011, quoted with permission

31   Terry Eagleton, "Cruel intentions: Is Evil Merely a Lack of Empathy" April 1, 2011, in review of; *Zero Degrees of Empathy: A New Theory of Human Cruelty*, Simon Baron-Cohen, quoted with permission from the *Financial Times*

32   Glenn Campbell, "Why Do People Do What They Do?" November 22, 2006, quoted with permission from www.FamilyCourtChronicles.com

33   Pryor, Mildred Golden, Singleton, Lisa Pryor, Taneja, Sonia, Humphreys, John H, "Workplace Fun and its Correlates: A Conceptual Inquiry," August 20, 2010, quoted with permission

34   Glenn Campbell, "Why Do People Do What They Do?" November 22, 2006, quoted with permission from www.FamilyCourtChronicles.com

35   Bill Vaughan 1915–1977

36   Philip Delves Broughton, "Simplicity and the Storm Before the Calm," December 27, 2010, quoted with permission from the *Financial Times*

37   Dale Dauten, *The Gifted Boss: How to Find, Create and Keep Great Employees*, ©1999, quoted with permission

38   Victor Kiam 1926–2001

39   Seth Godin, *Small is the New Big: And 183 Other Riffs, Rants, and Remarkable Business Ideas*, ©2006 by Penguin Group USA, quoted with permission.

40   Philip Delves Broughton, "The Hollywood Boss is No Work of Fiction," September 27, 2010, quoted with permission from the *Financial Times*

41   Stanley Bing, *What Would Machiavelli Do?: The Ends Justify the Meanness*, ©2002

42   Morgan Wetzel, "A Manager's Guide to Obtaining Power that Fails to Match Machiavelli," September 30, 2010, a review of; *Power, Why Some People Have It—and Others Don't*, Jeffery Pfeffer, quoted with permission from the *Financial Times*

43   Ralph Waldo Emerson 1803–1882

44   Morgan Wetzel, "A Manager's Guide to Obtaining Power that Fails to Match Machiavelli," September 30, 2010, a review of; *Power, Why Some People Have It—and Others Don't*, Jeffery Pfeffer, quoted with permission from the *Financial Times*

45   Oscar Wilde 1854–1900

46   Stanley Bing, *Sun Tzu was a Sissy, Conquer Your Enemies, Promote Your Friends, and Wage the Real Art of War*, Copyright ©2004 Reprinted by permission of HarperCollins Publishers

47   Stanley Bing, *Sun Tzu was a Sissy, Conquer Your Enemies, Promote Your Friends, and Wage the Real Art of War*, Copyright ©2004 Reprinted by permission of HarperCollins Publishers

48   Sun Tzu c. ~500 BC, *The Art of War*

49   Scott Adams, *Dilbert* ©2008 Used by permission of UNIVERSAL UCLICK. All rights reserved.

50   Albert Schweitzer 1875–1965

51   R. Earl Hadady

52   "The Allegory of the Cave" can be found in Book VII of Plato's *The Republic* written c. ~ 380 BC.

53   Gareth Morgan, *Images of Organization*, copyright ©1998 quoted with permission of the publisher Berrett-Koehler Publishers, Inc., San Francisco, CA. All rights reserved.

54   Philip Rosenzweig, *The Halo Effect: And the Eight Other Business Delusions That Deceive Managers*, ©2007

55   Words and Music by Michael McDonald and Kenny Loggins, *What A Fool Believes*, Copyright ©1978 Snug Music and Milk Money Music All Rights for Snug Music Administered by Wixen Music Publishing, Inc. All Rights Reserved Used by Permission of Hal Leonard Corporation and Alfred Publishing

NOTES

56   Conner O'Seanery, "Workplace Deception: Paying a Potential High Price," May/Jun, 2007, quoted with permission from Indiana Chamber of Commerce's *BizVoice* ® *Magazine*

57   Marshall Goldsmith, *What Got You Here Won't Get You There: How Successful People Become Even More Successful*, ©2007, quoted with permission

58   Conner O'Seanery, "Workplace Deception: Paying a Potential High Price," May/Jun, 2007, quoted with permission from Indiana Chamber of Commerce's *BizVoice* ® *Magazine*

59   Alison Boulter

60   Conner O'Seanery, "Workplace Deception: Paying a Potential High Price," May/Jun, 2007, quoted with permission from Indiana Chamber of Commerce's *BizVoice* ® *Magazine*

61   Francois de la Rochefoucauld 1613-1680

62   Conner O'Seanery, "Workplace Deception Paying a Potential High Price," May/Jun, 2007, quoted with permission from Indiana Chamber of Commerce's *BizVoice* ® *Magazine*

63   George Orwell 1903–1950

64   Harry Frankfurt *On Bullshit*, ©2005, quoted with permission from Princeton University Press

65   Harry Frankfurt *On Bullshit*, ©2005, quoted with permission from Princeton University Press

66   Harry Frankfurt *On Bullshit*, ©2005, quoted with permission from Princeton University Press

67   W.I. Thomas (1863–1947) and D.S. Thomas, *The Child in America: Behavior Problems and Programs*, ©1928

68   Robert K Merton, *Social Theory and Social Structure*, ©1968, quoted with permission from Simon and Shuster Publishing

69   Anaïs Nin 1903–1977

70   Leo Tolstoy 1828–1910

71   Samuel Johnson 1709–1784

72   William Shakespeare; *Hamlet* Act 1, scene 3

73   Nathanial Hawthorne 1804–1864

74   Stephen B, Karpman, M.D., "Fairy Tales and Script Drama Analysis," ©1968, quoted with permission

75   Lynne Forrest, "The Three Faces of Victim, An Overview of the Drama Triangle," ©2008, quoted with permission www.lynneforest.com.

76   Andrew Lange 1957–2010

77   Albert Einstein 1879–1955

78   Ken McCoy, "Perception v. Reality in the Business World," January 10, 2009, used with permission

79   Giancarlo Livraghi, *The Power of Stupidity*, ©2009, quoted with permission

80   W. Clement Stone 1902–2002

81   Harvey Leibenstein 1922–1994

82   Seth Godin, *Small is the New Big: And 183 Other Riffs, Rants, and Remarkable Business Ideas*, ©2006 by Penguin Group USA, quoted with permission

83   Herbert Simon 1916–2001

84   Andrew Hill, "Buffett's Exceptional Style of Leadership," February 28, 2011, quoted with permission from the *Financial Times*

85   Gareth Morgan, *Images of Organization*, copyright ©1998 quoted with permission of the publisher Berrett-Koehler Publishers, Inc., San Francisco, CA. All rights reserved.

86   Steven P. Borgatti, Paul Chellgren Endowed Chair of Management, "Organizational Culture with Examples from Liar's Poker," ©2004 Gatton College of Business and Economics, University of Kentucky, quoted with permission

87   Cameron, K. S., & Quinn, R. E., "Competing Values Framework," ©1999, quoted with permission from www.changingminds.org

88   Gareth Morgan, *Images of Organization*, copyright ©1998 quoted with permission of the publisher Berrett-Koehler Publishers, Inc., San Francisco, CA. All rights reserved.

NOTES

89   Gareth Morgan, *Images of Organization*, copyright ©1998 quoted with permission of the publisher Berrett-Koehler Publishers, Inc., San Francisco, CA. All rights reserved.

90   Giancarlo Livraghi, "Harpagon's Miseries," August 2011, quoted with permission

91   Giancarlo Livraghi, "Harpagon's Miseries," August 2011, quoted with permission

92   Giancarlo Livraghi, "Harpagon's Miseries," August 2011, quoted with permission

93   Morris Ruddick, "Kingdom Businesses," ©2005, used with permission of author, www.strategic-initiatives.org

94   Morris Ruddick, "Kingdom Businesses," ©2005, used with permission of author, www.strategic-initiatives.org

95   Gareth Morgan, *Images of Organization*, copyright ©1998 quoted with permission of the publisher Berrett-Koehler Publishers, Inc., San Francisco, CA. All rights reserved.

96   Sun Tzu, c. ~500 BC, *The Art of War*

97   Christian Lange, "Ritual in Business: Building a Corporate Culture through Symbolic Management," ©1991, quoted and modified with permission from *Institute of Industrial Engineering*

98   Gareth Morgan, *Images of Organization*, copyright ©1998 quoted with permission of the publisher Berrett-Koehler Publishers, Inc., San Francisco, CA. All rights reserved.

99   Giancarlo Livraghi, *The Power of Stupidity*, ©2009, quoted with permission

100   Gareth Morgan, *Images of Organization*, copyright ©1998 quoted with permission of the publisher Berrett-Koehler Publishers, Inc., San Francisco, CA. All rights reserved.

101   G B Singh, "Definition of Politics: The Ugly Game of Power," quoted with permission www.lifeslip.com

102   John C. Eldred, quoted with permission *Fast Company Magazine*, October 1998

103   Derek Loosvelt, "Why Fear Is Running Your Company (And Your Life)," *Vault Blogs*, April 13, 2011, quoted with permission

104   William Strong 1808–1895

105   Edwin A. Abbott (1838-1926), *Flatland: A Romance of Many Dimensions*, 1884

106   Edwin A. Abbott (1838-1926), *Flatland: A Romance of Many Dimensions*, 1884

107   Edwin A. Abbott (1838-1926), *Flatland: A Romance of Many Dimensions*, 1884

108   Manu Cornet, Organizational Charts, reprinted with permission www.bonkersworld.net/org-charts

109   Manu Cornet, Organizational Charts, reprinted with permission www.bonkersworld.net/org-charts

110   Robert I. Sutton, Ph.D., *The No Asshole Rule*, Copyright ©2007, by permission of Grand Central Publishing, All rights reserved.

111   Pryor, Mildred Golden, Singleton, Lisa Pryor, Taneja, Sonia, Humphreys, John H, "Workplace Fun and its Correlates: A Conceptual Inquiry," August 20, 2010, quoted with permission

112   Dr. Darrell White, "A Tribe of Adults: The Pond Theory of Management," October 2010, quoted with permission blog.skyvisioncenters.com

113   Robert Lindner

114   Manu Cornet, Organizational Charts, reprinted with permission www.bonkersworld.net/org-charts

115   *One Flew over the Cuckoo's Nest*, 1975 – Nurse Ratched is the cold, sociopathic tyrant who employs humiliation and unpleasant medical treatments to rule the patients with an iron-fist.

116   Erving Goffman, *Asylums: Essays on the Social Situation of Mental Patients and Other Inmates*, ©2007, quoted with permission from Transaction Publishers Inc.

117   Erving Goffman, *Asylums: Essays on the Social Situation of Mental Patients and Other Inmates*, ©2007, quoted with permission from Transaction Publishers Inc.

118   Inspired by a drawing by Hugh MacLeod, in which the original drawing layers are; sociopaths, clueless and losers. I have made modifications with permission www.gapingvoid.com

119   Gareth Morgan, *Images of Organization*, copyright ©1998 quoted with permission of the publisher Berrett-Koehler Publishers, Inc., San Francisco, CA. All rights reserved. www.bkconnection.com

120   Along with "Eurasia" and "Eastasia"

121   Venkatesh Rao, "The Gervais Principle, Or the Office According to *The Office*," October 7, 2009, quoted with permission www.ribbonfarm.com

122   Gareth Morgan, *Images of Organization*, copyright ©1998 quoted with permission of the publisher Berrett-Koehler Publishers, Inc., San Francisco, CA. All rights reserved. www.bkconnection.com

123   Gareth Morgan, *Images of Organization*, copyright ©1998 quoted with permission of the publisher Berrett-Koehler Publishers, Inc., San Francisco, CA. All rights reserved. www.bkconnection.com

124   Venkatesh Rao, "The Gervais Principle, Or the Office According to *The Office*," October 7, 2009, quoted with permission www.ribbonfarm.com

125   *Man Bites Dog*, 1992 (French: C'est Arrivé Près de Chez Vous, 'It Happened in Your Neighborhood')

126   L. Frank Baum (1856–1919), *The Wonderful Wizard of Oz*, 1900

127   Venkatesh Rao, "The Gervais Principle, Or the Office According to *The Office*," October 7, 2009, quoted with permission www.ribbonfarm.com

128   Green RE, Krause J, Briggs AW, et al., "A Draft Sequence of the Neanderthal Genome," May 2010, Science 328

129   Jennifer Miller, "The Power Trip: Nice People more Likely to Rise to Power," August 17, 2010, content is made available under the Creative Commons License

130   Kurt Nimmo

131   Marshall Goldsmith, *What Got You Here Won't Get You There: How Successful People Become Even More Successful*, ©2007, quoted with permission

132   Gary Namie, Ph.D. Research Director, 2010 Workplace Bullying Institute Survey–conducted by Zogby International, May 5, 2011,

133   www.workplacebullying.org for those interested there also is an organization called the Employee Empowerment Institute, www.employeeempowermentinstitute.com

134   Robert I. Sutton, Ph.D., *The No Asshole Rule*, Copyright ©2007 by permission of Grand Central Publishing, All rights reserved.

135   One who takes himself far too seriously; believing one's importance or influence is far greater than it really is. It's based on Charles Pooter, a fictional character in George and Weedon Grossmith's comic novel *Diary of a Nobody*, who displays an extreme example of self-importance.

136   Stuart Sorensen, "Understanding Primary Personality Disorder," August 22, 2011, quoted with permission <u>www.mental-health-today.com</u>

137   Manu Cornet, Organizational Charts, reprinted with permission <u>www.bonkersworld.net/org-charts</u>

138   George Santayana (1863–1952) this is an often misquoted quote (as I have done). The actual quote is: 'Those who cannot remember the past are condemned to repeat it.' and is also known as "Santayana's Law of Repeating Consequences."

139   Peter Vajda, PhD, "Pointing Fingers," May 1, 2009, quoted with permission

140   Robert I. Sutton, Ph.D., *The No Asshole Rule*, Copyright ©2007 by permission of Grand Central Publishing, All rights reserved.

141   David Chapman, "Are You Being Bullied at Work? Would You Like to Fight Back?" quoted with permission <u>www.kickbully.com</u>

142   Ambrose Bierce 1842–1913

143   Paul Wallis, "Sycophants–An Analysis," quoted with permission

144   Giancarlo Livraghi, *The Power of Stupidity*, ©2009, quoted with permission

145   W. D. Hamilton 1936–2000

146   Marshall Goldsmith, *What Got You Here Won't Get You There: How Successful People Become Even More Successful*, ©2007, quoted with permission

147   Marshall Goldsmith, "The Favoritism Test: Learn to Avoid the Pitfalls of Rewarding Sycophants in the Workplace," quoted with permission

148   Henry Pelifian, "The Sycophantic Culture," March 16, 2009, quoted with permission <u>www.dis-sidentvoice.org</u>

149   Lucy Kellaway, "Power Posing and Flattery Beat an MBA Any Day," October 3, 2010, quoted with permission from The *Financial Times*

NOTES

150   Kurt Vonnegut, *A Man without a Country*, ©2005, quoted with permission from Seven Stories Press (Vonnegut's argument was focused on political leaders but should be familiar to anyone who has worked in a sycophantic environment.)

151   Will Rodgers 1878–1935

152   Robert J. Herbold, *The Fiefdom Syndrome*, ©2004 quoted with permission from Random House - Doubleday

153   Robert J. Herbold, *The Fiefdom Syndrome*, ©2004 quoted with permission from Random House - Doubleday

154   Manu Cornet, Organizational Charts, reprinted with permission www.bonkersworld.net/org-charts

155   Manu Cornet, Organizational Charts, reprinted with permission www.bonkersworld.net/org-charts

156   Robert J. Herbold, *The Fiefdom Syndrome*, ©2004 quoted with permission from Random House - Doubleday

157   Peter R. Scholtes, "Leaders of People: Some are Wonderful, Some are Clueless, The Rest are Somewhere In Between," 1996, quoted with permission from Kelly Allen Association

158   Robert J. Herbold, *The Fiefdom Syndrome*, ©2004 quoted with permission from Random House - Doubleday

159   *Jerry Maguire* 1996

160   *One Flew Over the Cuckoo's Nest* is a 1975 American drama film based on the 1962 novel by Ken Kesey

161   Rick Brenner, "Devious Political Tactics: Divide and Conquer," July 20, 2005, quoted with permission

162   Actually written by William Safire, speechwriter to Richard Nixon

163   Spiro Agnew was known for his scathing criticisms of political opponents. He attacked his adversaries with relish, hurling unusual, often alliterative epithets; however, a bit of the pot calling the kettle black.

164   Sun Tzu, c. ~500 BC, *The Art of War*

165   Rick Brenner, Devious Political Tactics: Divide and Conquer, July 20, 2005, quoted with permission

166   Rick Brenner, Devious Political Tactics: Divide and Conquer, July 20, 2005, quoted with permission

167   Dr. Dale Roach, "Teamwork in the Workplace," July 2010, quoted with permission from Like A Team www.likeateam.com

168   Dr. Dale Roach, "Teamwork in the Workplace," quoted with permission from Like A Team www.likeateam.com

169   Patrick Lencioni, *The Five Dysfunctions of a Team: A Leadership Fable*, ©2002, quoted with permission

170   Patrick Lencioni, *Death by Meeting*, ©2004, quoted with permission

171   Patrick Lencioni, *Death by Meeting*, ©2004, quoted with permission

172   Patrick Lencioni, *Death by Meeting*, ©2004, quoted with permission

173   Giancarlo Livraghi, *The Power of Stupidity*, ©2009, quoted with permission

174   Robert J. Herbold, *The Fiefdom Syndrome*, ©2004 quoted with permission from Random House - Doubleday

175   Hugh MacLeod, *Ignore Everybody*, ©2009, quoted with permission from Penguin Group publishers

176   Harry S Truman, 33rd President of the United States, 1884–1972

177   Conversely the "constructive" script he calls "Waiting for Santa Claus."

178   Eric Berne, MD., *Games People Play*, copyright ©1964, Copyright renewed 1992 by Ellen Berne, Peter Berne, and Terence Berne. Used by permission of Random House, Inc. and the estate of Eric Berne

179   Robert I. Sutton, Ph.D., *The No Asshole Rule*, Copyright ©2007 by permission of Grand Central Publishing, All rights reserved.

180   Gareth Morgan, *Images of Organization*, copyright ©1998 quoted with permission of the publisher Berrett-Koehler Publishers, Inc., San Francisco, CA. All rights reserved.

181   Eric Garner, "Seven Barriers to Great Communication," February 28, 2006, quoted with permission www.managetrainlearn.com

182   These are Transactional Analysis terms. "Rackets" are learned patterns. "Stamps" are collections (hence stamps as in stamp collections) of bad memories, which some people tend to keep. It's as if people have a tendency to keep events which turned out badly, in their heads.

183   Andrew E. Schwartz, "Bad Communication: Is It Holding You Back? —Learn How to Break Free," July 2005, quoted with permission from Andrew E. Schwartz, (trainer, consultant, speaker, and entrepreneur) ©A. E. Schwartz & Associates with all rights reserved. www.aeschwartz.com

184   Marshall Goldsmith, *What Got You Here Won't Get You There*, ©2007, quoted with permission

185   Malcolm Gladwell

186   Steve Tobak, "Why Your Boss Doesn't Always Listen to You," January 25, 2010, quoted with permission

187   Steve Tobak, "Why Your Boss Doesn't Always Listen to You," January 25, 2010, quoted with permission

188   Nic Paton, "Bosses Blocking Workers' Careers," July 7, 2006 Quoted with permission, Copyright *Guardian News & Media Ltd* 2006

189   Seth Godin, "The Difference Between Management and Leadership," October 22, 2011, blog quoted with permission

190   Rahm Emanuel, former Chief of Staff for President Barack Obama

191   Michael Watkins, 'Are You a Pyromaniac?' March 30, 2007, quoted with permission from *Harvard Business Publishing Blog*

192   Michael Watkins, "Are You a Pyromaniac?," March 30, 2007, quoted with permission from *Harvard Business Publishing Blog*

193   Michael Watkins, "Are You a Pyromaniac?," March 30, 2007, quoted with permission from *Harvard Business Publishing Blog*

194   Michael Watkins, "Are You a Pyromaniac?," March 30, 2007, quoted with permission from *Harvard Business Publishing Blog*

195   Nathan Bennett, "Munchausen at Work," November 2007, quoted with permission *Harvard Business Review*

196   Giancarlo Livraghi *The Power of Stupidity*, ©2009, quoted with permission

197   Giancarlo Livraghi *The Power of Stupidity*, ©2009, quoted with permission

198   Leslie G. Ungar, "Executives Behaving Badly," February 19, 2009, quoted with permission. www.ezinearticles.com

199   Danny Miller, *The Icarus Paradox: How Exceptional Companies Bring About Their Own Downfall*, ©1992

200   Franklin P. Jones 1908–1980

201   Steve Becker, "Psychopaths' Cat and Mouse Game," February 21, 2008, quoted with permission www.powercommunicating.com

202   Steve Becker, "Psychopaths' Cat and Mouse Game," February 21, 2008, quoted with permission www.powercommunicating.com

203   Groucho Marx 1890–1977

204   Robin Stern, Ph.D., "Are You Being Gaslighted?," May 19, 2009, quoted with permission

205   Also reference: Hanlon's Razor; "Never attribute to malice that which is adequately explained by stupidity."

206   Geoff Crane, "Nine Destructive Project Manager Behaviors," quoted with permission www.edge.papercutpm.com

207   Geoff Crane, "Nine Destructive Project Manager Behaviors," quoted with permission www.edge.papercutpm.com

208   David Brinkley 1920–2003

209   Sir John Templeton 1912–2008

NOTES

210   George Santayana, "Santayana's Law of Repeating Consequences: Those who cannot remember the past are condemned to repeat it."

211   Leonard Bertain, "The Tribal Knowledge Paradox (Using the War on Waste to Align Strategy with Process)," ©2010

212   Excerpt from Seth Godin's daily blog, Quoted with permission www.sethgodin.com

213   *Eternal Sunshine of the Spotless Mind*, 2004 American science-fiction film about an estranged couple who have each other erased from their memories

214   Murphy's Law is actually Finagle's Law of Dynamic Negatives: "Anything that can go wrong, will; at the worst possible moment." O'Toole's Corollary of Finagle's Law is: "The perversity of the Universe tends towards a maximum."

215   Giancarlo Livraghi, *The Power of Stupidity*, ©2009, quoted with permission

216   Rick Brenner, "No Surprises," February 4, 2004, quoted with permission

217   Rick Brenner, "No Surprises," February 4, 2004, quoted with permission

218   Douglas R. Connant and Melle Norgaard, *TouchPoints: Creating Powerful Leadership Connections in the Smallest of Moments*, ©2011

219   Kathleen Schulweis, "Help for Abrasive Bullies and Their Targets: Using the Relationship Selling Method for Connecting," August 30,2010, quoted with permission

220   Actually called "pre ictal amnesia," it is the loss of the ability to recall information that had been previously encoded in memory prior to a specified or approximate point in time.

221   Art Petty, "Leadership Caffeine: It's Vujà Dé All Over Again," February 2010 quoted with permission www.artpetty.com

222   Abraham Wald (1902–1950), "A Method of Estimating Plane Vulnerability Based on Damage of Survivors" (1943)

223   Dave Barry

224   *Overland Monthly*, November, 1902

225   Julie Knechtel, "How to Attend a Meeting," from *Bored Room Chuckles*

226   Edward Tufte, "PowerPoint Is Evil, Power Corrupts: PowerPoint Corrupts Absolutely," November 2003, quoted with permission www.wired.com

227   , Giancarlo Livraghi, "The PowerPoint Disease." ©2004, quoted with permission

228   Seth Godin, *Small is the New Big: And 183 Other Riffs, Rants, and Remarkable Business Ideas*, ©2006, quoted with permission.

229   Hank Gillman, *You Can't Fire Everyone*, ©2011, quoted with permission from Penguin Group Publishers

230   C. Northcote Parkinson (1909-1993), "Parkinson's Law: The Pursuit of Progress," November 19, 1955

231   Hank Gillman, *You Can't Fire Everyone*, ©2011, quoted with permission from Penguin Group Publishers

232   Giancarlo Livraghi, *The Power of Stupidity*, ©2009, quoted with permission

233   Patrick Lencioni, *Death by Meeting*, ©2004, quoted with permission

234   Dave Barry, *Claw your Way to the Top: How to Become the Head of a Major Corporation in Roughly a Week*, ©1986, quoted with permission from Rodale Books

235   Dirty Harry, *The Dead Pool* (1988),

236   Lilliput and Blefuscu are two fictional island nations that appear in the first part of the 1726 novel *Gulliver's Travels*. Both kingdoms are empires– i.e., realms ruled by self-styled emperors.

237   Richard Harkness 1907–1977

238   Dwight Schrute, *The Office*

239   Scott Adams, *Dilbert*, ©2002, used by permission of UNIVERSAL UCLICK, All rights reserved.

240   George Bernard Shaw (1856–1950)

NOTES

241 Scott Adams, *The Dilbert Principle: A Cubicle's-Eye View of Bosses, Meetings, Management Fads & Other Workplace Afflictions*, Copyright ©1996 by United Features Syndicate, Inc. Reprinted by permission of HarperCollins Publishers

242 Sen. Arlen Specter (D-PA)

243 Mark McDonald, "Blame Storming—One of the Signs of Weak Management," July 20, 2009, quoted with permission

244 Lewis Carroll (1832–1898), *Alice's Adventures in Wonderland*, 1865

245 George Orwell (1903–1950), *Animal Farm*, ©1956 quoted with permission

246 Duke Energy Corporation, 526 S. Church St. Charlotte, NC 28202 quoted with permission

247 Olivier Serrat, "A Primer on Corporate Values," June, 2010, quoted with permission www.adb.org/documents

248 Marshall Goldsmith, *What Got You Here Won't Get You There: How Successful People Become Even More Successful*, ©2007, quoted with permission

249 Marshall Goldsmith, *What Got You Here Won't Get You There: How Successful People Become Even More Successful*, ©2007, quoted with permission

250 Olivier Serrat, "A Primer on Corporate Values," June 2010, quoted with permission www.adb.org/documents

251 Olivier Serrat, "A Primer on Corporate Values," June 2010, quoted with permission www.adb.org/documents

252 Robert I. Sutton, Ph.D., *The No Asshole Rule*, Copyright ©2007 by permission of Grand Central Publishing, All rights reserved.

253 Scott Adams, *The Dilbert Principle: A Cubicle's-Eye View of Bosses, Meetings, Management Fads & Other Workplace Afflictions*, Copyright ©1996 by United Features Syndicate, Inc. Reprinted by permission of HarperCollins Publishers

254 Peter Block, *Flawless Consulting*, ©1981, reprinted with permission of John Wiley & Sons, Inc.

255   Marshall Goldsmith, *What Got You Here Won't Get You There: How Successful People Become Even More Successful*, ©2007, quoted with permission

256   Mahatma Gandhi 1869–1948

257   Michael Mendelbaum, Professor of American Foreign Policy at The Johns Hopkins School of Advanced International Studies

258   *Outsourced*, ©2010 Courtesy of NBC Universal, quoted with permission

259   Samuel A. Culbert, "Get Rid of the Performance Review!" October 20, 2008, quoted with permission www.online.wsj.com

260   Samuel A. Culbert, *Get Rid of the Performance Review! How Companies Can Stop Intimidating, Start Managing–and Focus on What Really Matters*, ©2010 Pages 38/39 paragraph 4, Quoted with permission

261   Daniel Goleman, Richard Boyatzis and Annie McKee, *Primal Leadership: Realizing the Power of Emotional Intelligence*, ©2002, quoted with permission from Harvard Business Press,

262   Dale Dauten, *The Gifted Boss: How to Find, Create and Keep Great Employees*, ©1999, quoted with permission

263   J. Paul Getty 1892–1976

264   Ravi Mattu, "Look to Your Players, Not to the Rulebook," April 24, 2011, quoted with permission from the *Financial Times*

265   Steven Levy, *In the Plex: How Google Thinks, Works, and Shapes Our Lives*, ©2011, quoted with permission from Simon and Shuster publishers

266   Scott Adams, *The Dilbert Principle: A Cubicle's-Eye View of Bosses, Meetings, Management Fads & Other Workplace Afflictions*, Copyright ©1996 by United Features Syndicate, Inc. Reprinted by permission of HarperCollins Publishers

267   Tom Peters

268   Kip Tindell, CEO The Container Store

269   Scott Adams, Dilbert, ©2011, used by permission of UNIVERSAL UCLICK, All rights reserved.

NOTES

270   Ferdinand Lassalle 1825–1864

271   Ralph Waldo Emerson, "Compensation" appears in his book *Essays*, first published in 1841

272   Lucy Kellaway, "Next Time Don't Give Hiring a Moment's Notice," November 15, 2010, quoted with permission from the *Financial Times*

273   "Seventy-one Percent of Employers Say They Value Emotional Intelligence over IQ," August 18, 2011, quoted with permission www.CareerBuilder.com

274   Peter Salovey, Ph.D. and John D. Mayer, Ph.D., *Emotional Intelligence*, ©1990, quoted with permission

275   "Seventy-one Percent of Employers Say They Value Emotional Intelligence over IQ," August 18, 2011, quoted with permission www.CareerBuilder.com

276   Samuel A. Culbert, *Get Rid of the Performance Review! How Companies Can Stop Intimidating, Start Managing–and Focus on What Really Matters*, ©2010 Page 99, Paragraph 3, quoted with permission

277   Samuel A. Culbert, *Get Rid of the Performance Review! How Companies Can Stop Intimidating, Start Managing–and Focus on What Really Matters*, ©2010, Page 95, Paragraph 1, quoted with permission

278   Kruger, Justin and David Dunning, "Unskilled and Unaware of It: How Difficulties in Recognizing One's Own Incompetence Lead to Inflated Self-Assessments," ©1999, *Journal of Personality and Social Psychology*

279   Marshall Goldsmith, *What Got You Here Won't Get You There: How Successful People Become Even More Successful*, ©2007, quoted with permission

280   Fungibility is the quality of being transferable, interchangeable or exchangeable. In the job context it means a job or function that can be performed by anyone and is not required to be performed in any given location. It can thus be performed anywhere in the world especially where the costs are lower. An example is the call center function. For American business most call center functions were transferred to India where costs are significantly lower than in the US.

281   Trina Isakson, "Introverts v. Extroverts in the Workplace," October 26, 2009, quoted with permission www.brazencareerist.com

282   Allen B. Downey, "The Tyranny of the Extroverts," 2003, quoted with permission www.allen-downey.com

283   Philip Delves Broughton, "Leadership is Not Just for the Extroverts," November 29, 2010, quoted with permission from the *Financial Times*

284   Philip Delves Broughton, "Leadership is Not Just for the Extroverts," November 29, 2010, quoted with permission from the *Financial Times*

285   Robert I. Sutton, Ph.D., *The No Asshole Rule*, Copyright ©2007 by permission of Grand Central Publishing, All rights reserved.

286   Gary Namie, PhD, *The Bully at Work: What you can do to Stop the Hurt and Reclaim you Dignity on the Job*, ©2003, quoted with permission www.workplacebullying.org

287   Scott Adams, *Dilbert* ©2011, used by permission of UNIVERSAL UCLICK, All rights reserved.

288   Ray Williams, "Generation Y is Poised to Dominate the Workplace," June 14, 2009, quoted with permission from Ray Williams Associates, Inc. www.raywilliams.ca

289   Lucy Kellaway, "Better to Save Face than Take a Long Look in the Mirror," November 29, 2010, quoted with permission from the *Financial Times*

290   Daniel Goleman, Richard Boyatzis, and Annie McKee, *Primal Leadership: Realizing the Power of Emotional Intelligence*, ©2002, quoted with permission from Harvard Business Press

291   Steven Levy, *In the Plex: How Google Thinks, Works, and Shapes Our Lives*, ©2011, quoted with permission from Simon and Shuster publishers

292   Robert Benchley 1889–1945

293   Lyndon B Johnson, 36th President of the United States 1908–1973

294   Robert I. Sutton, Ph.D., *The No Asshole Rule*, Copyright ©2007, by permission of Grand Central Publishing, All rights reserved.

295   Friedrich Nietzsche 1844–1900

296   Pryor, Mildred Golden, Singleton, Lisa Pryor, Taneja, Sonia, Humphreys, John H, "Workplace Fun and its Correlates: A Conceptual Inquiry," August 20, 2010, quoted with permission

297   Pryor, Mildred Golden, Singleton, Lisa Pryor, Taneja, Sonia, Humphreys, John H, "Workplace Fun and its Correlates: A Conceptual Inquiry," August 20, 2010, quoted with permission

298   Niven's Laws from "Known Space: The Future Worlds of Larry Niven," www.larryniven.net

299   The authors contend that dissonant leaders lack empathy and are thus out of synch with the group. So the question is; does the lack of empathy result in a dissonant leader or does dissonant leadership spawn the lack of empathy?

300   Daniel Goleman, Richard Boyatzis and Annie McKee, *Primal Leadership: Realizing the Power of Emotional Intelligence,* ©2002, quoted with permission from Harvard Business Press

301   Rhymer Rigby, "The Workplace is Like a Cold Bed: the Warmth Will Spread—How to Cultivate the Right Attitude," April 24, 2011, quoted with permission from the *Financial Times*

302   Peter Drucker 1909–2005

303   William Arthur Ward 1921–1994

304   Pryor, Mildred Golden, Singleton, Lisa Pryor, Taneja, Sonia, Humphreys, John H, "Workplace Fun and its Correlates: A Conceptual Inquiry," August 20, 2010, quoted with permission

305   A Hobson's choice is a free choice in which only one option is offered; take the option or not— i.e., "take it or leave it." The phrase originates with Thomas Hobson (1544–1631), a livery stable owner in Cambridge, England. To rotate the use of his horses, he offered customers the choice of either taking the horse in the stall nearest the door or taking none at all.

306   Vadim Kotelnikov, "What is Values-Based Leadership," quoted with permission from www.1000ventures.com

307   Vadim Kotelnikov, "What is Values-Based Leadership," quoted with permission from www.1000ventures.com

308   Tom Antion, "Public Speaking: Self-Effacing Humor," November 2005 quoted with permission www.amazingpublicspeaking.com

309   Hank Gillman, *You Can't Fire Everyone,* ©2011, quoted with permission from Penguin Group Publishers

310   It's named after the attempts to avoid blame for the failure to prepare to defend the US Naval Base at Pearl Harbor, Hawaii from Japanese attack.

311   Rodrigo Canales, B. Cade Massey and Amy Wrzesniewski, "Promises Aren't Enough: Business Schools Need to Do a Better Job Teaching Students Values," August 22, 2010, quoted by permission of the *Wall Street Journal*, Copyright ©2011 Dow Jones & Company, Inc. All Rights Reserved Worldwide. License number 2672060602391

312   Lucy Kellaway, "Power Posing and Flattery Beat an MBA Any Day," October 3, 2010, quoted with permission from the *Financial Times*

313   Lucy Kellaway, "Chief Executives are Worse Than They Think," March 13, 2011, quoted with permission from the *Financial Times*

314   Lucy Kellaway, "The Real Reason CEOs Cry All the Way to the Bank," September 13, 2010, quoted with permission from the *Financial Times*

315   George Orwell (1903–1950), *Animal Farm*, ©1956 quoted with permission

316   Albert J. Bernstein, Ph.D., "15 Signs Your Workplace is Dysfunctional," February 11, 2009, reproduced with permission www.careerbuilder.com

317   Hugh MacLeod, "Business Porn," November 2005, reprinted with permission, www.gapingvoid.com

318   Scott Adams, "The Perfect Stimulus: Bad Management," November 6-7, 2010, quoted with permission of the *Wall Street Journal*, Copyright ©2011 Dow Jones & Company, Inc. All Rights Reserved Worldwide. License number 2663181429495

319   Lucy Kellaway, "My Measure of a Good Employer is better than Botox," January 31, 2011, quoted with permission from the *Financial Times*

320   Scott Adams, *Dilbert*, ©2011, used by permission of UNIVERSAL UCLICK, All rights reserved.

321   "Ozymandias" is a sonnet by Percy Bysshe Shelley (1792–1822) and is another name for Ramses the Great, Pharaoh of the nineteenth dynasty of ancient Egypt. Ozymandias has come to define the inevitable complete decline of all leaders, and of the empires they build, however mighty in their own time